C000179211

World Building

Advances in Stylistics

Series Editor: Dan McIntyre, University of Huddersfield, UK

Editorial Board:

Beatrix Busse, University of Berne, Switzerland
Szilvia Csábi, Eötvös Loránd University, Hungary
Monika Fludernik, University of Freiburg,Germany
Lesley Jeffries, University of Huddersfield, UK
Jean Boase-Beier, University of East Anglia, UK
Peter Verdonk, University of Amsterdam (Emeritus), The Netherlands
Larry Stewart, College of Wooster, USA
Manuel Jobert, Jean Moulin University, Lyon 3, France

Other titles in the series:

Corpus Stylistics in Principles and Practice
Yufang Ho
Chick Lit: The Stylistics of Cappuccino Fiction
Rocío Montoro
D. H. Lawrence and Narrative Viewpoint
Violeta Sotirova
Discourse of Italian Cinema and Beyond
Roberta Piazza
I.A. Richards and the Rise of Cognitive Stylistics
David West
Oppositions and Ideology in News Discourse
Matt Davies
Opposition in Discourse
Lesley Jeffries
Pedagogical Stylistics
Michael Burke, Szilvia Csábi, Lara Week and Judit Zerkowitz
Sylvia Plath and the Language of Affective States
Zsófia Demjén
Style in the Renaissance
Patricia Canning
Stylistics and Shakespeare's Language
Mireille Ravassat
Text World Theory and Keats' Poetry
Marcello Giovanelli
The Stylistics of Poetry
Peter Verdonk
World Building in Spanish and English Spoken Narratives
Jane Lugea

World Building

Discourse in the Mind

Edited by Joanna Gavins and
Ernestine Lahey

Bloomsbury Academic
An imprint of Bloomsbury Publishing Plc

B L O O M S B U R Y

LONDON · OXFORD · NEW YORK · NEW DELHI · SYDNEY

Bloomsbury Academic

An imprint of Bloomsbury Publishing Plc

50 Bedford Square
London
WC1B 3DP
UK

1385 Broadway
New York
NY 10018
USA

www.bloomsbury.com

BLOOMSBURY and the Diana logo are trademarks of Bloomsbury Publishing Plc

First published 2016
Paperback edition first published 2018

Joanna Gavins, Ernestine Lahey and Contributors, 2016

Joanna Gavins and Ernestine Lahey have asserted their right under the Copyright, Designs and Patents Act, 1988, to be identified as the Editors of this work.

All rights reserved. No part of this publication may be reproduced or transmitted in any form or by any means, electronic or mechanical, including photocopying, recording, or any information storage or retrieval system, without prior permission in writing from the publishers.

No responsibility for loss caused to any individual or organization acting on or refraining from action as a result of the material in this publication can be accepted by Bloomsbury or the author.

British Library Cataloguing-in-Publication Data
A catalogue record for this book is available from the British Library.

ISBN: HB: 978-1-4725-8-653-7
PB: 978-1-3500-5-606-0
ePDF: 978-1-4725-8-654-4
ePub: 978-1-4725-8-655-1

Library of Congress Cataloging-in-Publication Data
A catalog record for this book is available from the Library of Congress.

Series: Advances in Stylistics

Typeset by Newgen Knowledge Works (P) Ltd., Chennai, India

Contents

List of Figures

Notes on Contributors

Alice Bell's (Sheffield Hallam University) research interests are stylistics, cognitive poetics, narratology, Possible Worlds Theory, and digital literature. Her publications include *The Possible Worlds of Hypertext Fiction* (Palgrave Macmillan, 2010), *Analyzing Digital Fiction* (Routledge, 2014) and articles in *Narrative, Journal of Narrative Theory, Storyworlds* and *Style*.

Sam Browse is a lecturer in the Department of Humanities at Sheffield Hallam University. His research draws on cognitive frameworks from stylistics, narratology and psychology to investigate the rhetorical effects of political discourse. He has taught on a wide range of subjects, including stylistics, discourse analysis, critical theory, grammar and narrative theory.

Joanna Gavins is Reader in Literary Linguistics at the University of Sheffield, where she teaches courses in stylistics, linguistics and cognitive poetics. She is the author of *Reading the Absurd* (EUP, 2013), *Text World Theory: An Introduction* (EUP, 2007), and co-editor (with Gerard Steen) of *Cognitive Poetics in Practice* (Routledge, 2003). She has published widely on text-worlds, stylistics and cognitive poetics, and is Editor of the John Benjamins series *Linguistic Approaches to Literature*. She is Director of the Text World Theory Special Collection at the University of Sheffield.

Alison Gibbons is Senior Lecturer in English at Sheffield Hallam University. She is the author of *Multimodality, Cognition, and Experimental Literature* (Routledge, 2012) and co-editor of *Mark Z. Danielewski* (MUP, 2010) and the *Routledge Companion to Experimental Literature* (2012). Alison's research interests centre on stylistic and cognitive-poetic approaches to contemporary fiction and to innovative forms of narrative, including immersive and multimodal genres.

Marcello Giovanelli is Assistant Professor in English Education at the University of Nottingham, UK. He has research interests in educational linguistics, pedagogical stylistics and cognitive poetics. His recent publications include *Text World Theory and Keats' Poetry* (Bloomsbury, 2013) and *Teaching Grammar, Structure and Meaning* (Routledge, 2014).

Antonina Harbus is Professor of English and Head of Department at Macquarie University, Sydney, Australia. Her research on medieval and more recent English literary texts combines linguistic and literary analysis with ideas and methods from cognitive science. Her most recent book is *Cognitive Approaches to Old English Poetry* (Brewer, 2012).

David Herman is Professor of the Engaged Humanities in the Department of English Studies at Durham University. The author of *Storytelling and the Sciences of Mind* (2013), *Basic Elements of Narrative* (2009), and other books, he is currently working to bring ideas from narrative studies into dialogue with scholarship on animals and human-animal relationships.

Ernestine Lahey is Assistant Professor in Linguistics and Stylistics at University College Roosevelt, The Netherlands. Her research interests and main areas of publication include (cognitive) stylistics, Text World Theory, (literary) landscape representation and Canadian literature. She is currently working on a monograph on the poetics of landscape representation.

Jane Lugea is Senior Lecturer in Applied Linguistics at the University of Huddersfield. Her doctoral thesis, completed at Queen's University Belfast, adapted Text World Theory for the analysis of Spanish discourse and is currently being prepared for publication as a monograph. She is Publicity Officer for the Poetics and Linguistics Association (PALA) and Assistant Editor of the popular language magazine, *Babel*.

Agnes Marszalek is a PhD student in English Language at the University of Glasgow and a co-opted member of the PALA Committee. Her interests include humour, cognitive stylistics and psychological approaches to text analysis. Her current research, funded by the Carnegie Trust for the Universities of Scotland, focuses on the reader's experience of narrative humour.

Nigel McLoughlin is Professor of Creativity and Poetics at the University of Gloucestershire. He has published five collections of poetry, the latest of which is *Chora: New and Selected Poems* (Templar Poetry, 2009). In 2011, he was awarded a UK National Teaching Fellowship.

Jeremy Scott writes, teaches and researches on the border between literature and language studies at the University of Kent. As well as his own fiction, he has published on contemporary British and Irish fiction, on travel literature and on stylistics-based approaches to creative practice. A new short story, 'Black Shuck', appeared in *New Writing* magazine in July 2013, and a monograph, *Creative Writing and Stylistics*, was published by Palgrave Macmillan in 2014.

Peter Stockwell is Professor of Literary Linguistics at the University of Nottingham, UK, and a Fellow of the English Association. He has published 18 books and editions, and over 80 articles in cognitive poetics, stylistics, sociolinguistics and applied linguistics, and is consultant editor for the Routledge English Language Introductions series.

Sara Whiteley is a lecturer in Language and Literature at the University of Sheffield. Her research interests lie in the fields of cognitive stylistics and discourse analysis. She co-edited the *Cambridge Handbook of Stylistics* (Cambridge University Press, 2014) and is co-author of *The Discourse of Reading Groups: Integrating Cognitive and Sociocultural Perspectives* (Routledge, forthcoming 2016).

Isabelle van der Bom is a researcher in the School of English at the University of Sheffield. Her work focuses on providing a text-worlds approach to the study of linguistic identity in discursive interaction. Her fields of research include stylistics, cognitive poetics, discourse studies, language and gender and politeness.

World Building in Discourse

Joanna Gavins and Ernestine Lahey

1.1 Worlds, language and the mind

Over the last few decades, the disciplines of stylistics, narratology and cognitive poetics have all seen a notable proliferation of research taking a particular perspective on the experience of producing and receiving discourse. This research, while encompassing diverse analytical approaches and employing varied technical terminology, can be seen to be united in its view of language as essentially world-building in nature. The fundamental foundation for this perspective on discourse is the notion that all texts, whether literary or non-literary, are understood by language users through the construction of a mental representation or 'world' in the mind – a world which is greatly dependent on the linguistic cues provided by the text itself, but also vitally grounded in the context of the discourse. A succinct summary of the basic principles underpinning this view is provided by Marie-Laure Ryan in her discussion of the world-building nature of literary narrative:

> The idea of a textual world presupposes that the reader constructs in imagination a set of language-independent objects, using as a guide the textual declarations, but building this always incomplete image into a more vivid representation through the import of information provided by real-life experience or derived from other texts ... For the text to construct a world, or fragments of a world, it must offer something to see (or hear, or feel) to the sense of the mind. (Ryan 1998: 138)

Language thus provides a blueprint for the imagination, a set of textual prompts that allows human beings to build rich conceptual models of their own reality and of alternative realities. The researchers who view discourse through this lens all share a common aim to understand how world-building of this kind operates and to examine the relationships which exist between the real world, the text and mental representation. This book is intended to bring together some of the most recent work in this area of linguistics and to showcase the capabilities of worlds-based approaches to discourse.

The roots of all the varying analytical frameworks which regard language as world-building can be traced to the possible worlds theories of modal logic pioneered by philosophers such as Saul Kripke (1972), Nicholas Rescher (1975) and David Lewis (1986). Their view of language as an ontological system able to refer to and create accessibility relations between a plurality of worlds was of immediate and direct interest to theorists attempting to describe the imaginative ontologies of literary discourse. It was widely adapted for this purpose, particularly in the 1980s and 1990s (see Maître 1983; Pavel 1986; Ronen 1994; Ryan 1991; Semino 1997). The influence of possible-worlds logic extends far beyond the literary and narrative theory of the late twentieth century, however, and continues to lend its ontological structure and terminology to more recent cognitive-linguistic models of literary and non-literary discourse processing, such as Text World Theory (see Gavins 2007; Werth 1999), as well as to worlds-based approaches to contemporary narratology (Herman 2002). All of these various strands of worlds-theories are represented in this book, where we have attempted to draw together not only a diverse array of analytical frameworks, but also to demonstrate the equally wide range of discourse types now commonly explored from these perspectives. Although it is not possible to provide a comprehensive overview of the theoretical background to each of the analytical methods included in this volume, in the following section we present a summary of some of the basic building blocks and key terms upon which our contributors base their chapters.

1.2   Some basic architecture

The real world of everyday human experience forms the central matrix point for all worlds-based frameworks and theories. In Possible Worlds Theory, this world is known as 'the actual world' – the world from which all other imagined possibilities and alternatives are generated, and against which their truth status and relative accessibility are assessed. In more recent usage-based linguistic approaches, such as Text World Theory, the real-world situation in which language occurs is called 'the discourse-world'. The differing terminology here reflects the focus of the text-world framework on language as an interactive and negotiated event, where Possible Worlds Theory tends to be limited to an analysis of the ontological structures such language produces. The discourse-world from a Text World Theory perspective, then, is seen as fundamentally socially and culturally situated; the language produced by the discourse participants within it is recognized as being greatly influenced by their personal and shared knowledge and experiences. Text World Theory is thus as much grounded in the experiential principles of cognitive linguistics and cognitive psychology as it is in the ontology of possible-worlds semantics.

The second point upon which all worlds theories agree is the world-building capacity of language itself. As participants produce discourse in the real world – as we talk to one another, read a novel or a poem, watch a film or a play – we create mental representations of states of affairs, based on the language we encounter. These mental representations have been variously termed 'possible worlds' (see Ryan 1991), 'text-worlds' (see Werth 1999), 'storyworlds' (see Herman 2002), 'mental spaces' (see Fauconnier and Turner 2003), 'narrative worlds' (see Gerrig 1993) and 'frames' (see Emmott 1997) by an assortment of researchers, from differing but closely related disciplines, all with their own specific analytical aims. For some analysts, the 'text-as-world' metaphor simply provides a neat, but broadly applied description of the cognitive activity which enables us to comprehend discourse. For many of these theorists, particularly those interested in literary fiction, the metaphor also allows useful ontological distinctions between how we experience the real world and the imaginative activity of reading to be drawn and understood. For others, particularly those with disciplinary roots in stylistics, discourse analysis and cognitive linguistics, a more detailed account of the relationships between specific linguistic items and their resultant conceptual structures is the core objective.

For example, through the application of Possible Worlds Theory to literary language, narrative theorists have been able to produce complex and detailed accounts of the ontological structures underpinning an array of fictional texts. Under these approaches, a literary work is seen as producing a 'textual universe', in which the 'textual actual world' represents the base reality of the narrative's characters, but from which countless other 'textual possible worlds' can also be created. Narratologists working in this field can not only plot and understand the structural design of whole novels or interactive fictions, but they can also evaluate the accessibility relations – the varying degrees of closeness or distance – which exist between multiple textual worlds.

Contemporary Text World Theory extends its analytical focus further still, not only through its interest in all forms of discourse, both literary and non-literary, but in its aim to understand the experiential dimensions of world-building through language. From this point of view, text-worlds are constructed from deictic markers in a text, known as 'world-building elements'. These specify the temporal and spatial boundaries of a mental representation, as well as any entities present in the world (known as 'enactors' in this framework). Further detail can be added to a world through 'function-advancing propositions', which describe events, actions or states. Crucially, however, all of this textual information is fleshed out from the discourse participants' background knowledge, which allows text-worlds to become highly immersive and cognitively rich mental spaces. Text-world theorists, then, aim to account for the precise relationships between specific linguistic features and the worlds they create, while at the same time situating this understanding in the discourse-world environment which shapes all language production and reception.

The concept of accessibility between worlds persists across many worlds-based theories and is perhaps the most broadly influential notion to have emerged from early possible-worlds logic. Once again, all worlds frameworks agree on the crucial point that a discourse has the potential to produce a multitude of worlds and that human beings have the ability to shift their attention and comprehension between these worlds unproblematically. In Text World Theory, changes in the temporal or spatial parameters of a text-world are known as 'world-switches', but texts can also contain shifts between worlds which involve an accompanying shift in our ontological position as readers or listeners. For example, focalization in narrative involves viewing the textual world through the perspective of a textual entity, a text-world enactor whose reliability cannot be guaranteed. The worlds created from such points of view, the contents of which are unverifiable using information available in the discourse-world, are referred to in Text World Theory as 'enactor-accessible'. Certain other linguistic features, such as modality and hypotheticality, also function by creating worlds that exist at a remote or unrealized distance from their matrix worlds. These remote worlds are known as 'modal-worlds' and can be produced by, among other things, free indirect discourse, focalization, conditionals and modality. It is possible for a single text to contain hundreds of modal-worlds and world-switches, some of them embedded within one another many times over, creating intricate cognitive structures and effects (see Gavins 2007 for a full explanation).

All of the terms and concepts mentioned here will arise again and again over the coming chapters of this volume, as our contributors make their own choices over which apparatus best suits their analytical needs. What is important to remember is that the differing approaches represented in their chapters do not stand in contradiction or conflict with one another. Rather, the variety of frameworks, theories and terms included in this book can be seen to have developed over many decades of productive interdisciplinary collaboration, borrowing and cross-pollination, all of which has greatly enriched and improved the overall functionality of worlds-based approaches to discourse and is likely to continue long into the future.

1.3   The chapters of this book

The contributors to this volume were chosen because their work involves the application of one or more contemporary theories of discourse based on the 'text-as-world' metaphor. Some of the chapters to follow apply their chosen frameworks relatively strictly, adhering closely to the terminology and architecture of the theories as set out by their founding scholars and applying these straightforwardly in their textual analyses. Others draw more selectively from a theory or theories, borrowing terms such as 'text-world', 'possible world' and 'storyworld', but employing these as heuristic devices rather than explicitly subscribing to any single specific analytical method. The flexibility with which these terms are used in contemporary discourse analysis is testament to the influence and scope of worlds-based approaches within mainstream discourse linguistics today. Whatever their chosen approach, all the contributions to this volume extend the boundaries of the worlds-based perspective on language, as in their totality they address a remarkable diversity of discourse types and contexts: from narrative prose fiction to poetry, from newspaper discourse to oral narrative and from dramatic discourse to pedagogy.

   To date, the majority of linguistic analyses of the world-building nature of language have been carried out on narrative texts (for key examples, see Alber 2009; Bell 2007, 2010; Bell and Alber 2012; Bell and Ensslin 2012; Emmott 1997; Gavins 2003, 2005, 2007, 2010, 2013; Gerrig 1993; Gibbons 2011; Herman 1994, 2011, 2002; Hidalgo Downing 2000a, 2000b; Ronen 1994; Ryan 1991; Werth 1994, 1995a, 1995b, 1999; Whiteley 2011a, 2011b, 2014), and several chapters in this volume demonstrate the capabilities of a worlds-approach to this type of discourse. Alice Bell's chapter, for example, opens our collection with a possible-worlds analysis of metalepsis in digital fiction. Bell examines the effects created when entities positioned outside the diegesis of a text transcend ontological boundaries and intrude upon a textual world distinct from their own. Her exploration of Andy Campbell and Judi Alston's (2010) web-based narrative, *Nightingale's Playground*, demonstrates not only the ideal suitability of Possible Worlds Theory to the analysis of experimental digital texts, but also the unique ability of digital fiction itself to enable particular ontological transgressions. Ernestine Lahey's chapter also focuses on contemporary literary narrative, but this time selected from the contrasting genre of popular fiction. Her discussion centres around Dan Brown's globally best-selling novels *Angels and Demons* (2000), *The Da Vinci Code* (2003), *The Lost Symbol* (2009) and *Inferno* (2013), and specifically the construction of the main character, Robert Langdon, in these texts. Lahey combines contemporary Text World Theory with the traditional rhetorical notion of *ethos* in order to examine the stylistic means through which Brown presents Langdon as a reliable and authoritative character in his novels. Lahey also uses her findings to suggest important amendments to current Text World Theory and its treatment of the relationship between the discourse-world and text-world in particular.

Sara Whiteley's contribution to the volume focuses on the concept of literary resonance in narrative and examines how this effect is created in Kazuo Ishiguro's novel *The Unconsoled*. Whiteley makes use of Stockwell's (2009) taxonomy of textual attractors in her investigation of the text-worlds of Ishiguro's text. She argues that the positioning of certain attractors in the worlds of the text has a direct effect on readers' responses to the novel, often conflicting with or frustrating their discourse-world desires for particular narrative outcomes. David Herman, meanwhile, approaches the mental representations we create from literary narrative as 'storyworlds', and in his contribution to the volume he explores a range of narrative worlds through which animal minds are modelled. His highly interdisciplinary chapter blends ideas from narratology, stylistics, ethology and anthropology. Herman makes particular use of the biologist Jakob von Uexküll's notion of '*Umwelt*' to explore literary representations of animals' experiences of their lived environment, crossing species boundaries at the same time as disciplinary boundaries.

In recent years, the literary-analytical boundaries of worlds theories have been expanded through the application of a range of frameworks to dramatic discourse (see e.g. Courtney 1990; Elam 2003; Lahey and Cruickshank 2010; Lugea 2013; McIntyre 2006; Palfrey 2014; Vassilopolou 2008; Yacavone 2014). Several of our contributors continue this development through their explorations of the worlds of theatre and film. Alison Gibbons, for example, focuses her chapter on contemporary immersive theatre. She combines a centrally text-world approach with Conceptual Integration Theory (Fauconnier and Turner 2003) to examine the radical audience participation involved in Punchdrunk's production, *The Drowned Man*. Like Bell, she explores the ontological impli-cations of this discourse and argues that audience members' actions in the discourse-world of immersive theatre have the potential to result in trans-world projections across ontological domains. Jane Lugea, on the other hand, examines an absurdist play, *You and Me*, which presents challenges for Text World Theory not only through its dramatic realization of an absurd aesthetic, but also through its bilingual code-switching between English and Catalan discourse. Lugea is furthermore concerned with how these aspects of the play interact with its presentation of two elderly main characters and their unreli-able, senile mind styles. Agnes Marszalek adopts a broader worlds-based per-spective in her exploration of the worlds constructed in a series of humorous film scripts. She views the creation of humour in filmic texts as fundamen-tally contextually bound and examines the stylistic techniques through which a 'humorous mode' of interpretation is cued. Marszalek goes on to argue that experiencing an emotional reaction of amusement in response to humorous narrative worlds is dependent on a reader or viewer having been previously emotionally oriented towards a 'humorous mood'.

Poetic texts, too, have now become a common focus for worlds-based analy-ses (see e.g. Gavins 2007, 2010b, 2012, 2013, 2014, 2015; Giovanelli 2013; Harbus 2012; Hidalgo Downing 2002; Lahey 2003, 2006, 2010; McLoughlin 2013, 2014; Nahajec 2009; Semino 1996, 1997; Stockwell 2005, 2011a, 2011b, 2014, 2016) and, in our collection, Peter Stockwell uses Text World Theory to facilitate a discus-sion of authorial intention in poetry. He examines Isaac Rosenberg's famous poem, 'Break of Day in the Trenches', linking the deictic configuration of its text-worlds to the strongly preferred responses to the text evident across both scholarly and non-scholarly readings. However, through a consideration of dif-fering versions of the poem, Stockwell also reveals that authorial intention is essentially a readerly construct – the modelling of a mind, driven by a text, but crucially situated within a reader's historical and cultural context.

In his examination of Eavan Boland's poetry, Nigel McLoughlin combines Text World Theory with new insights from mobilities research (following Sheller and Urry 2006). McLoughlin is interested in the stylistic means through which Boland enacts imaginative travel in her work, and her tendency to col-lapse spatial and temporal boundaries as she does so. This, McLoughlin argues, can create what he terms 'twin text-worlds', locating poet and reader in concur-rent moments. Joanna Gavins also explores a contemporary poetic work, in her analysis of the text-worlds of Jacob Polley's unnerving poem 'Hide and Seek'. Gavins views Polley's work as an example of apophatic poetry, but claims that this aesthetic is not achieved through the use of negation alone. She argues instead for a fully coherent view of poetic worlds, from which perspective individual stylistic elements can be seen to interanimate with each other to produce a whole-text poetic effect. Antonina Harbus, meanwhile, demonstrates the potential historical reach of worlds-based approaches to poetic analysis. Her research centres on Old English poetry and her chapter for this volume looks at translated extracts from the Anglo-Saxon text, *Beowulf*. Harbus explores the stylistic features of the worlds of *Beowulf* which enable contemporary readers to build mental representations of this poem, in spite of its temporal and cultural remoteness, and to experience emotional responses to the text.

Some of the most recent and important advancements in worlds-based theories have been made through their application to non-literary discourse (see e.g. Browse 2013; Chilton 2004; Gavins 2007; Gavins and Simpson 2015; Hidalgo Downing 2000c; Marley 2008; van der Bom 2015). This innovative work is showcased in two chapters in our collection. The focus of Sam Browse's chapter is on metaphor use in newspaper op-ed articles on the recent global financial crisis. Browse examines disparate metaphors used to describe a single event, suggesting that such shifting expression reflects similarly shifting perspectives and conceptualizations. Browse's interests lie centrally in 'megametaphor', Werth's (1994, 1999) term for persistent metaphorical structures which can extend across whole stretches of discourse. Browse argues for a situated approach to such structures – one which is sensitive to the essential interrelationships which exist between metaphors and the array of other text-worlds among which they are positioned. Isabelle van der Bom's chapter, on the other hand, represents another important extension of Text World Theory to account for non-literary discourse through the analysis of oral narratives. Van der Bom's research is based on data collected from Chinese migrants from Hong Kong and their descendants settled in the city of Sheffield, and is concerned with how these discourse participants represent themselves and their identities in face-to-face interviews. Van der Bom argues that Text World Theory has an important contribution to make to sociolinguistic identity studies and her analysis of an oral narrative produced by a British-born Chinese volunteer at a Chinese school shows how identity is constructed across multiple conceptual layers in discourse.

Two more of our chapters, one by Marcello Giovanelli and one by Jeremy Scott, extend the parameters of Text World Theory in other ground-breaking directions and provide examples of how this framework can be applied in a teaching context and a creative writing context, respectively. Giovanelli centres his discussion around a case study of a teacher introducing her class of 11- and 12-year-olds to the poem 'The Red Wheelbarrow' by William Carlos Williams. Giovanelli examines how the teacher's knowledge of Text World Theory fed into her design and delivery of classroom tasks; he makes a compelling argument that her framing of the poem through a text-world perspective enabled the students to explore and better understand the self-projection involved in poetry, rather than limiting their engagement with the text to a simple dissection of its linguistic structures. Scott's chapter combines Possible Worlds Theory, Text World Theory and other cognitive models of writing and reading as useful perspectives on the day-to-day practice of creative writing. Scott suggests that creative practitioners and their work generally benefit from interactions with sound theoretical infrastructure and he goes on to argue that worlds-based theories can provide an invaluable mechanism for guiding and refining creativity.

What is most striking about these chapters in their assembled form is not only the diversity of discourse genres they collectively tackle, but also the expansive and multifarious critical perspectives these analyses enable. This is as much a result of the wide range of professional backgrounds from which our contributors come as it is of their diverging choices of topic; *World Building* represents the leading edge research of narratologists and stylisticians, sociolinguists and discourse analysts, creative writers and experienced teachers. This collection of essays exemplifies both the extraordinary current reach and the boundless future potential of worlds-based theories of discourse. It stands both as a testament to their prevailing influence across an expanse of different disciplines, and an invitation to future researchers to participate in and shape the further evolution of world-building yet to come.

References

Alber, J. (2009), 'Impossible Storyworlds and What to Do with Them', *StoryWorlds: A Journal of Narrative Studies*, 1: 79–96.

Bell, A. (2007), ' "Do You Want to Hear about It?" Exploring Possible Worlds in Michael Joyce's Hyperfiction, *Afternoon, A Story*', in M. Lambrou and P. Stockwell (eds), *Contemporary Stylistics*, London: Continuum: 43–55.

Bell, A. (2010), *The Possible Worlds of Hypertext Fiction*, Basingstoke: Palgrave Macmillan.

Bell, A. and Alber, J. (2012), 'Ontological Metalepsis and Unnatural Narratology', *Journal of Narrative Theory*, 42.2: 166–92.

Bell, A. and Ensslin, A. (2012), ' "Click = Kill". Textual You in Ludic Digital Fiction',
    StoryWorlds: A Journal of Narrative Studies, 4: 49–73.

Browse, S. (2013), *(Mega-)metaphor in the Text-Worlds of Economic Crisis: Towards
    a Situated View of Metaphor in Discourse*, Unpubished PhD Thesis, University of
    Sheffield.

Chilton, P. (2004), *Analysing Political Discourse: Theory and Practice*, London:
    Routledge.

Courtney, R. (1990), *Drama and Intelligence: A Cognitive Theory*, Montreal and
    Kingston: McGill-Queen's University Press.

Elam, K. (2003), *The Semiotics of Theatre and Drama*, London: Routledge.

Emmott, C. (1997), *Narrative Comprehension*, Oxford: Clarendon Press.

Fauconnier, G. and Turner, M. (2003), *The Way We Think: Conceptual Blending and
    the Mind's Hidden Complexities*, New York: Basic Books.

Gavins, J. (2003), ' "Too Much Blague?" An Exploration of the Text Worlds of Donald
    Barthelme's *Snow White*', in G. Steen and J. Gavins (eds), *Cognitive Poetics in
    Practice*, London: Routledge: 29–44.

Gavins, J. (2005), '(Re)thinking Modality: A Text-World Perspective', *Journal of
    Literary Semantics*, 3.2: 79–82.

Gavins, J. (2007), *Text World Theory: An Introduction*, Edinburgh: Edinburgh
    University Press.

Gavins, J. (2010a), ' "Appeased by the Certitude": The Quiet Disintegration of the
    Paranoid Mind in *The Mustache*', in B. Büsse and D. McIntyre (eds), *Language and
    Style*, Basingstoke: Palgrave Macmillan: 402–18.

Gavins, J. (2010b), ' "And Everyone and I Stopped Breathing": Familiarity and
    Ambiguity in the Text-World of "The Day Lady Died" ', in M. Lambrou and
    P. Stockwell (eds), *Contemporary Stylistics*, Basingstoke: Palgrave Macmillan: 133–43.

Gavins, J. (2012), 'Leda and the Stylisticians', *Language and Literature*, 21.4: 345–62.

Gavins, J. (2013), *Reading the Absurd*, Edinburgh: Edinburgh University Press.

Gavins, J. (2014), 'Defamiliarisation', in P. Stockwell and S. Whiteley (eds), *The
    Cambridge Handbook of Stylistics*, Cambridge: Cambridge University Press: 126–211.

Gavins, J. (2015), 'Text World Theory', in V. Sotirova (ed.), *The Bloomsbury
    Companion to Stylistics*, London: Bloomsbury Academic: 444–57.

Gavins, J. and Simpson, P. (2015), 'Regina v John Terry: The Discursive Construction
    of an Alleged Racist Event', *Discourse and Society*, 26.6: 712–32.

Gerrig, R. J. (1993), *Experiencing Narrative Worlds: On the Psychological Activities of
    Reading*, New Haven: Westview Press.

Gibbons, A. (2011), *Multimodality, Cognition, and Experimental Literature*, London:
    Routledge.

Giovanelli, M. (2013), *Text World Theory and Keats' Poetry: The Cognitive Poetics of
    Desire, Dreams and Nightmares*, London: Bloomsbury Academic.

Harbus, A. (2012), *Cognitive Approaches to Old English Poetry*, Cambridge: D.S.
    Brewer.

Herman, D. (1994), 'Textual "You" and Double Deixis in Edna O'Brien's *A Pagan Place*', *Style*, 28.3: 378–410.

Herman, D. (2002), *Story Logic: Problems and Possibilities of Narrative*, Lincoln, NE: University of Nebraska Press.

Herman, D. (2011), 'Post-Cartesian Approaches to Narrative and Mind', *Style*, 45.2: 265–71.

Hidalgo Downing, L. (2000a), 'Negation in Discourse: A Text World Approach to Joseph Heller's *Catch-22*', *Language and Literature*, 9.3: 215–39.

Hidalgo Downing, L. (2000b), *Negation, Text Worlds, and Discourse: The Pragmatics of Fiction*, Stamford, CT: Ablex.

Hidalgo Downing, L. (2000c), 'World Creation in Advertising Discourse', *Revista Alicantina de Estudios Ingleses*, 13: 67–88.

Hidalgo Downing, L. (2002), 'Creating Things That Are Not: The Role of Negation in the Poetry of Wislawa Szymborska', *Journal of Literary Semantics*, 31: 113–32.

Kripke, S. (1972), *Naming and Necessity*, Oxford: Blackwell.

Lahey, E. (2003), 'Seeing the Forest for the Trees in Al Purdy's "Trees at the Arctic Circle"', *BELL: The Belgian Journal of English Language and Literature*, 1: 73–83.

Lahey, E. (2006), '(Re)thinking World-Building: Locating the Text-Worlds of Canadian Lyric Poetry', *Journal of Literary Semantics*, 35.2: 145–64.

Lahey, E. (2010), 'Megametaphorical Mappings and the Landscapes of Canadian Poetry', in M. Lambrou and P. Stockwell (eds), *Contemporary Stylistics*, London: Continuum: 157–67.

Lahey, E. and Cruickshank, T. (2010), 'Building the Stages of Drama: Towards a Text World Theory Account of Dramatic Play-Texts', *Journal of Literary Semantics*, 39.1: 67–91.

Lewis, D. (1986), *On the Plurality of Worlds*, Oxford: Blackwell.

Lugea, J. (2013), 'Embedded Dialogue and Dreams: The Worlds and Accessibility Relations of *Inception*', *Language and Literature*, 22.2: 133–53.

Maître, D. (1983), *Literature and Possible Worlds*, Middlesex: Middlesex University Press.

Marley, C. (2008), 'Truth Values and Truth-Commitment in Interdiscursive Dating Ads', *Language and Literature*, 17.2: 137–54.

McIntyre, D. (2006), *Point of View in Plays: A Cognitive Stylistic Approach to Viewpoint in Drama and Other Text-Types*, Amsterdam: John Benjamins Publishing.

McLoughlin, N. (2013), 'Negative Polarity in Eavan Boland's "The Famine Road"', *New Writing: The International Journal for the Practice and Theory of Creative Writing*, 10.2: 219–27.

McLoughlin, N. (2014), 'The Marvellous as We Know It: A Text World Analysis of Seamus Heaney's "Squarings: Lightenings VIII"', *New Writings: The International Journal for the Practice and Theory of Creative Writing*, 11.2: 228–39.

Nahajec, L. (2009), 'Negation and the Creation of Implicit Meaning in Poetry', *Language and Literature*, 18.2: 109–27.

Palfrey, S. (2014), *Shakespeare's Possible Worlds*, Cambridge: Cambridge University Press.

Pavel, T. (1986), *Fictional Worlds*, Cambridge, MA: Harvard University Press.

Rescher, N. (1975), *A Theory of Possibility: A Constructivistic and Conceptualistic Account of Possible Individuals and Possible Worlds*, London: John Wiley & Sons.

Ronen, R. (1994), *Possible Worlds in Literary Theory*, Cambridge: Cambridge University Press.

Ryan, M.-L. (1991), *Possible Worlds, Artificial Intelligence and Narrative Theory*, Bloomington, IN: Indiana University Press.

Ryan, M.-L. (1998), 'The Text as World versus the Text as Game: Possible Worlds Semantics and Postmodern Theory', *Journal of Literary Semantics*, 27.3: 137–63.

Semino, E. (1996), 'Possible Worlds in Poetry', *Journal of Literary Semantics*, 25.3: 189–224.

Semino, E. (1997), *Language and World Creation in Poems and Other Texts*, Harlow: Longman.

Sheller, M. and Urry, J. (2006), 'The New Mobilities Paradigm', *Journal of Environment and Planning*, 38: 207–26.

Stockwell, P. (2005), 'Texture and Identification', *European Journal of English Studies*, 9.2: 143–53.

Stockwell, P. (2009), *Texture: A Cognitive Aesthetics of Reading*, Edinburgh: Edinburgh University Press.

Stockwell, P. (2011a), 'Authenticity and Creativity in Reading Lamentation', in R. Pope, J. Swann and R. Carter (eds), *Creativity in Language*, Basingstoke: Palgrave Macmillan: 203–16.

Stockwell, P. (2011b), 'Ethics and Imagination in Literary Reading', in R. Jones (ed.), *Discourse and Creativity*, London: Pearson: 35–51.

Stockwell, P. (2014), 'Creative Reading, World and Style in Ben Jonson's "To Celia"', in B. Dancygier, M. Borkent and J. Hinnell (eds), *Language in the Creative Mind*, Stanford, CA: CLSI: 157–72.

Stockwell, P. (2016), *The Language of Surrealism*, Basingstoke: Palgrave Macmillan.

van der Bom, I. (2015), *Text World Theory and Stories of Self*, Unpublished PhD Thesis, University of Sheffield.

Vassilopolou, K. (2008), '"Why Get Upset over a Few Cases of Rhinoceritis?": Possible Worlds in the Theatre of the Absurd', in G. Watson (ed.), *The State of Stylistics*, Amsterdam: Rodopi: 155–75.

Werth, P. (1994), 'Extended Metaphor: A Text-World Account', *Language and Literature*, 3.2: 79–103.

Werth, P. (1995a), 'How to Build a World (in a Lot Less than Six Days and Using Only What's in Your Head)', in K. Green (ed.), *New Essays on Deixis: Discourse, Narrative, Literature*, Amsterdam: Rodopi: 49–80.

Werth, P. (1995b), ' "World Enough and Time": Deictic Space and the Interpretation of Prose', in P. Verdonk and J.-J. Weber (eds), *Twentieth Century Fiction: From Text to Context*, London: Routledge: 181–205.

Werth, P. (1999), *Text Worlds: Representing Conceptual Space in Discourse*, Harlow: Longman.

Whiteley, S. (2011a), 'Talking about "An Accommodation": The Implications of Discussion Group Data for Community Engagement and Pedagogy', *Language and Literature*, 20.3: 236–56.

Whiteley, S. (2011b), 'Text World Theory, Real Readers and Emotional Responses to *The Remains of the Day*', *Language and Literature*, 20.1: 23–42.

Whiteley, S. (2014), 'Ethics', in P. Stockwell and S. Whiteley (eds), *The Cambridge Handbook of Stylistics*, Cambridge: Cambridge University Press: 393–407.

Yacavone, D. (2014), *Film Worlds: A Philosophical Aesthetics of Cinema*, New York: Columbia University Press.

'I felt like I'd stepped out of a different reality': Possible Worlds Theory, Metalepsis and Digital Fiction

Alice Bell

2.1 Introduction

This chapter offers a possible-worlds approach to metalepsis (Bell and Alber 2012) and, through its application to digital fiction, profiles a transmedial approach to this narratological device. It begins with an overview of the theory of metalepsis before arguing that conceptualizing metalepses as transgressions between worlds as opposed to the more abstract concept of diegetic levels more accurately accounts for what readers are asked to imagine happens when they encounter a metalepsis. It then shows how Possible Worlds Theory – and the concepts of counterparthood and transworld identity in particular – provides a systematic and replicable means of analysing metalepsis.

By combining the possible-worlds approach with a stylistic and multimodal analysis of Andy Campbell and Judi Alston's (2010) *Nightingale's Playground* this chapter shows how metalepses are enacted in digital fiction, not just through verbal language as is typical in print texts, but also through non-textual elements such as sound, images and interactive interface elements. Further, it shows that digital fiction allows metalepses to take place across the actual-fictional world boundary so as to insert the reader within the fiction in a way that is simply not possible in print. The chapter concludes that Possible Worlds Theory is able to model metalepses more accurately than other narrative theories that do not have an ontological focus. Yet while it can facilitate both a transmedial and media-specific analysis, it requires some modification for its application to digital fiction.

2.2   What is metalepsis?

A metalepsis, as initially defined by Genette (1980) is 'any intrusion by
the extradiegetic narrator or narratee into the diegetic universe (or by the
diegetic characters into a metadiegetic universe, etc.), or the inverse' (234–
5). Metalepsis is thus a term that describes the movement of entities between
what are, according to actual world logic, distinct realms. Metalepses can be
'descending' (Pier 2005) in which a fictional entity moves from a diegetic level
to a hierarchically lower one as in, for example, Woody Allen's short story 'The
Kugelmass Episode' (1980), in which university professor Kugelmass hires a
magician to help him enter the fictional world of *Madame Bovary*. Alternatively
when a fictional entity moves from a diegetic level to a hierarchically higher
level, the metaleptic jump is 'ascending' (Pier 2005). This happens in, for example, Flann O'Brien's (1939) *At Swim-Two-Birds*, when the characters that are
invented by the fictional author, Dermot Trellis, check themselves into his hotel
to torture him.

Metalepses, as Herman (1997) notes, can also 'dissolve the border not just
between diegetic levels, but also between the actual and the non-actual – or
rather between two different systems of actuality' (134). Thus 'metalepsis' is
also used to describe instances in which authors appear in their own works
(e.g. Chen 2008; Kukkonen 2011) such as Jonathan Coe's appearance at the end
of his novel *The Terrible Privacy of Maxwell Sim* (2010), and also in instances
of second-person address to the reader (e.g. Fludernik 2003: 389; McHale
1997: 89–95) such as the address to 'you' at the beginning of Italo Calvino's
(1979) *If On A Winter's Night a Traveller*. Crucially, in all cases of metalepses,
an entity moves across an ontological boundary.

2.2.1   Metalepsis and ontology

Following the original Genettean definition, some narratologists analyse
metalepses in terms of transgressions between diegetic or narrative levels (e.g. Cohn 2012; Fludernik 2003). This form of analysis can be applied
to texts, such as 'The Kugelmass Episode' and *At Swim-Two-Birds*, in which
metalepses take place across boundaries that exist within the fictional world
only because diegetic levels can be analysed within this space. However, other
metalepses, such as the appearance of the author within their work or the use
of second-person address, do not suit this model as well because the actual
world is not properly accounted for in a diegetic level model. When Jonathan

Coe appears in *The Terrible Privacy of Maxwell Sim*, a diegetic level analysis would propose that a fictionalized version of Coe exists as a quasi-narrator figure in an extradiegetic level. This narrator then intrudes into the diegetic level below him. However, this does not accurately model what readers are asked to imagine happens when Coe appears in his novel; they are supposed to believe that Coe in the text is Coe, the author from the actual world and that an ontological boundary has been violated. While the ontological peculiarity of the device is especially pronounced in instances in which the actual-to-fictional boundary is crossed, all cases of metalepsis ask readers to imagine that entities have moved between worlds. The characters from Dermot Trellis's novel move from the world *in* which they were created to the world *from* which they were created; Kugelmass moves from a fictional world in which Emma from *Madame Bovary* was created to an embedded fictional world in which she exists.

Adopting the term 'world' as opposed to 'level' in textual analysis seeks to address the narrative mechanics of metalepsis more authentically by emphasizing the ontological nature of the device. However, it is also significant for the method of analysis because it allows tools that are specifically designed to analyse the relationship between worlds to be utilized. In line with the methodological remit of stylistic analysis, I suggest that established concepts and terminology from Possible Worlds Theory, a systematic and comprehensive framework that is designed specifically to analyse worlds and the interactions between them, can be adopted (Bell and Alber 2012).

2.3   Possible Worlds Theory as an approach to fiction

As a theory that is founded on propositional modal logic, Possible Worlds Theory is primarily concerned with the relationship between the 'actual world' – the world we belong to – and 'possible worlds' – worlds that are constructed through imagination, hypothetical situations, dreams, wishes and so on. While Possible Worlds Theory originates in philosophical logic (e.g. Hintikka 1967; Kripke 1972; Lewis 1973; Plantinga 1974), it can also be used in a narratological context (Ryan 1991) because the world described by a fictional text represents a particular type of possible world: a textual actual world. As a methodological approach, Possible Worlds Theory provides appropriate terminology for labelling different ontological domains and is extremely proficient at analysing complicated ontological configurations. It is therefore especially effective for analysing fictions that play self-reflexively with ontological structures (e.g. Ashline 1995; Bell 2010; Punday 1997; Ryan 2001) including metaleptic texts (cf. Pier 2011). Most relevant to the study of metalepsis are the possible-worlds concepts of 'transworld identity' and 'counterparthood' which can be used to explain the process whereby individuals can be cross-identified between different worlds (e.g. Margolin 1990; Pavel 1979) and thus can ultimately be used to explain the ontological mechanics of metalepsis.

2.3.1   Possible Worlds Theory, counterparthood and transworld identity

While 'transworld identity' and 'counterparthood' both originate in possible-worlds philosophical logic, they each have a distinct and, crucially, contradictory theoretical heritage: the 'abstractionist' and 'concretist' schools of possible-worlds logic respectively (Nolan 2002). Historically, when Possible Worlds Theory has been applied to literary texts, this inconsistency has been largely ignored. However, when using Possible Worlds Theory to analyse metalepsis, it is imperative that concepts from both schools are available but also, as the section below explains, kept distinct.

From a 'concretist' perspective (e.g. Lewis 1973) possible worlds comprise tangible domains which materially exist; they have the same ontological status as the actual world. According to this view, the individuals that populate possible worlds exist in the same way that the individuals that populate the actual world exist; constituents of both possible worlds and actual worlds are concrete. An entity in the actual world cannot be the *same* entity as that in a possible world because it is impossible for them to exist simultaneously with the same ontological status (i.e. actual) in two different worlds. As Lewis (1983) explains, 'worlds do not overlap ... No possible individual is part of two worlds' (39). From Lewis's concretist perspective, therefore, it is impossible for the same individual to exist within a number of different possible worlds. Each individual within each possible world is a 'counterpart' of the others as opposed to the same individual travelling between domains.

Conversely, from an 'abstractionist' perspective (e.g. Hintikka 1967; Kripke 1972; Plantinga 1974), possible worlds represent the way things might have been rather than how they actually are within an alternative ontological domain. While the actual world is a concrete domain, possible worlds comprise imaginary conceptions only. Accordingly, their constituents, including the individuals that populate them, are also only imaginary. According to this philosophical position, the same individual *can* travel between and thus exist within a number of different ontological contexts. As Kripke (1972) explains 'in talking about what would have happened to Nixon in a certain counterfactual situation, we are talking about what would have happened to him' (44). Kripke refutes that the same individual exists in different ontological domains as a counterpart and instead the same individual is seen to travel between the potentially infinite numbers of possible worlds. Individuals therefore possess what abstractionists refer to as 'transworld identity'.

While originating in philosophical logic, these two concepts can be used in a narratological analysis of metalepses. For instance, in the descending metalepsis in 'The Kugelmass Episode' described above, when Kugelmass pursues Emma Bovary, readers are asked to imagine that Kugelmass has left one textual actual world and moved to another textual actual world; in possible-worlds terminology, Kugelmass possess transworld identity.

In other instances of metalepsis, the concept of 'counterparthood' is required because readers need to keep two versions of an individual in mind at the same time. In *The Terrible Privacy of Maxwell Sim* when Jonathan Coe talks to protagonist Maxwell about the creative process of writing the novel, readers are asked to believe that Jonathan Coe from the actual world now also exists in the textual actual world described in the novel. However, in order that readers can recognize the figure that sits in the train carriage as Jonathan Coe, they have to know that Jonathan Coe also exists as the author of that text in the actual world. Jonathan Coe's descending metaleptic jump is therefore not an example of transworld identity because he has not made a permanent transition from actual to the textual actual. Instead it is an example of counterparthood: Jonathan Coe exists in the actual world as the author of *The Terrible Privacy of Maxwell Sim* and Jonathan Coe also exists in the textual actual world as a character with the same ontological status as the other characters. The two Jonathan Coe figures are thus counterparts of one another.

2.4   Metalepsis and non-print media

The preceding section presents a systematic and replicable approach to metalepsis in fiction which can, in theory, be applied to any fictional narrative containing a metaleptic jump. Until relatively recently, research on metalepsis has primarily focused on printed narratives and thus on exclusively verbal manifestations of this device. Yet as Kukkonen (2011) notes 'metalepsis ... occurs in a variety of multimodal media' (18) and different media 'allow for different ways of depicting the fictional and the real world, of drawing and identifying the boundary between them and of realizing different types, effects and functions of the transgression of these boundaries' (18–19) (cf. Ryan 2006). Within recent studies that analyse non-print texts, analyses show how the affordances of various media facilitate different kinds of metalepsis. This chapter will contribute to that research by analysing metalepsis in digital fiction.

Digital fiction is 'fiction that is written for and read on a computer screen, that pursues its verbal, discursive and/or conceptual complexity through the digital medium, and that would lose something of its aesthetic function if it were removed from that medium' (Bell et al. 2010). Digital fiction is therefore 'born digital'; it is created for and through digital media rather than being converted from print. It includes hypertext fiction, kinetic poetry, flash fiction, and some videogames. Digital fictions are often multimodal, so that in addition to text, they may use images, film, sound or animation to depict the textual actual world. Further, in almost all digital fictions the reader has an overt role in constructing the narrative (e.g. by selecting hyperlinks or by responding to textual cues) so that the reader must interact with the narrative throughout the reading experience.

Using the possible-worlds approach outlined above, this chapter provides two examples of metalepsis in a Web-based digital fiction called *Nightingale's Playground*. It will show how metalepses can be enacted multimodally and how the digital context allows multimodality to work alongside the reader's interactive role. By analysing two examples of media-specific metalepsis, this essay will also examine the extent to which the possible-worlds approach can be used to analyse metalepsis in non-print media.

2.5   Metalepsis in *Nightingale's Playground*

Andy Campbell and Judi Alston's *Nightingale's Playground* is an eerie first-person Web-based narrative. Split into four parts, the narrative focuses on protagonist Carl and in particular his relationship with his old school friend Alex Nightingale. The narrative reveals that the two friends bonded while playing the 1980s cult 8-bit videogame *The Sentinel*, in which players have to get closer to the all-seeing, all-powerful 'Sentinel' without being noticed. As *Nightingale's Playground* progresses and readers learn more about Carl and his past, his narrative seems to become less reliable as some parts of the text suggest that Alex may not have existed at all. However, the narrative leaves it ambiguous as to whether Carl has imagined part of his past and is therefore psychologically unwell or whether something supernatural, and related to the Sentinel from the videogame, has happened that has meant that Alex and everyone else's memory of him has been erased. The work uses text, static and moving images and sound effects and, as is typical in digital fiction, the reader must click on objects onscreen to reveal text. Thus, engaging with what Ensslin (2014) has defined as a 'literary-ludic' feature, readers must take part in the textual game: they can also only progress to the next part of the narrative once all sections of a particular sequence have been visited.

2.5.1 Analysis 1: The metaleptic cursor and counterparthood

Entering the first 'chapter' of the text, titled Consensus Trance I, the reader is presented with a darkened bedroom scene as shown in Figure 2.1.

  The bedroom looks decrepit and contains a minimal amount of furniture – just an old mattress and wooden chair. The wall has pieces of wallpaper missing and the carpet is worn. The room has no light apart from that coming from the window; the shadows that this causes make the room quite difficult to see clearly. A red suitcase on a stripped bed suggests either that someone has just arrived or that they are leaving. Either way, this is not a particularly homely or welcoming environment.

Figure 2.1 Bedroom scene in Consensus Trance I in *Nightingale's Playground*

As with many other digital fictions, the reader is given instructions on the first screen using the second-person: 'Use the mouse to pan around and click on narratives you have read.' Here the imperative gives the reader two commands with the verbs drawing attention to their two different roles: 'pan' to their exploratory function and 'click' to their interactive role. As the reader moves the cursor, the screen pans around and the visual point of view – or what Ciccoricco (2012) following Thon (2009) has called 'point of action' – shifts. This exploratory function means that the reader is given partial responsibility for the visual perspective. The narrative that they uncover is verbal however; when the reader clicks on particular areas of the room, she discovers text and the narrative advances.

As the reader explores the surroundings by moving the mouse, she is also able to delve into the narrator's space and his belongings. For example, clicking on the red suitcase in the room, the visual perspective moves with the reader to the case before zooming in to give her a closer look. The narrator then tells us that 'I took some things out of the case for a closer look'. In order that the reader can see the contents of the case, the reader has to click the mouse on the case again. The case then opens and the point of view zooms in again so that we can see items inside it more closely. Clicking on individual objects within the case such as a calculator and a videogame case, we get more textual information about those objects from the narrator in the first person. There is a mixing of roles and perspectives here. The point of view is narrated verbally by the protagonist in the past tense, but the visual perspective is both his and ours in the present tense.

The reader's relationship to the textual actual world in *Nightingale's Playground* can be explained by utilizing Ryan's (1991, 2008) possible-worlds concept of 'recentring', a theory developed to explain readers' relationships to fictional worlds in general. Ryan (2008) suggests that 'through their act of make-believe, readers, spectators, or players transport themselves in imagination from the world they regard as actual towards an alternative possible world – a virtual reality – which they regard as actual for the duration of their involvement in the text, game, or spectacle ... I call this projection into a virtual body an imaginative recentering' (251, cf. Ryan 1991: 21–3). Recentring is thus an epistemological process by which readers imagine and therefore, to some extent, believe that the textual actual world described by a text really does exist; for the duration of their reading, readers 'recentre' or deictically relocate (cf. McIntyre 2006) into that textual actual world. Ryan (1991) explains, 'we know that the textual universe, as a whole, is an imaginary alternative to our system of reality; but for the duration of the game, as we step into it, we behave as if the actual world of the text textual universe were *the* actual world' (23).

As Ryan also acknowledges in the first quotation above, recentring occurs whenever readers encounter a fictional narrative of any kind – they can be 'readers, spectators, or players' – and this means that the concept of recentring can apply to and also be analysed in a range of media. Accordingly, recentring is not always stimulated verbally but can also be stimulated by a range of modes (cf. van Looy 2005). In *Nightingale's Playground*, readers are recentred via verbal, visual and audible cues. In some cases, the recentring is instigated via one mode exclusively. For example, when the narrator tells us that 'Yesterday I went to a school reunion in the hope of meeting up with my old best friend Alex Nightingale', readers regard the adverb 'yesterday' as referring to a temporal point in the textual actual world, rather than the actual world, but there are no corresponding visuals to confirm that. By contrast, when Carl tells us that he 'ended up in this Hellish place', readers process the proximal demonstrative, 'this', as referring to the room that is depicted visually on the screen. The reader is recentred multimodally therefore by text and image working together.

Irrespective of the modes at work which recentre the reader epistemologically and cognitively, the reader of any text is of course corporeally and thus ontologically external from the textual actual world in the actual world. The external position in this digital reading experience is emphasized further for the reader because of her interactive function. By moving and clicking the mouse, she is reminded that she is involved in constructing and reading a fiction. However, because the reader's choices are symbolized onscreen by the cursor which she uses to explore and inspect the textual actual world (e.g. the bedroom, the suitcase, etc.), a trace of the reader can also be seen within it.

The digitalized trace of the reader is especially apparent when she explores some of the items closely – as in the suitcase. As explained above, in order to learn more about the contents of the suitcase, she moves the mouse onto that item so that the visual point of view moves and zooms to that item. This draws the reader's visual perspective into the textual actual world. However, as a reader she has to do this from her position at the computer in the actual world. The distinction between these two spaces and the reader's two different roles is signalled visually throughout this particular work by the border that surrounds the visual representation of the textual actual world on the screen. As Figure 2.1 shows, the space on which the reader has influence and in which the narrative unfolds is contained within a gilded picture frame, with the exterior that surrounds it containing the title and instructions only, acting as a kind of permanent front matter for the narrative. Thus, the reader is able to influence her view of the world by moving the mouse in the actual world, but we also get a digital trace of the reader within the textual actual world via the cursor. The cursor therefore acts as a visual and ontological manifestation of the recentred reader in the textual actual world.

Analysing the role of the mouse in human-computer interaction in general, Bizzocchi and Woodbury (2003) suggest 'we are so accustomed to this correlation [between hand movements and associated cursor movements] that it is perfectly transparent – we don't think about it, we don't question it, we don't even notice it' (558). However, when reading a digital literary text and one that allows readers to explore a graphical representation of the textual actual world, the cursor is ontologically salient because it grants the reader access to a distinct and autonomous ontological domain. Theorizing the ontologically intrusive nature of the cursor in digital fiction, Ryan (2006) suggests that the cursor is 'the representation of the reader's virtual body in the virtual world' (122). Ensslin's (2009) concept of 'double-situatedness' also implies dual ontology. She argues that 'on the one hand, user-readers are "embodied" as direct receivers, whose bodies interact with the hardware and software of a computer. On the other, user-readers are considered to be "reembodied" through feedback which they experience in represented form, for example through visible or invisible avatars (third-person or first-person graphic or typographic representations on screen)' (158). Both theorists thus suggest that the cursor is a version or a copy of the reader in an alternate space.

In *Nightingale's Playground*, the reader-as-cursor does not have the same ontological status as the characters in the textual actual world; the reader's presence is via the cursor rather than a character-like avatar as is typical in some videogames. However, as Ciccoricco (2012) notes, 'the mouse pointer is in effect a literal, analog representation of the reader's movement in the text' (262) and the reader-as-cursor does have a presence and some influence within the textual actual world of *Nightingale's Playground*. It thus represents a form of metalepsis because the reader appears to have crossed an ontological boundary, albeit in a digital form. From a theoretical perspective, within Possible Worlds Theory, which relies on strict ontological categorizations based in philosophical logic, an entity belongs either to the actual world (and/or associated possible worlds) or to the textual actual world (and/or associated textual possible worlds), to both actual and textual actual, but, crucially, not in-between domains. Thus entities (such as the onscreen cursor) that are not completely textual-actual but that have a presence and influence in that realm compromise the theory to some extent.

Yet while the logical foundations of Possible Worlds Theory prohibit such ontological ambiguity, as the analysis above has shown, it is entirely possible within a digital literary context. Ronen (1994) regards logical violations as an unavoidable component of all types of fiction. She argues that 'the literary interpretation of possibility is ... bound to make use of possible world notions in a way that intensifies the autonomy of fictional worlds at the expense of doing justice to the *logical* meaning of possibility' (61, my emphasis). She therefore suggests that all fictional worlds compromise possible-worlds logic to some extent because the concerns of fiction are not those of possible-worlds logic. Most obviously, fictional texts construct worlds that readers interpret and enjoy rather than measure propositions against. From a cognitive point of view also, readers are adept at conceptualizing ontological configurations which do not necessarily obey the logic laws of the actual world so that ontological peculiarities such as the reader's role within the textual actual world of *Nightingale's Playground*, while perhaps uncanny, are part of that fictional experience and not necessarily problematic to process. The ontologically transgressive cursor simply represents a new, media-specific feature of storytelling, facilitated by the affordances digital technologies have brought. We might see the space that the reader occupies as the narrational part or mediating part of the textual actual world.

While the reader-as-cursor does not have the same ontological status as other entities within the textual actual world, she does have a presence and some influence within it. She exists in a digital form within the textual universe. At the same time, as reader of the fiction she also exists, corporeally, in the actual world. Like the case of Jonathan Coe appearing in his own fiction, analysed above, the reader is also present in two different ontological domains at the same time and she enacts a form of descending metalepsis. Yet unlike in Coe's print text, where the author appears verbally, the reader appears visually. Using the possible-worlds approach to metalepsis, we can make the analysis more systematic by seeing the cursor as a *counterpart* of the reader. Readers are situated in the actual world but they are ultimately doubly-situated because of their presence within the textual actual world or, rather, this is a form of digital counterparthood.

Kukkonen (2011) hypothesizes that 'narrative research into hypertext forms ... will certainly reveal a wealth of what I would call "interactional metalepsis"' (18) and the metaleptic cursor would seem to offer one such case. Since all digital fictions utilize some form of onscreen navigational aid, the cursor-as-reader counterpart relation and associated digital metalepsis is not necessarily exclusive to *Nightingale's Playground* (see Bell 2014 for another example of a metaleptic cursor). However, the verbal and, crucially, visual point of view within the text does allow the reader to permeate the textual universe and intrude into this fictional space in a way that is certainly not possible in print. It reveals how the cursor represents an exclusively digital metaleptic jump and also that Possible Worlds Theory can, with some modification, be combined with media-specific analysis (Hayles 2002) to analyse it.

2.5.2   Analysis 2: Audible metalepsis and transworld identity

In addition to the verbal and visual representation that the reader receives of the textual actual world, *Nightingale's Playground* also contains a permanent audio accompaniment. Some audio, on the opening sequences, is 'non-diegetic', which is 'mood music ... represented as being outside the space of the narrative' (Stam, 1992: 62, cf. Horowitz and Loone, 2014: 76 who consider sound in computer games). In the sequence depicted in Figure 2.1 above, for example, eerie background music plays which, when combined with the visual darkness of the room, creates a rather sinister atmosphere for the narrative. Other audio is diegetic or 'sounds represented as emerging from a source within the story, and temporally simultaneous with the image it accompanies' (Stam, 1992: 62). These sound effects are not just creating atmosphere, therefore, but instead are intended to represent for the reader what the narrator can or could hear at the time. Readers are to believe that the sounds originate ontologically in the textual actual world. Examples in *Nightingale's Playground* include the sound of street noise when the reader's visual point of view is directed through a window; rain falling outside when a storm is shown on screen; and the sound of a busy urban landscape when the reader is given a view of a high street (see Figure 2.2).

In each case of the three examples mentioned above, textual narration accompanies the image. In the high street scene in Figure 2.2, we learn from the text that the narrator was in a confused mental state. He says 'I didn't realize at first that I'd brought the red case into town with me' and later that 'I felt like I'd stepped out of a different reality. Everyone droning around oblivious'. The narrative here is past tense and thus so is Carl's recollection of what happened on this particular day. That the reader can hear the street scene is

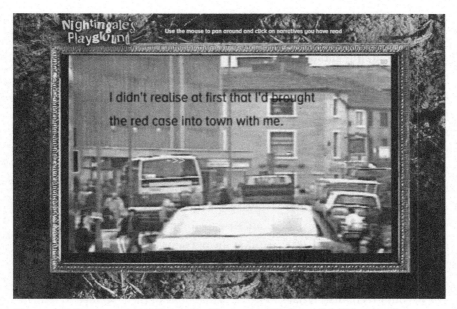

Figure 2.2 Street scene in Consensus Trance 1 in *Nightingale's Playground*

therefore ontologically and temporally anomalous because it suggests that we are witnessing his memory and/or Carl's past bleeding into the present.

The various diegetic sounds in *Nightingale's Playground* ultimately constitute a form of ascending metalepsis because in each case a noise that originates in the textual actual world crosses the ontological boundary to reach the reader in the actual world (cf. Keazor 2011). While sound effects are used in various audio-visual media, such as cinematic film, and are therefore not necessarily uncommon, in this digital fiction the diegetic sounds are intermittent and thus the metalepsis is foregrounded at particular points in the narrative. It is as though part of the textual actual world leaks into the actual world, crossing what McHale (1987) calls the 'semipermeable membrane' (34) through which both worlds seem to be temporarily but uncannily accessible to one other. More specifically, because a perceptible sound moves from the textual actual to the actual world – rather than there being two versions of those noises – the noises possess transworld identity. In this case, therefore, an inanimate entity, not a character or narrator, encroaches into the actual world and so possesses transworld identity. That this digital fiction shows inanimate metaleptic components is significant from a theoretical point of view because most studies of metalepsis focus on the movement of a character and/or narrator between ontological domains and thus on sentient components from a textual actual world. This example shows, however, that digital fiction allows inanimate objects to perform metaleptic jumps across world boundaries.

This ascending audible metalepses implies that the textual actual world can intrude into the reader's physical-sensory space. However, that the reader has access to the narrator's past world, via his memory, also means that she is intruding on the characters' private and personal (corporeal) space. The audible metalepses, like the metaleptic cursor, thus accentuate the reader's voyeuristic position in relation to the textual actual world. What is particularly unsettling about the cases of metalepsis in *Nightingale's Playground* is that by being able to access Carl's world via sound effects and exploring the textual actual world as a 'doubly-situated' counterpart, we are witness to if not corroborating with what is potentially a disturbed mind. As explained earlier, as we move through *Nightingale's Playground*, we learn that the narrator might not be as reliable as we might have initially thought. While Carl remembers his old school friend Alex Nightingale, his other school friends don't know who Alex Nightingale is. The narrator recounts, 'What's weird … is that none of them seemed to remember Alex at all.' Later in the narrative, Carl reports an interaction between him and his grandmother: 'I felt a chill down my back. She sounded a bit like Alex.' The narrator thus suggests that his grandmother might not be what she appears to be. He recounts elsewhere that his grandmother advises 'that there were things in the world, happenings, that she didn't understand, and neither would I, and neither would anyone else, and that sometimes it was best to just leave them alone.' In the context of Carl's narrative, this cautionary statement seems sinister rather than friendly familial reassurance, but the reality of this remains ambiguous.

In *Nightingale's Playground* readers are positioned visually, verbally and, sometimes, ontologically with the narrator, but we are not sure whether we can trust his perspective. The ontological status of Carl's tale is thus questionable. Further, while we are privy to the narrator's musings and allowed to explore the textual actual world to some extent, the reader is actually unable to explore it comprehensively because she belongs to a different ontological domain. There is a tension between epistemological access to intimate thoughts and the simulated ontological access to the textual actual world, and the actual ontological exclusion from the textual actual world. The reader is powerless within the textual actual world beyond what the narrator and the machine code will allow. Ultimately, readers do not find out what has really happened to Carl and/or Alex.

2.6 Conclusion

Metalepsis can be found in a range of different media including print and digital fiction, film, television, theatre, videogames and comics. This chapter has shown metaleptic jumps can manifest textually, visually and audibly and that a multimodal analysis is needed if these different forms of representation are to be captured. In particular, the analysis of two different kinds of media-specific metalepsis has shown that the affordances of Web technology can produce varying types of ontological violation. Sound effects act as ascending metalepses which suggest that elements from the textual actual world are able to cross into the actual world. While audible metalepsis could be found in other types of text that incorporate sound, the analysis of the cursor has shown that *Nightingale's Playground*, and digital fictions in general, contains a metaleptic feature that is exclusively digital.

This chapter has also profiled a possible-worlds approach to metalepsis. In particular, the concepts of transworld identity, in which an entity moves from one world to another, and counterparthood, in which an entity exists in two different worlds at the same time, can be applied to both descending and ascending metalepses. The analysis of the metaleptic cursor shows how the actual-to-textual-actual boundary can be breached in digital media in a way that is simply not possible in other media such as print or cinema. However, the visual trace of the reader in the text means Possible Worlds Theory needs to accommodate the appearance of the reader in an in-between, or mediated, ontological space if it is to become a truly transmedial approach. The analysis of sound effects also shows that the same actual-to-textual-actual boundary can be breached by inanimate as well as animate objects. The theory of transworld identity from Possible Worlds Theory must thus be expanded to accommodate the metaleptic movement of inanimate objects, as opposed to just characters, across world boundaries.

As the examples throughout this chapter have shown, all forms of metalepses inevitably challenge theories of narrative, and in this case Possible Worlds Theory, because they flout the real-world logical and spatial parameters on which these theories rest. Echoing the way that the reader interacts with the text throughout their reading experience, digital fictions appear to allow two worlds to dissolve into each other. Representing a form of media-specific metalepses therefore, they demonstrate some of the innovative narrative possibilities that digital technologies can bring to fiction.

Acknowledgement

The collaborative research on metalepis and unnatural narrative, with Dr. Jan Alber, that informs this chapter was originally funded by the British Academy (Small Research Grant Ref: SG100637).

References

Allen, W. (1980), 'The Kugelmass Episode', *Side Effects*, New York: Random House: 41–55.
Ashline, W. L. (1995), 'The Problem of Impossible Fictions', *Style*, 29.2: 215–34.
Bell, A. (2010), *The Possible Worlds of Hypertext Fiction*, Basingstoke: Palgrave Macmillan.
Bell, A. (2014), 'Media-Specific Metalepsis in *10:01*', in A. Bell, A. Ensslin and H. Rustad (eds), *Analyzing Digital Fiction*, New York: Routledge: 21–38.
Bell, A. and Alber. J. (2012), 'Ontological Metalepsis and Unnatural Narratology', *Journal of Narrative Theory*, 42.2: 166–92.
Bell, A., Ensslin, A., Pressman, J., Laccetti, J., Ciccoricco, D. and Rustad, H. (2010), 'A [S]creed for Digital Fiction', *Electronic Book Review* <http://www.electronicbookreview.com/thread/electropoetics/DFINative> [accessed 14 April 2015].
Bizzocchi, J. and Woodbury, R. F. (2003), 'A Case Study in the Design of Interactive Narrative: The Subversion of the Interface', *Simulation & Gaming*, 34.4: 550–68.
Calvino, I. (2007 [1979]), *If on a Winter's Night a Traveller*, London: Random House.
Campbell, A. and Alston, J. (2010), *Nightingale's Playground* <http://nightingalesplayground.com/> [accessed 14 April 2015].
Chen, F. F. (2008), 'From Hypotyposis to Metalepsis: Narrative Devices in Contemporary Fantastic Fiction', *Forum for Modern Language Studies*, 44.4: 394–411.
Ciccoricco, D. (2012), 'Focalization and Digital Fiction', *Narrative*, 20.3: 255–76.
Coe, J. (2010), *The Terrible Privacy of Maxwell Sim*, London: Penguin.
Cohn, D. (2012), 'Metalepsis and Mise en Abyme', *Narrative*, 20.1: 105–14.
Ensslin, A. (2009), 'Respiratory Narrative: Multimodality and Cybernetic Corporeality in "Physio-cybertext"', in R. Page (ed.), *New Perspectives on Narrative and Multimodality*, London: Routledge: 155–65.
Ensslin, A. (2014), *Literary Gaming*, Cambridge, MA: MIT Press.
Fludernik, M. (2003), 'Scene Shift, Metalepsis and the Metaleptic Mode', *Style*, 37.4: 382–400.
Genette, G. (1980), *Narrative Discourse: An Essay in Method*, trans. J. E. Lewin, Ithaca, NY: Cornell University Press.
Hayles, K. (2002), *Writing Machines*, Cambridge, MA: MIT Press.

Herman, D. (1997), 'Towards a Formal Description of Narrative Metalepsis', *Journal of Literary Semantics*, 26.2: 132–52.

Hintikka, J. (1967), 'Individuals, Possible Worlds, and Epistemic Logic', *Nous*, 1: 33–62.

Horowitz, S. and Loone, S. R. (2014), *The Essential Guide to Game Audio: The Theory and Practice of Sound for Games*, Abingdon: Focal Press.

Keazor, H. (2011), 'Metalepsis in Music Videos', in K. Kukkonen and S. Klimek (eds), *Metalepsis in Popular Culture*, Berlin, Germany: Walter de Gruyter: 104–26.

Kripke, S. (1972), *Naming and Necessity*, Oxford: Blackwell.

Kukkonen, K. (2011), 'Metalepsis in Popular Culture: An Introduction', in K. Kukkonen and S. Klimek (eds), *Metalepsis in Popular Culture*, Berlin, Germany: Walter de Gruyter: 1–21.

Lewis, D. (1973), *Counterfactuals*, Oxford: Blackwell.

Lewis, D. (ed.) (1983), 'Postscripts to "Counterpart Theory and Quantified Modal Logic"', in *Philosophical Papers: Volume 1*, Oxford: Oxford University Press: 39–46.

McHale, B. (1987), *Postmodernist Fiction*, London and New York: Routledge.

McHale, B. (1997), *Constructing Postmodernism*, London and New York: Routledge.

McIntyre, D. (2006), *Point of View in Plays: A Cognitive Stylistic Approach to Viewpoint in Drama and Other Text-Types*, Philadelphia, PA: John Benjamins Publishing.

Margolin, U. (1990), 'Individuals in Narrative Worlds: An Ontological Perspective', *Poetics Today: Narratology Revisited II*, 11.4: 843–71.

Nolan, D. (2002), *Topics in the Philosophy of Possible Worlds*, London: Routledge.

O'Brien, F. (1967 [1939]), *At Swim-Two-Birds*, London: Penguin.

Pavel, T. G. (1979), 'Fiction and the Casual Theory of Names', *Poetics*, 8.1–2: 179–91.

Pier, J. (2005), 'Metalepsis', in D. Herman, M. Jahn, and M.-L. Ryan (eds), *The Routledge Encyclopedia of Narrative Theory*, London: Routledge: 303–4.

Pier, J. (2011), 'Afterword', in K. Kukkonen and S. Klimek (eds), *Metalepsis in Popular Culture*, Berlin, Germany: Walter de Gruyter: 268–76.

Plantinga, A. (1974), *The Nature of Necessity*, Oxford: Clarendon Press.

Punday, D. (1997), 'Meaning in Postmodern Worlds: The Case of *The French Lieutenant's Woman*', *Semiotica*, 115.3–4: 313–43.

Ronen, R. (1994), *Possible Worlds in Literary Theory*, Cambridge: Cambridge University Press.

Ryan, M. L. (1991), *Possible Worlds, Artificial Intelligence and Narrative Theory*, Bloomington, IN: Indiana University Press.

Ryan, M. L. (2001), *Narrative as Virtual Reality: Immersion and Interactivity in Literature and Electronic Media*, Baltimore, ML: John Hopkins University Press.

Ryan, M. L. (2006), *Avatars of Story*, Minneapolis, MN: University of Minnesota Press.

Ryan, M. L. (2008), 'Fictional Worlds in the Digital Age', in S. Schreibman and R. Siemens (eds), *A Companion to Digital Literary Studies*, Oxford: Blackwell: 250–66.

Stam, R. (ed.) (1992), *New Vocabularies in Film Semiotics: Structuralism, Poststructuralism and Beyond*, London: Routledge.

Thon, J.-N. (2009), 'Perspectives in Contemporary Computer Games', in
    P. Hühn, W. Schmid and J. Schönert (eds), *Point of View, Perspective, and
    Focalization: Modelling Mediation in Narrative*, Berlin: de Gruyter: 279–300.
van Looy, J. (2005), 'Virtual Recentering: Computer Games and Possible Worlds
    Theory', *Image and Narrative*, 12 <http://www.imageandnarrative.be/inarchive/
    tulseluper/vanlooy.htm> [accessed 14 April 2015].

Author-Character *Ethos* in Dan Brown's Langdon-Series Novels

Ernestine Lahey

3.1 Introduction

Dan Brown (1964–) is an American novelist best known for his series of four thrillers featuring protagonist Robert Langdon: *Angels and Demons* (2009 [2000]), *The Da Vinci Code* (2004 [2003]), *The Lost Symbol* (2010 [2009]) and *Inferno* (2013). Each book sees Langdon – professor of 'symbology' at Harvard University – unwittingly thrust into the middle of a mysterious criminal plot which can only be unravelled with the help of his expert knowledge of ancient codes and symbols. The reader follows Langdon through an action-packed twenty-four-hour period, during which he cracks one cryptic code after another while revealing more and deeper layers of conspiracy and corruption within some of the world's most powerful organizations.

The novels in the Langdon series are among the best-selling books since records began (Mayer 2013; Rogers 2011, 2012). In what follows I argue that one of the reasons for the success of Brown's Langdon-series novels has to do with his enactment of a rhetorical *ethos* for his protagonist Robert Langdon. I furthermore argue that this enactment of character *ethos* has implications for Brown's own ethical appeal at the level of the discourse-world. My arguments will be supported by analysis combining traditional 'steam stylistic' (Carter 2010: 61) and text-world theoretical approaches. Text World Theory's facility for allowing a schematic representation of the worlds of a discourse (i.e. through diagramming) makes the theory a powerful analytic tool for stylistic analysis because it allows the analyst to see and track the relations between the different epistemic and deictic contexts prompted by a discourse. The importance of this capability of the theory is demonstrated in my analysis in Section 3.5 below.

My analysis reveals a need to rethink two aspects of contemporary Text World Theory. First, I question the applicability of the notion of the 'empty' text-world in cases of fixed focalization. Current Text World Theory suggests that the effect of fixed internal focalization is the formation of an epistemic modal focalization-world which serves as the matrix world from which all other worlds in the network derive (Gavins 2001: 133; Lahey 2004: 26). This is because where internal fixed focalization occurs, the resulting focalization-world represents the only point of access readers have to the contents of the narrative. All world-building and function-advancing propositions are provided via this focalization-world, rendering the text-world level redundant, or 'empty'. However, in the analysis that follows I suggest a rethinking of the role of empty text-worlds in the context of speech and thought presentation. Specifically, I argue that where speech and thought presentation indicate a level of reliability greater than that afforded to the matrix focalization-world, the deictic and epistemic modal-worlds prompted by speech and thought will be anchored in the backgrounded 'empty' text-world.

Second, I argue that the construction of text-worlds influences the construction of the discourse-worlds which surround them. Such upward influence from the text-world to the discourse-world level is not predicted by contemporary Text World Theory, in which the text-world is always considered to be a product of the discourse-world, rather than an element in its formation. As such this chapter not only presents a stylistic account of Brown's work, but also offers an important reconsideration of the theoretical foundations of Text World Theory.

3.2   *Ethos*

In his *Rhetoric*[1] Aristotle warns that it is not enough for a speech to appeal to reason; it must also convince the audience of the credibility of the speaker him/herself: '[W]e must have regard not only for the speech's being demonstrative and persuasive, but also to establishing the speaker himself as of a certain type and bringing the [audience] into a certain condition' (*Rhetoric* II.1, 1378a). *Ethos* (also known as an 'ethical appeal') is established when a speech suggests three qualities of the speaker: his or her good sense, high moral character (sometimes translated simply as 'virtue') and benevolence or good will (*Rhet.* II.1, 1378a).

---

[1] References to Aristotle's *Rhetoric* in this chapter are from two sources: a 1991 translation by Hugh Lawson-Tancred, and a 2004 re-issue of an early twentieth-century translation by W. Rhys Roberts (see References section). Lawson-Tancred's translation uses the title *The Art of Rhetoric*, while Roberts's translation employs the more commonly used short title, *Rhetoric*. I use the short form in all of my references to the work here, regardless of edition/translation.

Ethos may be enacted in myriad ways in a discourse. In addition to direct demonstration of the three elements noted above, *ethos* may also be established indirectly through the use of strategies associated with the other two rhetorical appeals – the appeal to reason (*logos*) and the emotional appeal (*pathos*) – as well as through the use of an appropriate style (Kinneavy and Warshauer 1994: 180). Furthermore, the grounds of argumentation for ceremonial discourse (also known as display oratory or *epideixis*) can also be exploited in enacting an ethical appeal. Ceremonial discourse is concerned with praise and blame; the aim is to highlight the virtues of an individual or, in blame-oriented speeches, to amplify his or her vices (*Rhet.* I.9, 1367b–1368a). That *ethos* should intertwine with the grounds of argumentation for ceremonial discourse is therefore logical, as both *ethos* and praise-type ceremonial discourses require a thorough understanding of the virtues that define 'the good' within a given community. In ceremonial discourses the virtues constitute the primary grounds for persuasion (in praise-type speeches). In the case of *ethos*, 'high moral character' is manifested when a speaker demonstrates an awareness of commonly held virtues. Contemporary treatments of *ethos* make this intersection with ceremonial discourse evident, citing extensively from Aristotle's chapter on display oratory (Altes 2014; Amossy 2002; Corbett and Connors 1999; Kinneavy and Warshauer 1994; Smith 2004).

Given the length of the texts under consideration and the space restrictions of this chapter, my coverage of *ethos* in Brown's novels is necessarily selective. While Langdon's *ethos* is manifested through Brown's handling of all the elements mentioned above, I attend to just three aspects of *ethos* which are especially prominent across the four novels. First, I analyse manifestations of Langdon's good sense, focusing specifically on his knowledge and expertise, especially as reflected through his reputation within the scholarly community. Second, I consider descriptions of Langdon's physical appearance. Physical attractiveness is mentioned in contemporary treatments of ceremonial discourse (see, e.g. Corbett and Connors 1999: 129), and is deemed an asset by Aristotle, who refers to beauty as a 'bodily virtue' and lists it among the elements of both human happiness and 'the good' (*Rhet.* I.5, 1360b; I.6, 1362a–1362b). Finally, I discuss Brown's depiction of Langdon's humility. Humility is one of the 'supreme virtues' of Western civilization, and is therefore a key resource for *ethos* (see the definition of high moral character above) (Corbett and Connors 1999: 127).

I am also especially concerned in what follows with one particular stylistic strategy used by Brown that foregrounds the three aspects of *ethos* outlined in the preceding paragraph. This strategy involves the juxtaposing of complimentary information about Langdon's character with diminishing modification to, or evaluations of, this information. Although subtle, this strategy is complicit in Brown's elaboration of all three of the *ethos* elements noted above, and is furthermore pervasive throughout the four novels.

3.3   Good sense

Of the core elements of *ethos* identified by Aristotle – good sense, high moral character and good will – good sense is most heavily emphasized in Brown's characterization of his hero, Robert Langdon. Good sense is demonstrated when one shows sufficient understanding of the subject at hand, a capability to advise on an effective course of action in a particular situation and an awareness of the particulars of the situation in which the discourse occurs (e.g. the surrounding political and social climate) (Kinneavy and Warshauer 1994: 178–9). Langdon's good sense is most obviously signalled through Brown's choice of profession for his hero. Langdon is a professor of symbology – an imaginary discipline that combines aspects of semiotics, history and art history – at Harvard University, one of the world's most respected academic institutions. This fact establishes Langdon as a credible hero in the context of these novels, in which expert knowledge of these fields is required to solve the mysteries around which the stories turn.

Brown capitalizes on Langdon's academic position by employing flashbacks to lectures Langdon has delivered at conferences and other scholarly events to showcase Langdon's extensive knowledge of his subject matter. These flashbacks also serve to highlight Langdon's good standing within the academic community. Excerpt 3.1 below from *Inferno* prefaces an extended flashback in which Langdon delivers a lecture at the Società Dante Alighieri Vienna:

Excerpt 3.1

As a noted student of Dante's work, Langdon had been asked to speak at a major event hosted by one of the world's oldest Dante societies – Società Dante Alighieri Vienna. The event was slated to take place at the Viennese Academy of Sciences. The event's primary sponsor ... had managed to secure the academy's two-thousand-seat lecture hall. (Brown 2013: 81)

Here Langdon's reputation as a 'noted' Dante scholar and his ability to fill a two-thousand-seat venue (a capacity well beyond the requirements of all but the most celebrated academic speakers) indicate that he is not only a respected but an in-demand figure. His celebrity status is even more overtly signalled in *The Da Vinci Code*:

Excerpt 3.2

[Langdon's] books on religious paintings and cult symbology had made him a reluctant celebrity in the art world [. . .].

Last month, much to Langdon's embarrassment, *Boston Magazine* had listed him as one of that city's top ten most intriguing people – a dubious honour that made him the brunt of endless ribbing by his Harvard colleagues. Tonight, three thousand miles from home, the accolade had resurfaced to haunt him at the lecture he had given.

'Ladies and gentlemen …' the hostess had announced to a full house at the American University of Paris's Pavillon Dauphine, 'Our guest tonight needs no introduction'. (Brown 2004: 18–19)

Excerpt 3.2 points to the esteem in which Langdon's academic work is held by his peers ('Langdon's books … had made him a reluctant celebrity in the art world'; 'Our guest … no introduction'), and again suggests his ability to attract a large audience to his lectures ('a full house'). Langdon's celebrity standing is a result of his scholarly efforts, a fact that is fundamental to his *ethos*. For Aristotle, '[n]oble … are [t]he things that win rewards and status, especially those that bring honour rather than money' (*Rhet.* I.9, 1366b). Langdon's books bring him respect within in the academic community, but their reach is limited (and thus we may assume they do not bring him much in the way of monetary rewards). The passage below from *Inferno* makes this last point more explicit.

Excerpt 3.3

'This is a great honour for me [. . .]. For Professor Langdon I would give a private tour at any hour. His little book *Christian Symbols in the Muslim World* is a favourite in our museum gift shop.'

Really? Langdon thought. *Now I know the one place on earth that carries that book.* (Brown 2013: 390, emphasis in original)

Excerpts 3.2 and 3.3 above also demonstrate a less obvious but recurrent stylistic technique that Brown uses in his construction of Langdon's *ethos* across all four Langdon-series novels. The technique involves the juxtaposing of complimentary facts about Langdon's character with diminishing modifications to, or evaluations of, these facts. Several examples of this technique can be seen in

Excerpt 3.2 above. The information that *Boston Magazine* has named Langdon as one of the city's most intriguing people is tempered by his embarrassment at this 'dubious' honour, which has come back to 'haunt' him during an event at The American University in Paris. The fact that Langdon is a celebrity in art history circles is likewise undercut: Langdon may be a celebrity, but he is a *'reluctant* celebrity'. In Excerpt 3.3, the information that one of Langdon's books is popular in a museum gift shop is counterbalanced by Langdon's surprise at (*'Really?'*) and self-deprecating response to (*'Now I know the one place on earth that carries that book'*) this information.

These juxtapositions do not involve clashing sense relations and therefore are not oxymora in the traditional sense (Gibbs, Jr. and Kearney 1994; Jeffries 2012: 1–2; Shen 1987). There is nothing paradoxical about responding to admiration with embarrassment or displeasure, nor is reluctance in any way antonymous to celebrity. What does typify the juxtapositions in Excerpts 3.2 and 3.3 above is that they involve either a clash in polarities (the positive or negative associations prompted by a word (Wilson, Wiebe and Hoffman 2005)), or else a disruption of expectations or schema-based knowledge (Jeffries 2012: 39).

Langdon's embarrassment at being honoured by *Boston Magazine* contrasts the positive semantic orientation of the word 'honour' with the negative associations of the words 'dubious' and 'embarrassed'. A similar contrast is produced through the juxtaposing of 'accolade' and 'haunt'. In the case of 'reluctant celebrity', the syntax of the adjective-noun pairing is partly responsible for the semantic dissonance of the juxtaposed elements. Following Grice, one assumes that a concept is modified for some particular purpose, namely to foreground an aspect of a concept that is not salient when unmodified (Estes and Ward 2002; Grice 1975: 150). Celebrity status is generally viewed positively: with celebrity typically come admiration, wealth and power, all valued assets in Western society. 'Reluctant celebrity' disrupts the expected schema for 'celebrity' by forcing a reassessment of celebrity status as less than desirable (Smith and Osherson 1984: 340).

The juxtapositions presented in Excerpt 3.3 also work to disrupt reader expectations. Langdon's response to the news of his book's popularity serves as a corrective to any assumptions a reader might entertain regarding the availability and popularity of his work elsewhere. Here the disruption operates at a local level. The reader who may have formed assumptions regarding Langdon's book's popularity in response to the speech of the museum employee finds these assumptions immediately invalidated by Langdon's own response in the very next move of the discourse. This kind of local disruption differs from that experienced as a result of 'reluctant celebrity' and 'dubious honour' above, both of which rely on modifications to discourse-external knowledge schemas for their dissonance.

In each of the juxtapositions discussed above, a positive assessment of Langdon's character is provided that bolsters his *ethos* by pointing to his good sense (e.g. 'honour' in 'dubious honour'). We might expect the diminishing evaluations which form the other pole of these juxtapositions to weaken the force of this appeal. However, Langdon's diminishing appraisals do not damage his *ethos*; on the contrary, they only serve to strengthen it further by highlighting his humility. I will return to this issue in Section 3.5 below.

3.4   Physical appearance

Descriptions of physical appearance can be powerful elements in *ethos* construction. Beauty is a 'bodily virtue' (*Rhet.* I.5, 1360b). It is indirectly implicated in Aristotle's grounds for argumentation in ceremonial discourse (*Rhet.* I.9, 1366a), and is explicitly mentioned in contemporary accounts of the same (see e.g. Corbett and Connors 1999: 129). Brown is clearly aware of the rhetorical force of physical description, as can be seen in the passage below from *Angels and Demons*.

Excerpt 3.4

Although not overly handsome in a classical sense, the forty-five-year-old Langdon had what his female colleagues referred to as an 'erudite' appeal – wisps of gray in his thick brown hair, probing blue eyes, an arrestingly deep voice, and the strong, carefree smile of a collegiate athlete. A varsity diver in prep school and college, Langdon still had the body of a swimmer, a toned, six-foot physique that he vigilantly maintained with fifty laps a day in the university pool. (Brown 2009: 21)

Langdon possesses the stock physical traits of the popular fiction hero: he is six feet tall, has thick hair and 'probing' eyes (Nash 1990: 111–12). However, relying again on his strategy of juxtaposition, Brown disassociates Langdon from a stereotyped brand of masculine beauty by describing him as 'not overly handsome in a classical sense' but as possessing an 'erudite appeal'. The adjective-noun pairing 'erudite appeal' has the same schema-disrupting effect as that seen above in 'reluctant celebrity'. In addition, while 'classically handsome' and 'erudite appeal' are not conventional opposites, Brown establishes them as opposites for the purposes of this discourse. This is accomplished through the use of what Davies refers to as a 'concessive opposition', a constructed oppositional structure triggered by the use of a concessive clause ('Although not handsome in a classical sense'), indicating that the information in the main clause ('erudite appeal') is unexpected (2008: 125–6; see also Jeffries 2012).

Exactly the same type of structure can be found in *The Da Vinci Code*. The flashback excerpted in Excerpt 3.2 above continues with the hostess of the event remarking: ' "Although Professor Langdon might not be considered hunk-handsome like some of our younger awardees, this forty-something academic has more than his share of scholarly allure" ' (Brown 2004: 20). The adjective-noun pairing 'scholarly allure' mimics 'erudite appeal' above, both syntactically and semantically, again suggesting the atypicality of the concept combination. Similarly, and also mirroring the structure of the juxtaposition in Excerpt 3.4 above, a concessive opposition is formed between 'hunk-handsome' and 'scholarly allure'. This opposition presents 'scholarly allure' as an unexpected attribute of male attractiveness, forcing a shift away from a stereotype based on physical beauty alone.

The juxtapositions 'classically handsome'/'erudite appeal' and 'hunk-handsome'/'scholarly allure' are novel surface-level manifestations of a familiar underlying dichotomy conventional in Western culture, between 'beauty' and 'brains'. Through his use of juxtaposition Brown challenges the stereotyped contrast between the two and suggests an alternative brand of attractiveness in which these traits are not mutually exclusive. In Langdon, beauty and brains coalesce; indeed, Langdon's appearance itself betrays his intellectual depths ('*erudite* appeal', '*scholarly* allure'). These passages of physical description therefore not only indicate Langdon's unique brand of male beauty, they also continue to signal his good sense – in both cases, Langdon's *ethos* benefits.

3.5   Humility

I noted in the introduction to this chapter that one of the advantages of Text World Theory for stylistic analysis is that it allows the analyst to track through the worlds of a discourse in a way that concretizes the deictic and epistemic relations between the various worlds of a text-world network. Such a capacity is crucial to my analysis of the third and final aspect of Langdon's *ethos* that I attend to in this chapter – depictions of his humility. As I argue in what follows, Brown's demonstration of Langdon's humility relies heavily on his manipulation of the accessibility (i.e. reliability) relations (Werth 1995: 61) associated with the worlds prompted by focalization and speech and thought presentation.

The chapters in which Langdon features as active participant are almost always focalized through his consciousness (exceptions include chapters focalized by the main female protagonist). This has implications for Langdon's *ethos* because it means the diminishing evaluations of his character presented in the juxtapositions discussed above are attributable to him. In Excerpt 3.2 the evaluative lexical choices 'reluctant', 'embarrassment', 'dubious' and 'haunt' reflect Langdon's perspective with regard to his inclusion on the *Boston Magazine* list and his attendant celebrity status. In Excerpt 3.3, free direct thought provides Langdon's self-deprecating stance towards his book's reach, while a positive assessment of his reputation and his book's popularity are provided via the direct speech of another character. Likewise, in Excerpt 3.4, the diminishing appraisal of Langdon's appearance ('Although not overly handsome in a classical sense') is Langdon's – the excerpt begins with Langdon studying his reflection in a window, signalling that the description which follows is filtered through his consciousness – while the attribution of 'erudite appeal' is assigned to the (indirect) speech of his female colleagues.

As noted in the introduction to this chapter, Text World Theory treats fixed internal focalization as resulting in the formation of an epistemic modal-world which acts as the matrix world from which all other worlds derive (Gavins 2001: 133; Lahey 2004: 26). The reason for this has to do with the level of accessibility afforded to the contents of focalized narratives. In Text World Theory 'accessibility' refers to the level of reliability a discourse participant may attribute to the propositions of a discourse. Because discourse participants are seen to be bound by pragmatic principles of cooperation (similar to Grice's well-known maxims for communication (Grice 1975)), any propositions offered up by them are expected to be reliable (i.e. truthful and coherent; not deliberately obscure or deceptive); worlds prompted by these propositions are therefore deemed 'participant-accessible'. However, enactors in text-worlds are constructs built up through discourse; as products of the discourse they inhabit a different ontological plane from that of the discourse participants and are not bound by the same pragmatic metaprinciples that hold in the surrounding discourse-world. For Werth, this meant that any worlds originating from the minds of enactors – those resulting from speech and thought but also from focalization – were not reliable and were therefore 'participant-inaccessible'.

Gavins (2001) was the first to note the likely incongruity between Werth's proposed accessibility restrictions for focalized narratives and the behaviour of readers when faced with such narratives. She writes:

> It seems unlikely that with a fixed narration, where the only access route to the text world is through the perspective of a character, the reader might resist incrementing the contents of that focaliser's mind into the Common Ground simply for lack of adequate evidence of its truth status .... It would seem far more probable that typical reader behaviour, when faced with such a text, would be to build a text world based on the information presented by the main narrator, regardless of whether that happens to be a participating character or not. (Gavins 2001: 153)

Gavins goes on to propose that the result of focalization is the construction of an epistemic-world which assumes a 'stand-in' text-world status due to its being the only world through which the reader may access the contents of the narrative. Since all world-building and function-advancing propositions will be provided via the epistemic focalization-world, the text-world level is rendered redundant, or 'empty' (Lahey 2004: 26). This shift in the status of the text-world occurs despite the limitations normally associated with other types of epistemic modal-worlds, which are enactor-accessible and therefore unreliable for the reader (Gavins 2001: 132, 153–5).

In Excerpts 3.3 and 3.4, Langdon's own appraisals of his character are confined to the matrix focalization-world, or else to epistemic modal-worlds anchored within it and triggered by free direct thought. Positive assessments of his character are located in the deictic- or modal-worlds corresponding to the direct or indirect speech of other characters. In Excerpt 3.3 for instance, Langdon's surprised and self-deprecating responses to the news of his book's popularity in the museum shop are expressed via (Langdon's) free direct thought. Free direct thought is epistemic-world-forming, since it gives access to the consciousness of an enactor. In this case, since the surrounding narrative is also focalized via Langdon, the epistemic-world prompted by his free direct thought is embedded within a pre-existing focalization-world (see Figure 3.1 below). However, the positive information about his character (in this case, that his book is popular in the museum shop) is provided via the direct speech of the museum employee. Direct speech cues a world-switch, since it (typically) involves the insertion of present-tense utterances into a past-tense narrative. Thus the information that Brown's book is popular in the museum book shop is anchored in a distinct deictic-world. Similarly, in Excerpt 3.4, Langdon's modest

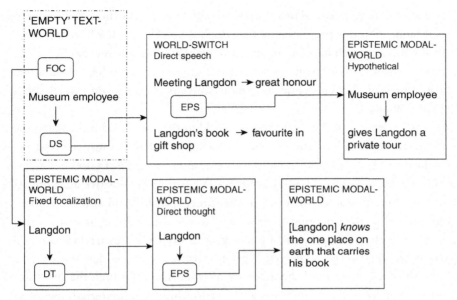

Figure 3.1 The world architecture of Excerpt 3.3

assessment of his physical appearance ('not overly handsome in the classical sense') occurs in the matrix focalization-world while the proposition that he possesses 'erudite appeal' is attributed to a modal-world built in response to the indirect speech of his female colleagues (for a complete overview of world creation in relation to speech and thought, see Gavins 2007).

While Langdon provides the controlling perspective on the narration, the reader may assume the same level of reliability with regard to direct speech that would be expected in a non-focalized narration. Because direct speech is an apparently verbatim account of what has been said, the reported clauses of direct speech must be seen as unmediated 'facts' of the fictional world. It is therefore more logical to treat direct speech as originating from the back-grounded, 'empty' text-world, rather than the matrix focalization-world (see Cruickshank and Lahey 2010, and Lugea 2013 and this volume for discussions of this problem in relation to dramatic discourse). Figure 3.1 demonstrates the suggested augmentation to current Text World Theory (TWT) practice in relation to Excerpt 3.3.

In Figure 3.1, the 'empty' text-world gives rise to two distinct 'branches' of worlds. The first is rooted in the focalization-world which represents the matrix world for most of the discourse; the second is anchored in the direct speech-world prompted by the speech of the museum employee. Both branches contain further embedded modal-worlds. In the focalization branch an embedded modal-world is prompted by Langdon's use of the epistemic verb 'know'. In the direct speech branch, the museum employee's comment that he 'would give a private tour at any hour' refers to an unrealized hypothetical situation, also represented as epistemically remote from its parent world (Werth 1997, 1999: 239–40).

The anchoring of the direct speech-world in the text-world rather than the focalization-world has ramifications for Langdon's *ethos*. Because the contents of the direct speech-world will be interpreted as more reliable than the contents of the focalization-world, more credence is given to the positive assessments of Langdon's character anchored in the direct speech-world and the embedded modal-world emerging from it than to the diminishing assessments of Langdon's character provided by Langdon himself via focalization and free direct thought. From a rhetorical perspective it is notable that the positive assessments of Langdon's character are often provided through the speech of others. For Aristotle testimony is a key non-technical (i.e. external) means of persuasion and an important element the establishment of character (*Rhet.* I.15, 1376a).

Turning to Excerpt 3.4, here the indirect mode of speech presentation means that Langdon (as focalizer and therefore default narrator) controls the reporting of his female colleagues' speech ('what his female colleagues referred to as an "erudite" appeal'). However, the use of inverted commas around the adjective modifier 'erudite' suggests that their words are faithfully represented. Thus, even though the indirect speech presented in Excerpt 3.4 results in a remote epistemic-world which is deemed less accessible than the focalization-world from which it arises (Gavins 2001: 114; Werth 1999: 240–1), the signal of faithfulness provided by the inverted commas means that the reader will be encouraged to treat the testimony of the female colleagues as reliable (and may resist Langdon's own diminishing appraisal).

Because Langdon's diminishing evaluations will be treated as less reliable than the positive evaluations of others, the reader may choose to reject them, in much the same way that a speaker may verbally challenge the modest protestations of an interlocutor. Such a challenge occurs in *The Lost Symbol*, where the following exchange takes place:

Excerpt 3.5

'This year, as is customary,' the assistant continued, 'the dinner will be preceded by a keynote address.' [. . .]

'The problem is this,' the man said. 'Our speaker has fallen ill and has just informed us she will be unable to give the address.' He paused awkwardly. 'This means we are desperate for a replacement speaker. And Mr. Solomon is hoping you would consider filling in.'

Langdon did a double take. 'Me?' [...] 'I'm sure Peter could find a far better substitute.'

'You're Mr. Solomon's first choice, Professor, and you're being much too modest. The institution's guests would be thrilled to hear from you, and Mr. Solomon thought you could give the same lecture you gave on Bookspan TV a few years back'. (Brown 2010: 37)

Here Langdon is asked to deliver a keynote address at a private gala of the Smithsonian Institution in Washington, DC. The passage contributes to Langdon's *ethos* in several ways. First, that Langdon is being asked to deliver the address in the first place (even if only as a second choice replacement) again demonstrates the force of his reputation as a public intellectual. This is bolstered further through the direct speech of another character (later revealed to be Mal'akh, the book's antagonist), who remarks that the guests of the gala would be 'thrilled' to hear from Langdon. Further support for Langdon's *ethos* is provided in the reference to 'the same lecture you gave on Bookspan TV a few years back', which makes readers aware of yet another of Langdon's important public appearances. Most relevant in the context of my arguments in this section, however, is the caller's assertion that Langdon, in suggesting that someone better could be found to deliver the lecture, is 'being much too modest'. This remark provides an explicit textual echo of the reader's own resistance to Langdon's diminishing appraisals of his character, which, because they are located in epistemically remote worlds, are seen as having little to do with the 'facts' of his character as revealed through the testimony of others.

By locating Langdon's diminishing appraisals of himself within the matrix focalization-world or a world embedded in it, Brown assigns responsibility for these evaluations to Langdon, thereby demonstrating Langdon's humility. I noted in the introduction to this chapter that humility is considered a 'supreme virtue' of Western civilization and is therefore implicated in *ethos* as a component of high moral character. Langdon's humility is crucial for the success of Brown's novels, because it allows Langdon to function as a member of the intellectual elite and at the same time as an 'ordinary guy', an American everyman.

As numerous commentators have argued, contemporary American culture is typified by a deep vein of anti-intellectualism that has grown deeper in the post-Cold War era and has been particularly reinvigorated in the wake of 9/11 and the presidency of George W. Bush (Canovan 1999; Formisano 2010; Long, Gardner and Long 1996; Shogan 2007; Wacquant 1996). While Brown's books have become international bestsellers, his primary audience is an American one; it is therefore important for Brown to present his academic hero in a way that allows him to be accepted by an American readership. Langdon must been seen as knowledgeable, since his expertise is a prerequisite to solving the mysteries around which the books turn. However, Brown must equally be careful not to construct Langdon as elitist or arrogant. Brown achieves the balance between these two competing goals in several ways, but most centrally through the use of juxtapositions which foreground Langdon's complete lack of arrogance with regard to his own character while simultaneously and subtly alluding to his strengths (often through the testimony of others). This delicate balancing act also demonstrates Brown's sensitivity to the prejudices of his primary audience, thereby strengthening his own *ethos*.

3.6   Brown's *ethos*

In face-to-face spoken discourse, participants share the same spatio-temporal context and have direct access to one another, such that they are able to draw inferences about each other based on factors in the shared discourse-world. However, the discourse-worlds of written communication are normally split, with writers and readers occupying distinct spatio-temporal locations (Werth 1995: 55). This means that reader-participants have no direct access to writer-participants in the discourse-world; as such, it is usually accepted that readers must base their judgements about their co-participants on previous experiences with or of them, and on information about them that might be available from other sources (Gavins 2007: 78).

However, a reader's perception of his or her co-participant's character must also be partially text-driven. The same process of 'mind-modelling' (Stockwell 2009; see also Zunshine 2006) that occurs when we conceptualize fictional characters surely also takes place in our modelling of authorial minds; in both cases the conceptualization begins with a default assumption of personhood and is subsequently and dynamically fleshed out by cues from within the discourse (see Stockwell, this volume). Indeed, from the perspective of classical rhetoric there is nothing new in this assertion. The importance of a text in illuminating the character of its producer is at the very heart of the classical Aristotelian definition of *ethos* discussed above. It follows from this that every aspect of Brown's novels – not just his characterization of Langdon, but also his treatment of other characters, as well as lexical choices and other aspects of his style – has the potential to influence readers' perceptions of him. While it certainly is the case that these perceptions will also be formed partly based on what readers know of Brown from other sources, the text plays a crucial role in the formation of these perceptions.

A second, more specific point concerns Langdon's role as the primary controlling perspective on the narrative in each of the novels. There is a tendency for readers confronted with a third-person narrative to equate the narrator with the author themselves. As Gavins notes:

> [A]lthough fictional narrators are textual constructs, the reader-participants in literary discourse-worlds often map their knowledge of real-world authors onto these text-world beings. [...] Basing one's mental representation of a narrator on discourse-world knowledge of the author of the text is a common reaction to third-person narration. (2007: 78)

The mapping Gavins describes is bi-directional; not only do readers tend to form an image of fictional narrators which largely conforms to what they know about their corresponding real-life authors, but we can expect readers' perceptions of authors to be shaped by their experience of the narrators those authors create. This situation is somewhat different in the case of internal fixed focalization because if there is a narrator present in such narratives, his or her existence may be purely theoretical; the complete control of a narrative by one or more of its characters means that any real sense of engagement with a narrator is erased. However, given that the focalizer operates in such cases as a stand-in for the absent narrator, a certain degree of identity mapping between focalizer and author can be expected to occur. Following the principle of minimal departure, we can expect mapping relations to be especially plentiful when the reader perceives a strong degree of correspondence between focalizer and author based on what is known about the author from other real-life sources (Ryan 1991: 51). Indeed, it is our tendency towards this kind of mapping between characters and authors that allows us to talk of fictional characters as alter egos of their creators, a term that has, incidentally, been used in relation to Langdon and Brown (Scott 2013).

There are numerous correspondences between Langdon and Brown. Both were born in Exeter, New Hampshire, on 22 June 1964 and reside in New England. Both are former students of art history. Brown and his fictional hero share the same style of dress. Langdon is always depicted wearing tweed jackets, casual chino-style trousers and loafers; a review of promotional and book-jacket photos of Brown reveals this to be Brown's preference as well (publicly at least). These and other similarities have led journalists to question Brown about the extent of the correspondence between him and his fictional character, to which Brown has responded that Langdon is 'the hero I wish I could be' (Scott 2013).

I suggest, following Aristotle, that a text – any text – represents the primary source for the *ethos* of its producer. Furthermore, in cases where specific and salient correspondences are perceived between an author and a character – as they may be between Langdon and Brown – the *ethos* of that character will be fundamental to the *ethos* of the author. It is important to note that I am not suggesting that identity mapping between a character and an author is the *only* source of *ethos* construction for an author. My contention here is simply that where particularly salient correspondences exist between real-life authors and their fictional characters, this mapping may form a critical component of readers' construction of an author's *ethos*. From a Text World Theory perspective what is significant about these arguments is the following: if the construction of authorial minds is partially text-driven this implies that the same textual prompts that cue the construction and elaboration of a text-world simultaneously cue the ongoing, dynamic (re)configuration of that text-world's containing discourse-world. This suggests a degree of upward influence from the text-world which is not predicted by current Text World Theory, which maintains that the text-world, as a product of the discourse-world, can never be an element in its formation.

3.7   Conclusion

Part of the success of Dan Brown's Langdon-series novels can be attributed to his enactment of a combined author-character *ethos* for his protagonist Robert Langdon and for himself. In this chapter I have shown some of the key ways in which this *ethos* is constructed stylistically, drawing links along the way between current thinking in stylistics and the classical approach to rhetoric as conceived of by Aristotle and developed by contemporary rhetoricians. One outcome of my analysis has been to suggest two augmentations to Text World Theory, one minor (concerning the reliability of direct speech-worlds) and one more sweeping (concerning the upward influence of text-worlds). However, since my focus here was primarily on the stylistics of *ethos* construction in Brown's novels, and only secondarily on a critical examination of Text World Theory as an analytic tool, it has not been possible to comprehensively test the applicability of these augmentations. Such testing would require an application of the augmented theory to many and more varied discourses. It is therefore hoped that this study may serve as an invitation for future work which may assess the validity of these proposed changes.

References

Altes, L. K. (2014), *Ethos and Narrative Interpretation: The Negotiation of Values in Fiction* [ebook], Lincoln and London, NE: University of Nebraska Press.

Amossy, R. (2002), 'How to Do Things With Doxa', *Poetics Today*, 23.3: 465–87.

Aristotle. (1991), *The Art of Rhetoric*, trans. H. Lawson-Tancred, London: Penguin.

Aristotle. (2004), *Rhetoric* [ebook], trans. W. R. Roberts, Mineola, NY: Dover.

Brown, D. (2004 [2003]), *The Da Vinci Code*, London: Corgi.

Brown, D. (2009 [2000]), *Angels and Demons*, London: Corgi.

Brown, D. (2010 [2009]), *The Lost Symbol*, London: Corgi.

Brown, D. (2013), *Inferno*, London: Bantam.

Canovan, M. (1999), 'Trust the People! Populism and the Two Faces of Democracy', *Political Studies*, 47.1: 2–16.

Carter, R. (2010), 'Methodologies for Stylistic Analysis', in D. McIntyre and B. Busse (eds), *Language and Style*, Houndsmills, Basingstoke: Palgrave MacMillan: 55–68.

Corbett, E. P. J. and Connors, R. J. (1999), *Classical Rhetoric for the Modern Student*, 4th ed., New York: Oxford University Press.

Cruickshank, T. and Lahey, E. (2010), 'Building the Stages of Drama: Towards a Text World Theory Account of Dramatic Play-Texts', *Journal of Literary Semantics*, 39.1: 67–91.

Davies, M. (2008), *Oppositions in News Discourse: The Ideological Construction of Us and Them in the British Press*, Unpublished PhD Thesis, University of Huddersfield.

Estes, Z. and Ward, T. B. (2002), 'The Emergence of Novel Attributes in Concept Modification', *Creativity Research Journal*, 14.2: 149–56.

Formisano, R. (2010), 'Populist Currents in the 2008 Presidential Campaign', *Journal of Policy History*, 22.2: 237–55.

Gavins, J. (2001), *Text World Theory: A Critical Exposition and Development in Relation to Absurd Prose Fiction*, Unpublished PhD Thesis, Sheffield Hallam University.

Gavins, J. (2007), *Text World Theory: An Introduction*, Edinburgh: Edinburgh University Press.

Gibbs, Jr., R. W. and Kearney, L. R. (1994), 'When Parting is Such Sweet Sorrow: The Comprehension and Appreciation of Oxymora', *Journal of Psycholinguistic Research*, 23.1: 75–89.

Grice, H. P. (1975), *Logic in Conversation*, New York: Academic Press.

Jeffries, L. (2012), *Opposition in Discourse: The Construction of Oppositional Meaning*, New York: Bloomsbury Academic.

Kinneavy, J. L. and Warshauer, S. C. (1994), 'From Aristotle to Madison Avenue: Ethos and the Ethics of Argument', in J. S. Baumlin and T. F. Baumlin (eds), *Ethos: New Essays in Rhetorical and Critical Theory*, Dallas, TX: Southern Methodist University Press: 171–90.

Lahey, E. (2004), 'All the World's a Subworld: Direct Speech and Subworld Creation in "After" by Norman MacCaig', *Nottingham Linguistic Circular*, 18: 21–8.

Long, C. D., Gardner, B. B. and Long, C. D. (1996), 'It Came from Hollywood: Popular Culture Casts Professors in a Negative Light', *Academe*, 82.4: 32–6.

Lugea, J. (2013), 'Embedded Dialogue and Dreams: The Worlds and Accessibility Relations of *Inception*', *Language and Literature*, 22.2: 133–53.

Mayer, A., 2013. 'How *The Da Vinci Code* Author Built Buzz for his Latest Book', CBC News <http://www.cbc.ca/news/arts/how-the-da-vinci-code-author-built-buzz-for-his-latest-book-1.1339833> [accessed 23 September 2013].

Nash, W. (1990), *Language in Popular Fiction*, London: Routledge.

Rogers, S. (2011), 'Top-Selling 100 Books of All Time', *Guardian Data Blog* <http://www.theguardian.com/news/datablog/2011/jan/01/top-100-books-of-all-time> [accessed 23 September 2013].

Rogers, S. (2012), 'The Top 100 Bestselling Books of All Time: How Does Fifty Shades of Grey Compare?' *Guardian Data Blog* <http://www.theguardian.com/news/datablog/2012/aug/09/best-selling-books-all-time-fifty-shades-grey-compare> [accessed 14 October 2013].

Ryan, M. L. (1991), *Possible Worlds, Artificial Intelligence, and Narrative Theory*, Bloomington: Indiana University Press.

Scott, J. (2013), 'Q&A with Dan Brown, Author of Inferno', *Retreat by Random House* <http://www.retreatbyrandomhouse.ca/2013/05/qa-dan-brown-author-inferno/> [accessed 27 November 2014].

Shen, Y. (1987), 'On the Structure and Understanding of Poetic Oxymoron', *Poetics Today*, 8.1: 105–22.

Shogan, C. J. (2007), 'Anti-Intellectualism in the Modern Presidency: A Republican Populism', *Perspectives on Politics*, 5.2: 295–303.

Smith, C. R. (2004), 'Ethos Dwells Persuasively: A Hermeneutic Reading of Aristotle on Credibility', in M. J. Hyde (ed.), *The Ethos of Rhetoric*, Columbia, SC: University of South Carolina Press: 1–19.

Smith, E. E. and Osherson, D. N. (1984), 'Conceptual Combination with Prototype Concepts', *Cognitive Science*, 8.4: 337–61.

Stockwell, P. (2009), *Texture: A Cognitive Aesthetics of Reading*, Edinburgh: Edinburgh University Press.

Wacquant, L. J. D. (1996), 'The Self-Inflicted Irrelevance of American Academics', *Academe*, 82.4: 18–23.

Werth, P. (1995), 'How to Build a World (In a Lot Less Than Six Days and Using Only What's in Your Head)', in K. Green (ed.), *New Essays on Deixis: Discourse, Narrative, Literature*, Amsterdam: Rodopi: 49–80.

Werth, P. (1997), 'Remote Worlds: The Conceptual Representation of Linguistic Would', in J. Nuyts and E. Pedersen (eds), *Language and Conceptualization*, Cambridge: Cambridge University Press: 84–115.

Werth, P. (1999), *Text Worlds: Representing Conceptual Space in Discourse*, Harlow: Longman.

Wilson, T., Wiebe, J. and Hoffman, P. (2005), 'Recognizing Contextual Polarity in Phrase-Level Sentiment Analysis', in *HLT 2005: Proceedings of the Conference on Human Language Technology and Empirical Methods in Natural Language Processing*, Stroudsburg, PA: Association for Computational Linguistics: n.p. <http://www.di.uniba.it/intint/IUM2-0809/WilsonetAl.pdf> [accessed 30 October 2014].

Zunshine, L. (2006), *Why We Read Fiction: Theory of Mind and the Novel*, Columbus, OH: Ohio State University Press.

Building More-Than-Human Worlds: *Umwelt* Modelling in Animal Narratives

David Herman

4.1   Introduction

In one of her earliest published essays, 'Undersea' (1937), Rachel Carson demonstrates her already highly developed skill at evoking the diverse experiential worlds of different kinds of animals – a skill that she would continue to perfect in her acclaimed book-length contributions to the genre of nature writing, including *Under the Sea-Wind* (2007 [1941]), *The Sea Around Us* (1951) and *The Edge of the Sea* (1998 [1955]). Carson's essay begins as follows:

Excerpt 4.1

Who has known the ocean? Neither you nor I, with our earth-bound senses, know the foam and surge of the tide that beats over the crab hiding under the seaweed of his tidepool home; or the lilt of the long, slow swells of mid-ocean, where shoals of wandering fish prey and are preyed upon, and the dolphin breaks the waves to breathe the upper atmosphere. Nor can we know the vicissitudes of life on the ocean floor, where the sunlight, filtering through a hundred feet of water, makes but a fleeting, bluish twilight, in which dwell sponge and mollusk and starfish and coral, where swarms of diminutive fish twinkle through the dusk like a silver rain of meteors, and eels lie in wait among the rocks. Even less is it given to man to descend those six incomprehensible miles into the recesses of the abyss, where reign utter silence and unvarying cold and eternal night. (Carson 1937: 55)

This paragraph, which denies even as it enacts the possibility of imagining the experiential worlds of animals living underwater, thereby brings into view what might be called the paradox of narrative prosthesis – a paradox that obtains in at least some narratives that cross the species boundary. In projecting so vividly what it might be like for undersea creatures to inhabit the niches to which their organismic profile makes them suited, and in driving home equally vividly how different these niches are from the ones humans characteristically occupy, Excerpt 4.1 affords means for modelling the experiences of other kinds of beings, with Carson all the while making a claim for cross-species incomprehensibility.

Exploring how resources built into narrative generate possibilities and paradoxes of this kind, my chapter suggests how key questions about the interrelations among mental capacities and dispositions, the structures of discourse, and processes of world-building take on a new inflection when they are asked about stories that engage with animal experiences. To this end, I synthesize stylistic and narratological research on speech and thought representation (e.g. Fludernik 1993; Leech and Short 2007; Toolan 2001), including discussions of 'mind style' (e.g. Fowler 1977; Halliday 1971; Semino 2007), with ideas about animals and human-animal relationships emerging from fields such as ethology (von Uexküll 2010) and anthropology (Descola 2013; Kohn 2013). Arguing for an expanded and diversified conception of the mind-narrative nexus, I link the narrative modelling of non-human subjectivity with von Uexküll's idea of the *Umwelt*, glossed by Thompson (2007) as 'an animal's environment in the sense of its lived, phenomenal world, the world as it presents itself to that animal thanks to its sensorimotor repertoire' (59; see also von Uexküll 2010: 53, 96). My aim is to investigate how narrative methods for presenting minds can be used to probe not only potential heterogeneities but also potential areas of commonality in the structure of experience across the species boundary.

Drawing on a variety of case studies to examine ways in which narratives project animal worlds, I also consider how those methods straddle the fiction/non-fiction divide. For this purpose, I use the technical term 'discourse domain' to explore how ascriptions of mental states and experiences to non-human agents flow, in a top-down manner, from domain-specific assumptions about what kinds of subjective experiences it is appropriate and warranted to attribute to others, non-human as well as human. My analysis thus raises questions about the scope of the presupposition embedded in the subtitle of the present volume: although in one sense discourse does take shape within the mind, in another sense minds take shape in discourse. In other words, discourse can be viewed as an ecology of mind-ascribing practices, a constellation of regions or domains marked by contrasting assumptions about the range of experiences available to particular kinds of beings.

4.2 Presenting experiential worlds beyond the species boundary

In narrative contexts, a key world-building activity entails using textual patterns to project the second-order mental and verbal world-making acts of characters. Such embedded worlds come into view when characters remember, imagine or explicitly recount (as intradiegetic narrators) further worlds-within-the-storyworld. To account for the discourse environments in which such nested worlds take shape, analysts have identified a continuum that stretches from verbal or mental performances that are more overtly mediated by a narrator to performances that are less overtly mediated in this sense (see e.g. Cohn 1978; McHale 1978; Stanzel 1984). One version of the scalar model is shown in Figure 4.1, where 'discourse' serves as a cover term for presentations of speech as well as thought.

Significantly, research in narratology and stylistics has not yet fully investigated the issues that arise when this model is brought to bear on presentations of the experiences of non-human animals in stories. Extending the model in this way, I suggest, highlights the need to rethink its conceptual underpinnings. In particular, I wish to emphasize the advantages of continuing to work with distinctions of the sort captured in Figure 4.1 but without seeking to map them onto a Cartesian geography of mind – onto increments of an external-internal scale stretching from the world out there to the mind in here.

Instead, analysts can bring the previous scholarship into relation with a different, non- or rather anti-Cartesian metric (see also Herman 2011). This metric

Narration > Narrative Representation of Speech, Thought, or Perceptual Act > Indirect Discourse > Free Indirect Discourse > Direct Discourse > Free Direct Discourse

N: She sat there quietly.
NRS/T/PA: She sat there quietly and talked about/thought about/glimpsed the picture of home on the wall.
ID: She sat there quietly and *said/thought that home seemed so far away.*
FID: She sat there quietly; *home seemed so far away now.*
DD: She sat there quietly and said/thought, *'Home is so far away now.'*
*FDD: She sat there quietly. *Home--so far away. Must try to return.*

*In contexts of thought presentation, some analysts reserve the term 'interior monologue' for relatively extended stretches of FDD (Prince 2003: 45)

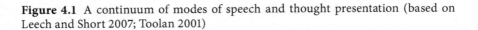

Figure 4.1 A continuum of modes of speech and thought presentation (based on Leech and Short 2007; Toolan 2001)

is based on the relative degree of detail used to project the interplay between agents and their environments. At one end of the spectrum are narratives, or segments within narratives, that provide a globalizing, summative account of agent-environment interactions; at the other end are narratives that stage the moment-by-moment construction of characters' experiential worlds, detailing how a being's subjective experience arises from the way it is functionally coupled with the environments it inhabits. From this perspective, the paradoxically prosthetic status of Excerpt 4.1 derives from the manner in which Carson's discourse reaches out towards both ends of the spectrum just described, stating the impossibility of presenting sea creatures' experiences with any degree of precision and yet providing specifics about what the world might be like for beings of that sort.

It is important to stress that although in some contexts increments on the scale shown in Figure 4.1 may be aligned with degrees of granularity in *Umwelt* modelling, in accordance with what Sternberg (1982) has termed 'the Proteus Principle', or the plural, fluctuating correspondences between linguistic form and representational function, there is no one-to-one correspondence between a particular technique of mind presentation and a specific level of detail in capturing experiential worlds. Granted, compared with Excerpt 4.1 Excerpt 4.2, which is taken from an account of a deer hunt by the American naturalist Charles Dudley Warner (1878), projects an experiential world that is more dense with mental ascriptions than those inhabited by Carson's crab, dolphin and eel. Warner uses techniques positioned farther to the right on the scale than N and NRTA or NRPA – these being the modes used in Carson's account. In 4.2 Warner recounts how a doe runs towards the hounds that are pursuing her in order to lead them away from her threatened fawn:

Excerpt 4.2

After running at high speed perhaps half a mile farther, it occurred to [the doe] that it would be safe now to turn to the west, and, by a wide circuit, seek her fawn. But, at the moment, she heard a sound that chilled her heart. It was the cry of a hound to the west of her. The crafty brute had made the circuit of the slash, and cut off her retreat. There was nothing to do but to keep on; and on she went, still to the north, with the noise of the pack behind her ... She bounded on; she stopped. What was that? From the valley ahead came the cry of a searching hound. All the devils were loose this morning. Every way was closed but one, and that led straight down the mountain to the cluster of houses. Conspicuous among them was a slender white wooden spire. The doe did not know that it was the spire of a Christian chapel. But perhaps she thought that human pity dwelt there, and would be more merciful than the teeth of the hounds. (Warner 1878: paragraph 20)

The first sentence of this excerpt hovers somewhere between Narrator's Report of a Thought Act (NRTA) and Indirect Thought (IT). Likewise, with its tag phrase, the final sentence has the surface structure of IT, although the hedge provided by the adverb 'perhaps', together with the propositional content of the sentence itself, detaches the suggestion of religious hypocrisy from the deer's own frame of reference. Other sentences in the excerpt, meanwhile, are situated still farther to the right on the scale in Figure 4.1. Thus the sentences featuring expressions such as 'the crafty brute', 'there was nothing to do but to keep on', 'what was that?' and 'all the devils were loose this morning' can be interpreted as instances of Free Indirect Thought (FIT), serving to model the subjectivity of the doe, to evoke the animal's landscape of consciousness (see Bruner 1990), even as they simultaneously project the landscape of action in which the deer seeks to evade the hounds.

Yet Excerpts 4.3 and 4.4, taken together with Excerpt 4.1, confirm that any alignment between increments on the scale and degrees of granularity in *Umwelt* modelling is contingent rather than necessary, with variable degrees of detail being afforded by a given increment. Like Excerpt 4.1, both 4.3 and 4.4 limit themselves to the portion of the continuum in Figure 4.1 that stretches between N and NRT/PA. Excerpt 4.3 is taken from Esther Woolfson's memoir about her and her family's experiences while living with several birds; it recounts what Woolfson observes when she first releases doves that she and her daughters have been caring for. Excerpt 4.4 derives from J. A. Baker's account of the ten-year period he spent pursuing and observing peregrine falcons, condensed into a diary format covering one year. This passage suggests how the birds' visual acuity enables them to encounter, in ways strikingly different from humans, the terrestrial environments over which they fly.

Excerpt 4.3

On the day of eventual release, I removed the door and, after considerable hesitation and anxious hovering (mine, not theirs), [the doves] walked out on to the small platform in front of the house, looked around them, seemed almost blinded by the possibilities in front of them, and then flew .... I did, in that moment, assume that this would be my final glimpse of them, but I was wrong. After some flight, a bit of brisk circling in the air above us, a period of what I assume was orientation, they flew back into their house, confirming remarkably, amazingly, the truth of the designation 'homing pigeon'....As I watched my doves' light, easy flight, I was delighted by them, by their certitude and reliability, the way they flew off into the sky and returned unfailingly each evening with the onset of dusk. (Woolfson 2008: 20–2)

Excerpt 4.4

The peregrine's view of the land is like the yachtsman's view of the shore as he sails into the long estuaries. A wake of water recedes behind him, the wake of the pierced horizon glides back on either side. Like the seafarer, the peregrine lives in a pouring-away world of no attachment, a world of wakes and tilting, of sinking planes of land and water. We who are anchored and earthbound cannot envisage this freedom of the eye. The peregrine sees and remembers patterns we do not know exist: the neat squares of orchards and woodland, the endlessly varying quadrilateral shapes of fields. He finds his way across the land by a succession of remembered symmetries. But what does he under-stand? Does he really 'know' that an object that increases in size is moving towards him? Or is it that he believes in the size he sees, so that a distant man is too small to be frightening but a man near is a man huge and therefore terrify-ing? He may live in a world of endless pulsations, of objects forever contracting or dilating in size. (Baker 1967: 35–6)

Excerpt 4.3 ascribes several perceptual or cognitive performances to the doves: experiencing apparent bewilderment at the range of navigational pos-sibilities open to them as they first survey the skies around them; achieving spatial orientation by rapidly flying in circles above Woolfson's own position as observer; and possessing certitude (and demonstrating reliability) when they unfailingly make their way home each evening after their aerial forays. It should also be noted that Woolfson hedges the first two of these ascriptions ('*seemed* almost blinded by the possibilities', 'a period of what *I assume* was'). The first part of Excerpt 4.4, by contrast, with its paradoxically prosthetic account of 'a pouring-away world of no attachment' made accessible by a 'freedom of the eye' ostensibly unknown to humans, models the peregrine falcon's experience of flight in much greater detail. Similarly, in the second part of the passage, the interrogatives set up a disjunction that exhausts the logical space of the bird's perceptual possibilities, with the hedging force of the modal auxiliary 'may', in the final sentence, offset by the vividness with which Baker takes up the imagined perspective of the falcon. Thus, although the excerpts from Carson, Woolfson and Baker all use techniques situated towards the left end of the scale from Figure 4.1, Baker's text, as excerpted in 4.4, shows greater particulariza-tion and prolificness when it comes to presenting animal experiences, revealing the Proteus Principle in action.

Two other sets of issues are especially relevant for inquiry into the narrative modelling of animals' experiential worlds. One grows out of questions about how previous research on the concept of mind style might be extended to engage with narratives about non-human minds; the other arises from work on the asymmetrical norms governing the use of methods to present characters' thoughts in contrast to their verbalized utterances. In Fowler's (1977) original account the term 'mind style' refers to the process whereby 'cumulatively, consistent structural options [such as choices in vocabulary and the use of transitive versus intransitive verbs], agreeing in cutting the presented world to one pattern or another, give rise to an impression of a "world-view" associated with a character or narrator' (Fowler 1977: 76). As such, the idea of mind style seems to encompass narrative practices associated with relatively fine-grained methods of modelling experiential worlds. Instead of projecting a globalizing outline of those worlds, in the manner of NRTA or NRPA (Narrator's Report of a Perceptual Act), for example, mind style refers to modes of textual patterning that encapsulate, or even iconically reproduce, an intelligent agent's moment-by-moment negotiation of its lived environment.

Significantly, although the pioneering work on mind style by Fowler and by Halliday (1971) as well as later research in this area (e.g. Bockting 1994; Semino 2007) has centred on differences among the minds of human characters in fictional narratives, Fowler's initial definition is neutral with respect to species identity as well as genre. He wrote: 'We may coin the term "mind-style" to refer to any distinctive linguistic presentation of an individual mental self' (Fowler 1977: 103). This definition accommodates the study of how textual patterns might be used to project species-specific modes of niche construction and also the niche-building activities of individual creatures – activities arising from the more or less idiosyncratic capacities, dispositions and life experiences of the individuals in question. Thus, excerpted from Carson's account of Silverbar the sanderling, one of the named seabirds who acts as a species representative in *Under the Sea-Wind*, Excerpt 4.5 could in principle be glossed as an instance of N; yet the paratactic stacking of clauses, combined with the repetition of 'pad, pad' in the second clause, can also be interpreted as iconically evoking the way Silverbar registers the accumulating details of the fox's appearance and behaviours as threats to her newly hatched chicks, before the final clause morphs into NRTA:

Excerpt 4.5

The gleaming eyes of the fox – the soft pad, pad of his feet on the shales – the twitch of his nostrils testing the air for scent of her chicks – became for her the symbols of a thousand dangers, formless and without name. (Carson 2007: 45)

For its part, Excerpt 4.6, again taken from Baker's *The Peregrine*, suggests how style can be used to project non-human ways of encountering the world even when there is no attempt to create an iconic matching of textual patterns with the unfolding of an animal's experience. In Excerpt 4.6, the bird's mind style emerges, not directly from the verbal texture of statements that reflect its manner of processing events in the storyworld, but indirectly from Baker's chosen format of a sequence of commands – commands that the author issues to any human who seeks to enter the world of a peregrine on its own terms. Here the imperatives invite readers to engage in a two-stage modelling process: in a first stage, the prescriptive statements project a set of behavioural protocols for humans who seek to gain recognition and acceptance by peregrines, and then in a second stage those protocols can be mapped onto the birds' way of making sense of the world around them.

> Excerpt 4.6
>
> Enter and leave the same fields at the same time each day, soothe the hawk from its wildness by a ritual of behavior as invariable as its own. Hood the glare of the eyes, hide the white tremor of the hands, shade the stark reflecting face, assume the stillness of a tree. A peregrine fears nothing he can see clearly and far off. Approach him across open ground with a steady unfailing movement. Let your shape grow in size but do not alter its outline. Never hide yourself unless concealment is complete. Be alone. Shun the furtive oddity of man, cringe from the hostile eyes of farms. Learn to fear. (Baker 1967: 13)

As Excerpt 4.6 demonstrates, when the mind being modelled in a narrative does not traffic in human language, the styles that can be used to stage the workings of that mind arguably become not more but less constrained, less bound to particular sorts of experiments with vocabulary, process types and syntax on which the early research in this area focused. In turn, because they may use a variety of strategies to project non-human ways of experiencing the world, animal narratives can not only be informed by but also inform existing conceptions of mind style.

But it is not just the range of textual phenomena falling under the scope of mind style that needs to be reconsidered when it comes to animal narratives; these narratives raise broader questions about how assumptions concerning what sorts of experiential worlds are available to various kinds of beings bear, in a top-down manner, on the strategies used to present (and interpret) different kinds of minds. At issue here is the way the textual patterns associated with mind styles and with the presentation of animal experiences more generally are interwoven with cultures' ontologies; such ontologies specify, in the form of common knowledge, what sorts of beings populate the world and how those beings' attributes relate to the attributes ascribed to humans. Thus, for Descola (2013), ontologies are 'schemes of coding and parceling out phenomenal reality by means of which [people] have learned to couch and transmit their experience of things'; deriving 'from historical choices that privileged ... certain sets of relations to humans and non-humans', the schemes at issue allow particular, contingent ways of categorizing animals vis-à-vis humans 'to be experienced as naturally coherent' (66–7; see also Herman 2014; Kohn 2013). Grounded in such ontologies, norms that guide the production and interpretation of narratives about animal experiences, like the norms bearing on narratives about humans' ways of encountering the world, determine when, to what extent, and in what manner it is appropriate to ascribe mental states and experiences to others. Reciprocally, the patterns of ascription used in particular narratives can impinge on, and potentially recalibrate, normative assumptions about species of minds.

This set of issues intersects with questions about differences in the norms governing the presentation of thought versus speech. As shown in Figure 4.2, Leech and Short (2007) as well as Toolan (2001) have built on the scalar model presented in Figure 4.1 to suggest a fundamental contrast between the norms in question. According to this model, the norm for presenting speech is direct speech, such that 'any movement to the right of DS ... will produce an effect of freeness, as if the author has vacated the stage and left it to the characters', 'whereas any movement to the left of the norm will usually be interpreted as a movement away from verbatim report and towards "interference"' (Leech and

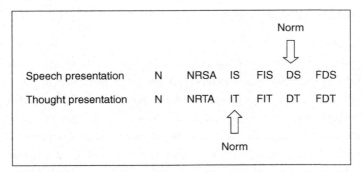

Figure 4.2 Contrasting norms for speech and thought presentation (based on Leech and Short 2007: 276; Toolan 2001: 139)

Short 2007: 268). By contrast, 'thoughts, in general, are not verbally formulated and so cannot be reported verbatim' (276). Hence shifts from one increment to another mean different things in the context of speech versus thought. Free Indirect Speech (FIS), for example, comes across as being subject to greater narratorial mediation or intervention than the norm for reported speech, or DS. But FIT comes across as a less mediated presentation of characters' mental activity when compared with the norm of IT.

This model, however, affords only a relatively low-resolution image of the wider ecologies of ascriptive practice bound up with thought presentation in particular. As Leech and Short (2007) themselves note, in novels the default mode of thought representation moved rightwards along this scale, from indirect thought to free indirect thought, as the nineteenth century gave way to the twentieth (277). Besides being subject to historical variability, norms for presenting characters' mental experiences are also subject to inter- and intracultural differences. Animal narratives highlight such variability because they point to a plurality of norms structuring engagements with experiential worlds, and suggest how contrasts among the norms at issue cross-cut the distinction between fictional and non-fictional accounts of animal life.

Consider Excerpt 4.7. Like Excerpt 4.5, Excerpt 4.7 concerns Silverbar's response to the marauding fox who threatens her chicks. Yet Excerpt 4.7 features more prolific and more fine-grained ascriptions of perceptions, beliefs, intentions and emotions to the animals involved than does the previous excerpt or, for that matter, other parts of Carson's narrative. In other words, 4.7 reflects an upward adjustment of the threshold for permissible levels of detail in *Umwelt* modelling. This adjustment arises, in turn, from the difficulty of parsing Silverbar's and the fox's complex interaction without building a scenario that makes sense of what's going on in terms of the animals' (interconnected) intentional and volitional states:

Excerpt 4.7

Now for the first time an abiding fear entered the heart of Silverbar ... After the fourth chick had hatched, Silverbar began to carry the shells, piece by piece, away from the nest ... A polar fox passed near her, making no sound as he trotted with sure foot over the shales. His eye gleamed as he watched the mother bird, and he sniffed the air, believing that she had young nearby. Silverbar flew to the willows further up the ravine and watched the fox uncover the shells and nose them. As he started up the slope of the ravine the sanderling fluttered toward him, tumbling to the ground as though hurt, flapping her wings, creeping over the gravel.

All the while she uttered a high-pitched note like the cry of her own young. The fox rushed at her. Silverbar rose rapidly into the air and flew over the crest of the ridge, only to reappear from another quarter, tantalizing the fox into following her. So by degrees she led him over the ridge and southward into a marshy bottom fed by the overflow of upland streams. (Carson 2007: 43–4)

The co-presence of different norms for mental-state attribution in the same narrative as well as across different kinds of accounts points to a more complex ecology of minds than that indicated in Figure 4.2. My analysis suggests that multiple norms bear on mind-ascribing practices in narrative contexts; rooted in different cultural or sub-cultural ontologies, these sets of norms encompass competing ways of allocating minds to animal agents (see Herman 2014). In an effort to account more fully for the variability and plurality of the relevant norms, I turn now to the concept of discourse domains, or arenas of practice that are governed by more or less distinctive interpretative paradigms and protocols for behaviour.

4.3   *Umwelt* modelling across discourse domains

Up to now, all of my examples have been taken from the realm of non-fiction, the genre that on the face of it would seem to be least hospitable to prolific ascriptions of subjective states to non-human agents. Yet my discussion suggests how, in fact, non-fiction features a variety of techniques for presenting animal minds and accommodates varying degrees of detail when it comes to *Umwelt* modelling. In seeking to make this case, I do not mean to shortshrift the way fictional narratives likewise afford resources for modelling animal experiences; a comprehensive study of animal narratives must engage with fictional as well as non-fictional accounts in order to capture the full range of methods used to project non-human experiences in storyworlds. That said, I have focused on non-fiction because I seek to dispute what remains, arguably, a pervasive assumption about animal narratives: namely, that *only* fictional accounts of animals support particularized, highly differentiated ascriptions of mental experiences to non-human agents. In lieu of any such a priori dichotomization of fictional and non-fictional animal minds, I propose a different, inductive research strategy, which requires documenting the diversity of attested mind-ascribing practices in narratively organized discourse about animals, including the multiple practices at work in non-fiction.

The concept of discourse domains can be used to further this argument for replacing a binarized model of animal minds – accessibility in fiction versus opacity (and otherness) in non-fiction – with a scalar or gradient model involving different degrees of projected relatedness, mutuality and rapport across the fiction/non-fiction divide. Along the lines of what Wittgenstein called (2009) 'language games' and Levinson (1979) labelled 'activity types', discourse domains are frameworks for conduct that organize participants' verbal and non-verbal comportment around recognized modes of activity grounded in shared norms, purposes and goals. Relevant activities include playing tennis, having an academic debate, or going on a walk with a dog – in short, activities that involve interacting with one or more human or non-human others in a particular setting and for specific kinds of reasons. Encompassing ascriptions of mental states both within and beyond the species boundary, discourse domains in this sense also cut across the divide between fictional and non-fictional narratives. For example, in a discourse domain marked by an emphasis on the biophysical bases for human and non-human behaviour, ascriptions of subjectivity will remain severely curtailed, for the full range of species in both fictional and non-fictional accounts. By contrast, other discourse domains are marked by more prolific, far-reaching and detailed ascriptions. Hence the similarly extensive and particularized modelling of experiential worlds in texts otherwise miles apart, such as Jane Austen's novels, contemporary romance fiction, textbooks on forensic psychology and manuals on the training of rescue dogs (see also Herman forthcoming).

Figure 4.3 presents a visualization of the idea of discourse domains vis-à-vis ascriptions of subjective experiences to others – with particular reference to ascriptions that cross the species boundary. Each dot (or data-point) in the background grid constitutes a mind-ascribing act, with those acts being organized into domains governed by more or less distinctive norms. The size of the circles corresponds to the relative pervasiveness of discourse domains in a given culture, allowing for cross-cultural comparisons as well as tracking of the diachronic development and transformation of domains within a particular culture. The norms associated with each domain bear in a top-down fashion on all the representational practices that fall within its purview, including non-narrative and narrative modes, narratives that feature animals as well as narratives that do not, and non-fictional as well as fictional accounts.

Figure 4.3 suggests that discourse domain trumps genre when it comes to modelling *Umwelten* in narrative contexts: in a given instance a non-fictional account may feature more fine-grained ascriptions of subjective experiences

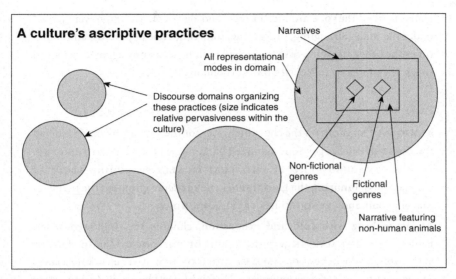

Figure 4.3 Discourse domains and mind-ascribing practices

to animals than would a fictional account, depending on the domain in which the narrative is anchored. This hypothesis is borne out by Excerpts 4.8 and 4.9, both of which, marked up in accordance with an annotation system to be discussed below, center on human-canine interactions. Excerpt 4.8 is taken from Jack London's 1903 novel *The Call of the Wild*, whereas 4.9 is excerpted from a recent non-fictional account of animal heroes (Stevens et al. 1997). In Excerpt 4.8, Buck, a sled dog, rescues John Thornton from the fast-moving river into which he has fallen. In Excerpt 4.9, a dog named Patches likewise acts as a rescuer, saving Marvin from drowning in a frigid lake.

Excerpt 4.8

<u>His master's voice</u> **acted on Buck like an electric shock**. He SPRANG TO HIS FEET AND RAN UP THE BANK AHEAD OF THE MEN TO THE POINT OF HIS PREVIOUS DEPARTURE.

Again the rope was attached and he was launched, and again he STRUCK OUT, BUT THIS TIME STRAIGHT INTO THE STREAM. **He had miscalculated once, but he would not be guilty of it a second time.** Hans paid out the rope, permitting no slack, while Pete kept it clear of coils. BUCK HELD ON TILL HE WAS ON A LINE STRAIGHT ABOVE THORNTON; THEN HE TURNED, and with the speed of an express train HEADED DOWN UPON HIM. Thornton saw him coming, and, as Buck struck him like a battering ram, with the whole force of the current behind him, he reached up and closed with both arms around the shaggy neck.

Hans snubbed the rope around the tree, and Buck and Thornton were jerked under the water. Strangling, suffocating, sometimes one uppermost and sometimes the other, dragging over the jagged bottom, smashing against rocks and snags, they VEERED IN TO THE BANK. (London 2009: 62–3)

Excerpt 4.9

ANXIOUSLY SEARCHING the churning waves for the spot where *his friend* had disappeared, Patches gave one **agonized** bark, THEN LEAPED INTO THE LAKE. He DOVE THROUGH 15 feet of water, FRANTICALLY SEARCHING ABOUT in the blackness. **Ignoring the glacial shock,** he suddenly glimpsed the thatch of Marvin's hair and CLENCHED HIS TEETH AROUND IT....

At last, **aching with cold and exhaustion,** choking on swallowed water, Patches BROUGHT MARVIN WITHIN REACH OF THE DOCK. Marvin clutched at the wood and Patches RELEASED HIS HOLD ON HIM. **It was up to Marvin now – Patches couldn't get out of the water alone.** **He felt himself being pushed to *safety* by *his friend*,** but once on shore he turned to see Marvin, overcome by shock, slipping under once more. **Marvin had blacked out!....**

Marving was fading fast. **If he slipped beneath the surface again he would surely die.** Patches PACED FRANTICALLY BEFORE THE DROWNING MAN, LICKED AT THE PALE, NEAR-FROZEN FINGERS AND WHINED. Then, **steeling himself against his own exhaustion,** he PLANTED HIS FOUR FEET FIRMLY ON THE ROUGH PLANKS, GRIPPED THE COLLAR OF MARVIN'S COAT IN HIS TEETH, AND PULLED. (Stevens et al. 1997: 20–1)

Because of the intricate inter-involvement of humans' and canids' evolutionary histories, in general the threshold for permissible ascriptions of mental states to dogs is higher than it is for ascriptions in accounts of many other sorts of human-animal interactions. But what is noteworthy here is that the non-fictional narrative projects a richer experiential world than does the fictional example. To facilitate a more precise comparison, I have marked up the two excerpts using

ALL CAPS mark locutions about observable actions by non-human animals that imply intentional or volitional states (e.g., 'STRAINING MIGHTILY')
underlining used for expressions that imply perceptual activity by an animal (e.g., '[Marvin] had disappeared')
italicized type used for expressions that index arrangements, situations, or practices to which non-human agents orient intentionally, whether individually or jointly with humans (e.g., '*master*', '*safety*', '*his friend*')
bold-faced type marks direct references to non-human mental states, including an animal's proprioceptive awareness of his or her own bodily condition or position
smaller bold marks free indirect discourse manifesting non-human subjectivity

Figure 4.4 Key to the annotation system used for Excerpts 4.8 and 4.9

the annotation system for which Figure 4.4 provides a key. The more marked-up a text that engages with non-human beings, the denser or more prolific the ascriptions of subjective experiences to the animal agents involved.

Excerpts 4.8 and 4.9 are almost exactly the same length: 184 and 187 words, respectively. The passages thus allow for an indicative comparison of the frequency and range of mental-state ascriptions across an equivalent span of text in the two narratives. The annotations reveal that both the number and the variety of ascriptions are greater in the non-fictional account than in London's novel, suggesting that it is not the fiction–non-fiction distinction per se but rather the norms organizing discourse domains that determine the degree to which detailed subjective experiences can be ascribed to animal agents in narratives.

Excerpt 4.8 does feature free indirect discourse ('He had miscalculated once …'). The passage also includes a direct reference to Buck's mental states, as well as references to his perceptual activity and to intentional actions on Buck's part. Per line of text, however, Excerpt 4.9 is considerably more marked up, and the passage also reveals more variation in the techniques used to project Patches's experiences. Reports that imply the dog's intentional activity are layered with multiple direct references to his mental (specifically, emotional) states; hence, in the first paragraph alone, mental-state descriptors include 'anxiously', 'agonized', 'frantically' and others. In addition, over the course of the excerpt, the narration moves in and out of the different ascriptive methods more rapidly than is the case in the passage from London. The second paragraph exemplifies these dynamic shifts in technique, moving from direct mental-state attribution, to implied intentionality on Patches's part, to free indirect discourse manifesting Patches's subjectivity, to further direct ascription intermixed with references to situations and relationships to which the dog orients intentionally ('safety', 'his friend'), to expressions suggesting Patches's perceptual activity, and then back to more free indirect discourse. The net result of the greater frequency and range of the ascriptions in Excerpt 4.9 as compared with Excerpt 4.8 is a text that builds a richer profile of non-human subjectivity than the profile that emerges from London's text. Indeed, it is plausible to hypothesize that, because London was embroiled in what became known as the 'nature fakers' debate, and sought to hedge his account of Buck's experiences to ward off charges of anthropomorphism made by the naturalist John Burroughs (1903; cf. London 1909), there is less scope for *Umwelt* modelling in his fictional text than in the non-fictional account of Patches's rescue of Marvin.

Previously I argued for the need to register the variability, and plurality, of the norms organizing thought presentation in particular. I can now restate this argument by connecting it more explicitly with the idea of discourse domains – and with the way contrasting domains link up, in turn, with different ontological commitments, more or less parsimonious or prolific allocations of possibilities for subjectivity beyond the realm of the human (Herman 2014; Kohn 2013). As suggested by Figure 4.5, what Leech and Short (2007) treated as singular norms associated with the semantics of reporting can now be redescribed, in contexts of thought presentation, as a range of 'bands' of permissible ascriptive practices. The various bands, cutting across the fiction/non-fiction divide, will be more or less inclusive of available methods for presenting minds. Hence the domains associated with behaviourist discourse disallow all but narration and perhaps the bare suggestion of NRTA or NRPA, whereas domains associated with the exploratory modelling of non-human worlds license the full range of ascriptive techniques when it comes to projecting animal experiences.

To be sure, Figure 4.5 raises further questions that will need to be addressed in future work. For example, how can the concept of discourse domains be used to capture the distinction between exploratory modelling of animal experiences, like Baker's (1967) and Carson's (2007), and naive or uncritical anthropomorphism, marked by the full spectrum of mind-presenting techniques but also the suppression or evacuation of potential differences in the structure of experience across the species boundary? Likewise, how can the approach be used to capture the potential bottom-up impact of specific narratives on normative assumptions about animal worlds? For instance, Gabriela Cowperthwaite's 2013 documentary film *Blackfish*, part of a larger constellation of narratives linking the deaths of several animal trainers to the treatment of orca whales

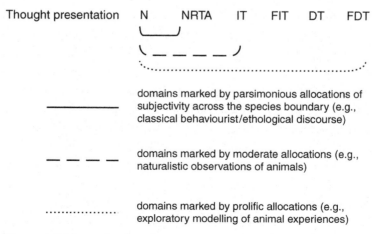

Figure 4.5 Norms for thought presentation across discourse domains

kept in captivity at marine mammal parks maintained by the SeaWorld corporation, has contributed to the call for legislation to free the whales, on the grounds that current practices violate the US Constitution's prohibition of slavery. How is it that such narratives (but not others) lead to the recalibration of ascriptive norms, or shifts in the discourse about particular species to different normative 'bands' – whereby the accounts at issue, once grounded in parsimonious allocations of subjective experience, now fall within the purview of norms based on moderate or even prolific allocations? Coming to terms with these and other questions posed by forms of storytelling that extend beyond the human will require new modes of inquiry, cutting across established disciplinary boundaries as well as species lines.

References

Baker, J. A. (1967), *The Peregrine*, London: Collins.

Bockting, I. (1994), 'Mind Style as an Interdisciplinary Approach to Characterisation in Faulkner', *Language and Literature*, 3.3: 157–74.

Bruner, J. (1990), *Acts of Meaning*, Cambridge, MA: Harvard University Press.

Burroughs, J. (1903), 'Real and Sham Natural History', *Atlantic Monthly*, (September) 91: 298–310.

Carson, R. (1937), 'Undersea', *Atlantic Monthly*, (September) 160: 55–67.

Carson, R. (1951), *The Sea Around Us*, Oxford: Oxford University Press.

Carson, R. (1998 [1955]), *The Edge of the Sea*, New York: Houghton Mifflin.

Carson, R. (2007), *Under the Sea-Wind*, New York: Penguin.

Cohn, D. (1978), *Transparent Minds: Narrative Modes for Presenting Consciousness in Fiction*, Princeton, NJ: Princeton University Press.

Descola, P. (2013), *The Ecology of Others*, trans. G. Godbout and B. P. Luley, Chicago, IL: Prickly Paradigm Press.

Fludernik, M. (1993), *The Fictions of Language and the Languages of Fiction*, London: Routledge.

Fowler, R. (1977), *Linguistics and the Novel*, London: Methuen.

Halliday, M. A. K. (1971), 'Linguistic Function and Literary Style: An Inquiry into the Language of William Golding's *The Inheritors*', in S. Chatman (ed.), *Literary Style: A Symposium*, New York: Oxford University Press: 330–65.

Herman, D. (2011), '1880–1945: Re-minding Modernism', in D. Herman (ed.), *The Emergence of Mind: Representations of Consciousness in Narrative Discourse in English*, Lincoln, NE: University of Nebraska Press: 243–72.

Herman, D. (2014), 'Narratology beyond the Human', *DIEGESIS: Interdisciplinary E-Journal for Narrative Research*, 3.2: 131–43.

Herman, D. (forthcoming), 'Animal Minds across Discourse Domains', in
    M. Burke and E. Troscianko (eds), *Dialogues between Literature and Cognition*,
    Oxford: Oxford University Press.
Kohn, E. (2013), *How Forests Think: Toward an Anthropology beyond the Human*,
    Berkeley, CA: University of California Press.
Leech, G. and Short, M. (2007), *Style in Fiction: A Linguistic Introduction to English
    Fictional Prose*, 2nd ed., Harlow: Longman.
Levinson, S. C. (1979), 'Activity Types and Language', in P. Drew and J. Heritage
    (eds), *Talk at Work: Interaction in Institutional Settings*, Cambridge: Cambridge
    University Press: 66–100.
London, J. (1909), 'The Other Animals', in *Revolution and Other Essays*, New York:
    Macmillan: 235–67 <http://london.sonoma.edu/Writings/Revolution/animals.
    html> [accessed 2 January 2015].
London, J. (2009 [1903]), *The Call of the Wild*, in *The Call of the Wild and Selected
    Stories*, New York: Signet Classics: 3–84.
McHale, B. (1978), 'Free Indirect Discourse: A Survey of Recent Accounts',
    PTL: A Journal for Descriptive Poetics and Theory of Literature, 3: 249–78.
Prince, G. (2003), *A Dictionary of Narratology*, 2nd ed., Lincoln, NE: University of
    Nebraska Press.
Semino, E. (2007), 'Mind Style Twenty-five Years On', *Style*, 41.2: 153–73.
Stanzel, F. K. (1984), *A Theory of Narrative*, trans. C. Goedsche, Cambridge:
    Cambridge University Press.
Sternberg, M. (1982) 'Proteus in Quotation-Land: Mimesis and the Forms of Reported
    Discourse', *Poetics Today*, 3.2: 107–56.
Stevens, P. D., with Vincent, Z., Crenshaw, N., Sobel, B. and Gavagan, D. (1988),
    'Patches', in Paul Drew Stevens (ed.), *Real Animal Heroes: True Stories of Courage,
    Devotion and Sacrifice*, New York: Dutton/Signet: 19–24.
Thompson, E. (2007), *Mind in Life: Biology, Phenomenology, and the Sciences of Mind*,
    Cambridge, MA: Harvard University Press.
Toolan, M. (2001), *Narrative: A Critical Linguistic Introduction*, 2nd ed., London:
    Routledge.
Uexküll, J. von (2010), *A Foray into the Worlds of Animals and Humans*, trans. J. D.
    O'Neil, Minneapolis, MN: University of Minnesota Press.
Warner, C. D. (1878), 'A-hunting of the Deer', in *The Complete Project Gutenberg
    Writings of Charles Dudley Warner* <http://www.gutenberg.org/ebooks/3136>
    [accessed 2 January 2015].
Wittgenstein, L. (2009), *Philosophical Investigations*, trans. G. E. M. Anscombe, P. M.
    S. Hacker and J. Schulte, Chichester: Wiley-Blackwell.
Woolfson, E. (2008), *Corvus: A Life with Birds*, London: Granta.

Building Hollywood in Paddington: Text World Theory, Immersive Theatre, and Punchdrunk's *The Drowned Man*

Alison Gibbons

5.1 Text World Theory and immersive theatre

Once considered an experimental niche of the narrative arts, immersive storytelling no longer seems peripheral but symptomatic of the cultural *jetztzeit* of the twenty-first century. Immersive theatre is a fast-growing subgenre of immersive storytelling (White 2013: 2). Immersive theatre comes in varied forms, but is characterized as theatre that is site-specific and requires audience involvement. Machon claims that it is 'discernable as that practice which actually allows you to be in "the playing area" with the performers, physically interacting with them' (2013: 67). The strategies of immersive theatre as a genre are not wholly new – White traces aesthetic sympathies in theatre and in live art performances back to the mid-twentieth century at least – but they are *in vogue* (see Machon 2009, 2013; White 2013). While Text World Theory approaches have predominantly focused on linguistic texts, recent studies have developed the framework in relation to mixed forms such as multimodal novels (Gibbons 2012) and mobile narratives (Gibbons 2014). To remain relevant to cultural and artistic experience today, Text World Theory must continue to advance by understanding the dynamics of immersive narratives.

Text World Theory is founded on a powerful conceptual metaphor of immersion: TEXT AS WORLD. This metaphor recognizes that processing any discourse involves constructing a mental representation which can be so vivid as to be comparable with the experience of the real world. Even so, in Text World Theory the ontological divide between discourse-world and text-worlds is resolute. While readers might experience various degrees of deictic and psychological projection into text-worlds (Whiteley 2011), those text-worlds maintain their integrity as fictional spaces distinct from the discourse-world. One of the major challenges that immersive theatre poses for Text World Theory then, relates to the ways in which the apparent actualization of the immersion metaphor alters projection relations between discourse-world and text-worlds. Pioneering the application of Text World Theory to immersive theatre, this chapter explores the cognitive implications of immersive theatre on text-world creation, focusing on Punchdrunk's (2013–14) London production *The Drowned Man: A Hollywood Fable*, which opened on 20 June 2013 and ran for just over a year, finishing 6 July 2014.

Cruickshank summarizes the challenges involved in analysing drama, acknowledging that the 'performance event in practice is ambiguous and inaccessible after the fact, and its interpretation individual and in flux at levels of both production and reception' (2014: 456). This is all the more apt in relation to immersive theatre where the free-roaming nature of audience participation means that no two audience members are likely to see all of the same scenes, let alone in the same order. The irreproducibility of live performance has often led stylisticians to focus on linguistic content. This is the approach taken by Cruickshank and Lahey (2010) in their application of Text World Theory to drama. Their discussion is important in extending the parameters of Text World Theory scholarship yet their decision to focus solely on the published play-text presents inevitable limitations. For instance, they add to Text World Theory's repertoire the concept of the 'staged world': 'Theatrical signals in the discourse (such as act and scene numbers, for example) will prompt a reader to build a conceptual space which corresponds to a performative enactment of the play' (2010: 76). However, since staged worlds are defined in ontological terms as text-worlds, Cruickshank and Lahey do not offer insight into the ways in which audience members experience these fictional text-worlds when they are actualized by their performance in the discourse-world.

This chapter advances the capabilities of Text World Theory in relation to theatre and performance by investigating the textual mechanisms employed to promote immersion and how such mechanisms position audience members in relation to text-worlds they are invited to explore physically. The discussion offers two important outcomes. First, it presents a nuanced understanding of the possible points of contact between text-worlds and the discourse-world that may be utilized across the narrative arts. Second, it promises to have wider significance for both Text World Theory and cognitive-poetic explorations of dramatic discourse and performance.

5.2   Welcoming the blended-world of performance

Punchdrunk's (2013–14) *The Drowned Man* was staged across four levels of a vast building in Paddington in central London. When prospective audience members purchased their tickets, they selected an arrival time, the purpose of which was to stagger audience entry into the performance spaces. To reach the performance areas, audience members stepped through a black curtain and walked through dark corridors emerging into a small dimly lit space where a member of the production team greeted them. Each audience member was given a white mask and instructed to wear it. They were told they were waiting for the elevator in which they would soon be taken to Temple Studios. Before this, their host Leland Madison Stanford would say a few words.

Leland Madison Stanford's Welcome Speech is a significant part of *The Drowned Man* from the point of view of Text World Theory analysis for two reasons. First, for the most part *The Drowned Man* is a contemporary dance performance. There is therefore little by way of linguistic text so the Welcome Speech provides a valuable opportunity to explicate the ways in which *The Drowned Man* builds worlds through language. Second, since the speech is delivered to audience members *before* they enter, it does vital work in constructing the parameters of the text-worlds to *The Drowned Man*. The Welcome Speech, which the audience hear as a voice recording, begins (Punchdrunk 2013–14):

> Good evening. This is Leland Madison Stanford. Welcome to Temple Studios. Thank you for coming here to celebrate the completion of our latest production, *The Drowned Man*.

Following speech conventions, the Welcome Speech begins with a greeting from speaker Leland Madison Stanford to the audience as receivers of the discourse. The first greeting in the Welcome Speech, 'Good evening', is what Firth describes as an 'affirmation' (1972). The affirmation imparts important world-building information; the noun within the affirmation changes as appropriate, marking out the temporality of the interaction. Used in these opening words, 'Good evening' matches the temporal parameters of the Welcome Speech (and its fictional context) with the audience's temporal reality. 'Evening' is therefore interpreted by real audience members as a timeframe they share with the absent and fictional character Stanford.

Stanford continues by introducing himself and offering another greeting: 'Welcome to Temple Studios'. The prepositional phrase in this second
greeting offers further world-building information, this time setting the scene.
The audience is then directly addressed with the formulaic politeness marker
'Thank you' while the proximal adverb 'here' functions to align the real building in Paddington with the fictitious Temple Studios. Stanford's mention of *The
Drowned Man* similarly creates resonances between discourse-world and text-
world. On one hand, it is a textual deictic reference to Punchdrunk's production
for which the real audience has purchased tickets; on the other, it reconstructs
The Drowned Man fictionally, as a movie being filmed within the studios.

The linguistic composition of these first few lines of the Welcome Speech
is crucial in terms of how they construct the text-worlds of *The Drowned Man*
relative to the discourse-world. From its opening, the Welcome Speech asks
the audience wilfully to suspend disbelief and to commit to a pretence: that
they are not theatre-goers but rather are about to celebrate the end of filming
with the cast at Temple Studios. In order to do so, audience members have to
create complex mental representations that project relationships between the
discourse-world and the text-world. Specifically, they must generate a blended-
world, as illustrated in Figure 5.1. Unusually for a theatrical performance, the
discourse-world is split. When the actor is physically present, the split does
not occur since actor and audience exist within the same spatiotemporal location. However, because the Welcome Speech is pre-recorded, the actor voic-
ing Stanford must have performed this elsewhere and prior to the audience's
present-time. The dotted line in the centre of Figure 5.1 represents the fictionality divide between discourse-world and text-world. As can be seen, this
ontological boundary remains intact. The blended-world, however, is vital in
creating the metaleptic illusion that the character Stanford is directly addressing and welcoming the audience in the discourse-world.

The blended-world is an innovation to Text World Theory proposed by
Gavins (2007: 146–64, 2013: 40–1) that incorporates the concept of blending from Conceptual Integration Theory (Fauconnier and Turner 2002).
Conceptual Integration Theory accounts for the way in which mental spaces
can merge to create new meanings. Input spaces are projected into a blended
space, and the process of completion results in an emergent blended structure
also containing any meanings unexplained within the blend or stemming
from unique experience. Gavins's conception of the blended-world enables a
Text World Theory account of metaphor since metaphors involve the conceptual mapping of mental constructs. Although Gavins initially claims that the

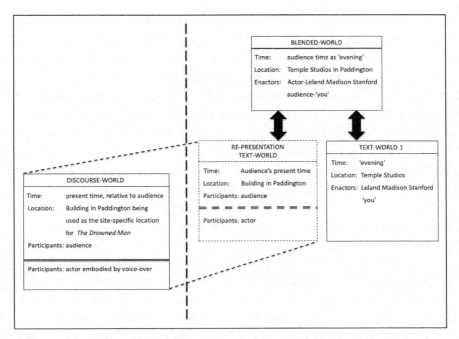

Figure 5.1 Ontological world structure for the opening to the Welcome Speech

blended-world 'comes into being whenever a metaphor occurs in a given text', she later adds that blended-worlds 'occur in discourse as the result of the conceptual merger of two otherwise independent text-worlds' (2007: 149). Metaphor is not present in the linguistic content of the Welcome Speech, but the metaleptic breach of text-world enactor talking to discourse-world participant relies upon metaphors of immersion such as TEXT AS WORLD and ARTWORKS ARE CONTAINERS in order to create the illusion of rupturing ontological boundaries. Audience members must use elements of the discourse-world and text-world as input spaces that merge to create the blended-world in which the audience is addressed by Stanford. Crucially, it is not the discourse-world itself that is used in the process of conceptual integration (this would, of course, be impossible) but a mental representation of the discourse-world. Figure 5.1 illustrates this, with the inclusion of what I am here calling a 're-presentation world': a world which re-presents the discourse-world as a text-world and thus as a mental construct.

Using Conceptual Integration Theory to account for the conceptual blending of discourse- and text-world in theatre and performance is by no means novel. In their original discussion of Conceptual Integration Theory, Fauconnier and

Turner use theatre as exemplar: 'Drama performances are deliberate blends of a living person with an identity. They give us a living person in one input and a different living person, an actor, in another. The person on stage is a blend of these two' (2002: 266). They continue, considering how the audience must also perform this conceptual integration in order to appreciate performance: 'For the spectator, the perceived living, moving, and speaking body is a supreme material anchor' (2002: 266). Theatre scholars have consequently adopted Conceptual Integration Theory to account for the cognitive complexities of performance as an art form and particularly the sense of ontological duplicity (Cruickshank 2014: 457; McConachie 2008; McConachie and Hart 2006).

Immersive theatre is often conceived as adding a further complexity to the basic conceptual integration network, which fundamentally consists of two input spaces, their generic mapping and the blended space (Fauconnier and Turner 2002: 45–6). Contemplating Punchdrunk's New York show *Sleep No More*, for instance, Worthen claims that it 'resists the straightforward blending of literary character to performer described by Fauconnier and Turner' (2012: 89) because it adds to the blend a grammar of choreographed dance. Shaughnessy agrees, appending to Worthen's statement that immersive theatre 'involves a complex fusion of simultaneous states of presence' (2013: 12). These 'simultaneous states of presence' are exposed by Text World Theory analysis. Where Conceptual Integration Theory deals only with inputs as conceptual spaces, Text World Theory's division of discourse-world and text-worlds shows the ontological status of the input spaces and therefore the ontological intricacies of the blended-world. Moreover, the deconstruction of world-building elements highlights Punchdrunk's linguistic strategies whereby the details of the text-world are created to match the discourse-world (its spatiotemporal parameters). Additionally, the acknowledgement in Text World Theory of the split discourse-world and the specific identification of discourse-world participants and text-world enactors reveals projection relations: audience members in the discourse-world psychologically project into the blended-world in which they self-implicate into the addressee role of apostrophic textual 'you'.

5.3   Encouraging participation through imagined text-worlds

Having established the blended-world, integrating discourse-world and initial text-world, the Welcome Speech continues to construct further text-worlds that include audience members through second-person address. The Welcome Speech serves a specific purpose in the context of the immersive theatre production: once audience members have created an emergent blend in which they self-implicate into the role of textual 'you', continued use of second-person address in further text-worlds is designed to encourage audience members to become dynamic participants through their physical discourse-world exploration of the performance spaces later. This section of the chapter will analyse the text-world composition of the Welcome Speech (see Figure 5.2) in order to show how it fosters audience members' motivation to explore the set of *The Drowned Man*. The Welcome Speech is quoted below in full (Punchdrunk 2013–14):

> Good evening. This is Leland Madison Stanford. Welcome to Temple Studios.
>
> Thank you for coming here to celebrate the completion of our latest production, *The Drowned Man*.
>
> Celebrations will begin in a few hours' time, after we have finished shooting the last few scenes on the schedule. Until then, you are all welcome to drink in the bar on the fairground set in studio three.
>
> You are also free to take a look around the studios where we have a number of other pictures currently in production. I must ask you to remain absolutely silent and to wear your masks at all times. I would also warn you to take special care if you choose to stray beyond the confines of the studio complex, as the surrounding neighborhood is unsafe after dark.
>
> Studio employees wearing black masks are posted throughout the building. Approach one if you need assistance, they will help you but they cannot guide you. I urge each of you to steer your own course, allowing your destiny to be determined by your own choices alone, and not by those of your companions.
>
> Tonight, your bearing shapes your fate. Thank you.

The second text-world of the Welcome Speech is generated through the shift to future tense in 'Celebrations will begin in a few hours' time' and maintained in the prepositional phrase 'after we have finished', which includes both retrospection in 'after' and anticipation of completed action with 'have finished' in present perfect. While the prepositional phrase 'Until then' returns, temporally and temporarily, to the first text-world, a spatial world-switch generates a third text-world with the stacked prepositional phrases in 'you are all welcome to drink in the bar on the fairground set in studio three'. Another spatial shift occurs in 'You are also welcome to take a look around the studios ...', producing

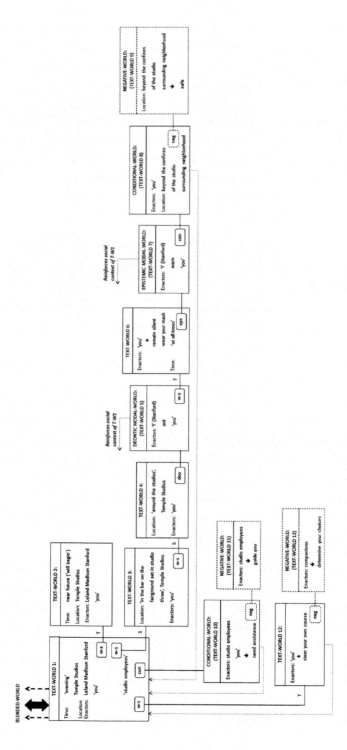

Figure 5.2 Total world structure for the Welcome Speech

a fourth text-world. Here, and throughout the Welcome Speech, words relating to a lexical set of movies and filming are prevalent ('production', 'set', 'studio', 'pictures'), reinforcing the fictional context of the text-worlds (Temple Studios).

At this point in the Welcome Speech, Stanford employs first-person singular 'I' in the declarative statement 'I must ask you ...'. The auxiliary generates a deontic modal-world including Stanford as first-person 'I' and textual 'you' as enactors, yet the verbalization process denoted by 'ask' additionally serves to reinforce the social context of Text-World 1 and by extension the blended-world. Full infinitives in the verb phrases 'to remain' and 'to wear' generate Text-World 6 through a temporal world-switch while Text-World 7 is another modal-world, this time epistemic, in the parallelism 'I would also warn you' which, of course, functions similarly to the structure it parallels in Text-World 5.

Text-World 8 is a conditional-world produced by the subordinating conjunction 'if'. As Gavins explains, in text-world composition, a conditional construction 'establishes an epistemic modal-world which has its status as an unrealized possibility made linguistically evident' (2007: 120). Audience members are thus prompted to mentally construct a text-world in which they 'choose to stray beyond the confines of the studio complex'. In the subordinate clause that follows, 'as the surrounding neighborhood is unsafe after dark', the negative prefix 'un-' triggers a negative-world. The content of the negative-world (a *safe* neighbourhood) has to be understood before its lack can be appreciated as a defining element (the *unsafe* neighbourhood) of the text-world from which the negation is linguistically construed. Text-World 8 is important since it compels audience members to imagine themselves as textual 'you', undertaking the action represented by the subordinate infinitive verb in the verb phrase 'choose to stray'. Moreover, the 'unsafe' character of this world may serve to prepare audience members for the potential feeling of vulnerability they might experience while exploring the set of *The Drowned Man*, particularly since promenade theatre is unconventional thus possibly beyond the comfort-zone of some audience members.

The next sentence in the Welcome Speech ('Studio employees wearing black masks are posted throughout the building') returns the audience to Text-World 1 and the blended-world, not least because they are standing waiting for the elevator with a studio employee dressed in black. The noun phrase 'the building' is a rare exception to the movie lexis Stanford's speech has so frequently employed, though of course this is for the important reason of audience safety and reassurance. It is a short-lived foregrounding of their current circumstances, since

Stanford's elaboration 'Approach one if you need assistance' produces another conditional world. This too functions to ensure the health and safety of audience members in the case of an emergency during the production. Such housekeeping notes might run the risk of shattering the illusion of the building in Paddington as Hollywood-style Temple Studios. However, Stanford continues, 'they will help you but they cannot guide you'. While the studio employees' acts of helping take place as a function-advancer within the conditional world, the syntactic negation in 'cannot guide you' generates a second negative-world.

Stanford's words 'I urge each of you', as with previous verbalization processes, remind the audience of the social context of the blended-world. Given that 'urge' is realized in present tense and not modified by a modal auxiliary (unlike 'I must ask' and 'I would also warn'), this statement does in fact return the audience to Text-World 1. It is a brief homecoming since the full infinitive verb form of 'to steer' presents a subordinate structure that implies future action (relative to the simple present tense of 'urge'). A temporal world-switch consequently occurs, inciting audience members to imagine themselves ('each of you') steering their 'own course' as well as performing the ensuing described action – 'allowing your destiny to be determined by your own choices alone'. The syntactic negation of the prepositional phrase 'by those of your companions' then activates a fleeting negative-world in which audience members do not make their own choices. Finally, the Welcome Speech ends by returning audience members, both in imaginative and linguistic terms, to the first text-world with the temporal adverb 'tonight' and the somewhat theatrical and sensational statement, 'your bearing shapes your fate'. Stanford closes with the gratitude expression 'Thank you', formally indexing the end of his speech.

Analyzing the text-world structure of the Welcome Speech discloses its linguistic devices. Words pertaining to the lexical set of movies are used as world-building information that, in addition to the play's subtitle *A Hollywood Fable* and to Stanford's clearly identifiable American accent, give the text-worlds a Hollywood character. Through self-implication with a textual 'you', audience members are required to project through a series of imagined text-worlds in which they 'look around' the studio and possibly 'stray' into fringe areas of the performance space. Moreover, in the latter half of the Welcome Speech, audience members as textual 'you' are the grammatical subjects of function-advancers in the form of verbs of motion: 'stray', 'steer'. In this way, Punchdrunk invites the audience to visualize themselves behaving as active participants in the performance and in such a way as to comply with Punchdrunk aesthetics (this includes: 'remain absolutely silent' and 'wear your mask at all times'). Another lexical set that can be noted towards the end of the Welcome Speech includes expressions that foreground autonomy: 'choose', 'choices', 'your own course', and the proximity of the synonymic adjectives 'own' and 'alone' in 'your own choices alone'. Coupled with this is a more mystic register ('destiny', 'bearing', 'fate') that elevates the power of audience member's prospective independent explorations to cosmic proportions.

To protect the blended-world from disintegration, the Welcome Speech offers frequent reminders of the social context of Text-World 1. These take the form of statements featuring verbalization processes: 'I must ask you', 'I would also warn you' and 'I urge you'. Moreover, since all of the text-worlds in the Welcome Speech develop outwards from Text-World 1 and since they all rely on the textual 'you' that is integrated with audience member in the blended-world, each new text-world is successively fed into the blend. These imagined worlds and the inquisitive behaviour they promote consequently exist for audience members as cognitive possibilities, actions they are motivated to perform once they are taken up to the performance spaces.

5.4 Recognizing the staged world and embracing or refusing the figured trans-world

When the Welcome Speech finishes, the door to the elevator opens and a female actor in 1960s eveningwear invites the audience inside. As Stanford did in the Welcome Speech, she directly addresses them creating another blended-world, again integrating the discourse-world and a text-world. This text-world includes the elevator, the female character (represented by the female actor), and a timeframe of the 1960s as suggested by her costume. When the audience leave the elevator, they can begin exploring the set of *The Drowned Man*. Some audience members choose to follow particular actors so that they witness all of his or her scenes, while others explore the building and therefore view a potentially more random collection of narrative episodes. Whatever technique an audience member chooses, there is no denying that the atypical nature of immersive theatre, with actors occupying the same spaces as audience members, impacts the ontological architecture of text-world dynamics. This is an effect of what Papaioannou, in relation to Punchdrunk's work, has described as 'experimenting with, and sometimes blurring, the boundaries between normality and irregularity; that is, between the safety of spectatorial distance and the unpredictability of proximity' (2014: 166).

Surprisingly, although actors and audience members are physically present within the same space, in the performance areas Punchdrunk deliberately segregates them in ontological terms. While Stanford and the female actor spoke directly to the audience, the dancers predominately engage with their fellow performers. Furthermore, the white masks worn by the audience mark them out as *not*-performers and thus distinct from the representational action. In a comment posted in response to the *Time Out* review of the show, for instance, Dewi clearly differentiates between fictional characters and the audience when s/he relays, 'A character comes in followed by a masked entourage' (*Time Out* 2013). Similarly, in response to an online survey about Punchdrunk's *Sleep No More* (Gibbons unpublished), one participant admitted that the 'masks themselves looked quite scary too. It's unfortunate as it made it easier to identify who was a performer and who was a spectator'. Conversely, other participants in this survey felt that the masks helped them to immerse within the fiction of the performance: one respondent commented that by 'wearing the masks the other audiences members became nothing more than parts of the scenes that I was walking through'; another felt that they 'allowed us to ignore others around us and concentrate on the performances and our environment'. In light of such comments, Fauconnier and Turner's conception of drama as a blend does not entirely encapsulate the ontological complexities engendered by the participatory nature of immersive theatre. They acknowledge, for instance, that the 'spectator can decompress the blend to recognize outer-space relations between these input spaces, as when we recognize the actor has not quite got the accent right or Hamlet trips over the stage lights' (2002: 266). This does not, however, account for the cognitive process of continuing to run the blend of performer-as-character while also being conscious of the theatrical context of the performance in the discourse-world.

At this point, it is helpful to revisit Cruickshank and Lahey's (2010) discussion of the staged world. They propose that when using Text World Theory to analyse play-texts, the framework must distinguish between two levels of dramatic representation, which they classify as 'staged worlds' and 'fictional worlds'. Although both are imagined text-worlds for readers, fictional worlds are forms of text-world concerned with the fictional narrative, the story and its characters, while the staged world is the *enactment* of that story by actors. In Cruickshank and Lahey's words, the 'reader of drama does not only imagine a world in which the fictional characters [...] exist: in having two simultaneous points of view (as reader and as imagined audience), they imagine a *stage* on which a fictional world in which [those characters] exist is *represented*' (2010: 75–6, emphasis in original).

Because they are talking about the reading of play-texts, Cruickshank and Lahey classify both as text-worlds. The staged world, however, in relating to the staged context might be understood to shift its ontological anchoring relative to either the reading or the audience experience. When reading a play-text, the staged world is, unavoidably, a text-world. When viewing a performance, it must transfer into a layer of representation in the discourse-world yet distinct from that discourse-world by the very fact of its designed and choreographed nature. This is perhaps what Worthen meant when speaking of the shortcomings of blending theory for Punchdrunk's brand of immersive theatre. Indeed he muses, 'much as the (wandering, gathering, dispersing) audience is visibly choreographed into the spectacle, dancing here embraces a wide variety of activities, some in a conventional modern-dance idiom and some not, but all challenging the lamination of movement and gesture to representation, to character, to writing' (2012: 90). Relating Cruickshank and Lahey's levels of text-world architecture to *The Drowned Man*, then, the performance takes place in the discourse-world with performers and audience members as participants. When audience members notice the style of and choreography behind the dancers' movements as well as when they notice other mask-wearing audience members, they are forced to acknowledge the staged world (which in viewing performance compared with reading play-text is a frame of representation anchored in the discourse-world). The actors' performative actions are also part of a blended-world, which exists as the physical dramatization of the fictional world (text-world).

The final aspect of Punchdrunk's *The Drowned Man*, and immersive theatre more generally, to be considered in this analysis is what happens when audience members are invited to participate in the action in some way. Papaioannou claims that 'the spectators become a part of the choreographic landscape by means of what they do, by inviting or being invited to physical and emotional contact, but also by means of how they try to avoid this from happening' (Papaioannou 2014: 166). His words are telling in that however audience members respond to a performative incitement, whether they commit to or resist participation, influences their relationship with the fictional text-world and the blended-world. Although Punchdrunk are famed for private one-on-one encounters (often implied in critical reviews to be an audience member's ultimate aspiration in Punchdrunk shows), this analysis will focus on a moment of invitation to a single audience member but within a more public scene.

During *The Drowned Man*, performers occasionally gesture to audience members to collude with them – perhaps to hold their hand or to embrace them – and I have witnessed two opposing reactions: alarmed embarrassment which is often accompanied by a physical movement away from the performer and towards the apparent safety of fellow audience members; or an eagerness for and an openness towards interaction. Holding the gaze of a performer and/ or taking their hand is an act of performative complicity, producing what Vincs (2013: 136) has referred to as a 'gem moment' of increased engagement. In such moments, however fleeting, an audience member feels entirely absorbed in the interaction. Moreover, their own physical deed in the discourse-world is inter-relating with represented fictional text-world through a performative action (in the staged world).

I attended Punchdrunk's *The Drowned Man* in December 2013 and during the performance experienced a gem moment. One of the central plotlines in *The Drowned Man* is a love story between William and Mary. Mary, however, has been unfaithful and William's increasing jealousy eventually leads him to murder her. Realizing that she is dead, William looks stunned and stumbles towards the audience, muttering her name several times and looking to members of the audience. During the performance I attended, the performer playing William looked directly at me, and slowly moved to embrace me. I echoed the gesture. The moment did not last long but during our embrace, the performer as the character William whispered into my ear, 'Why do you look so pale?' Having previously called out 'Mary', this utterance – audible only to me and not my fellow audience members – addressed me as 'Mary' or at least as a phantom or hallucinatory enactor of Mary seen by William. The textual 'you' spoken by the performer is therefore doubly-deictic (Herman 1994, 2002), addressing both a fictional 'you' (the enactor of Mary) within a text-world and an apostrophic 'you' (an audience member who has physically responded) in the discourse-world. Additionally, because I responded physically my acceptance of the address, and the performative role it signified, generated what I have elsewhere called a 'figured trans-world' (Gibbons 2012: 77–81, 2014: 415). Figured trans-worlds are created when a reader or participant 'is required and/or directed by the text into a performative role in the discourse-world, a role that calls upon corporeal activity and insinuates, to a greater or lesser extent, active reader involvement in the narrative' (2012: 80). What differentiates the figured trans-world from the blended world is the participant's active and corporeal role. That is, not only do they psychologically project into the role of a text-world character, but their performative movement recasts trans-world projection as embodied action. Thus in *The Drowned Man*, my own performative act in the discourse-world is an example of figuration, mapping my movements onto a character in the fictional text-world. Audience members who retreat from such invitations are not only taking a physical step back but also a figurative one, disengaging with the figured trans-world offered by the performer.

While textual 'you' and double deixis contribute to creating blended-worlds in linguistic and psychological terms, a figured trans-world requires physical participation. In the case of immersive theatre where the dynamics of performance and encouraged audience participation seek to literalize the TEXT AS WORLD metaphor, such physical interaction exists in the discourse-world and contributes movement to the staged-world. Moreover, the concretized form of trans-world projection that is encapsulated in the figured trans-world becomes part of the complex network of worlds as input spaces in immersive theatre. It is therefore used as additional information that is fed into a blended-world in which performers act out characters who interact with characters embodied by audience members.

In Figure 5.3, the figured trans-world is represented in dotted lines since it is founded on merely the illusion of interaction between discourse-world and text-world through the concretized form of trans-world projection on the part of audience member. This action and the details of the discourse-world are of course filtered through a re-presentation world. However, I have not included it nor have I included the staged world in Figure 5.3 since neither feature as a recognized layer of representation for the audience member in this moment. Nevertheless, both the re-presentation of the discourse-world and the text-world continue to be fed into a blended-world that encapsulates the integrated experience of these multiple world parameters in immersive theatre. The ontological divide between fictional text-world and discourse-world is not destroyed, only distorted in the audience member's experience of immersive theatre, and it is this distortion that offers poignancy and strength to a participant's impression of being immersed in the text-worlds of immersive theatre.

5.5   Conclusion

Using Text World Theory to approach the theatrical play-text, Cruickshank and Lahey (2010) progressed the framework's understanding of drama. Their focus on the readerly experience of the linguistic composition of the play-text, however, meant that their proposed augmentations had limitations for live

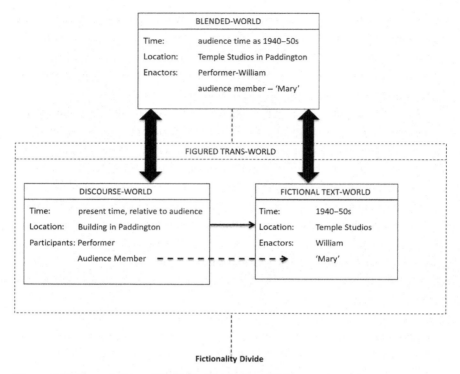

Figure 5.3 Figured Trans-Worlds in *The Drowned Man*

performance. By exploring what might be thought of as a radical example of audience participation in the form of immersive theatre, namely Punchdrunk's *The Drowned Man*, this chapter has advanced the capabilities of Text World Theory in relation to theatre and performance. Not only has the applicability of the framework for performance analysis been established, the chapter has also demonstrated the value of Text World Theory in explicating the ontological world relations of performance. The chapter explicitly develops Cruickshank and Lahey's concept of the staged world by suggesting that it shifts its ontological foundations in context: it is a text-world construct in the reading of a play-text but a discourse-world frame in performance.

My analysis of *The Drowned Man* builds upon existing cognitive approaches in theatre studies by employing Fauconnier and Turner's (2002) Conceptual Integration Theory, which shows that actors and characters are blended. However, using Gavins's (2007) adaptation of blending for Text World Theory in the form of the blended-world, my analysis proves that a Text World Theory account of conceptual integration provides a more nuanced understanding of the ontological dynamics of immersive theatre: using worlds as input spaces distinguishes the ontological status of those world-inputs (text-world and/or re-presentation of discourse-world). Analysis of audience participation offered further insight into the ontological architecture of immersive theatre by showing how an audience member's performative action in a moment of increased engagement creates trans-world projection relations. The figured trans-world maps audience member onto character-enactor, and is converted into further input for the blended-world. Figured trans-world projection and its incorporation into the emergent structure of the blended-world is a key factor in enabling audience members to feel actively involved in immersive theatre.

Because the Text World Theory analysis presented in this chapter has concerned itself with performance and the way in which audience-participants experience text-worlds from the position of and in relation to their discourse-world context, the terms 'participant' and/or 'audience member' have mostly been used notionally. Like Iser's (1974) and Booth's (1983) 'implied reader', the participant(s) in this analysis are largely implied. Empirical investigations of real audience members' responses are therefore required to ascertain the psychological validity of immersive theatre experiences. Even so, the outcome of the Text World Theory analysis presented in this chapter is an enhanced understanding of the experiential and ontological dynamics of world-creation, both linguistically and performatively. It therefore progresses stylistic accounts of dramatic discourse and enriches cognitive-poetic understandings of ontology and experience across the narrative arts.

References

Booth, W. C. (1983), *The Rhetoric of Fiction*, Chicago, IL: University of Chicago Press.

Cruikshank, T. (2014), 'Performance', in P. Stockwell and S. Whiteley (eds), *The Cambridge Handbook of Stylistics*, Cambridge: Cambridge University Press: 456–66.

Cruickshank, T. and Lahey, E. (2010), 'Building the Stages of Drama: Towards a Text World Theory Account of Dramatic Play-Texts', *Journal of Literary Semantics*, 30.1: 67–91.

Eglinton, A. (2010), 'Reflections on a Decade of Punchdrunk Theatre', *Theatre Forum*, 37: 46–55.

Fauconnier, G. and Turner, M. (2002), *The Way We Think: Conceptual Blending and the Mind's Hidden Complexities*, New York: Basic Books.

Firth, R. (1972), 'Verbal and Bodily Rituals of Greeting and Parting', in J. S. La
    Fontaine (ed.), *The Interpretation of Ritual: Essays in honour of A. I. Richards*,
    London: Tavistock Publications: 1–38.
Gavins, J. (2007), *Text World Theory: An Introduction*, Edinburgh: Edinburgh
    University Press.
Gavins, J. (2013), *Reading the Absurd*, Edinburgh: Edinburgh University Press.
Gibbons, A. (2012), *Multimodality, Cognition, and Experimental Literature*, London:
    Routledge.
Gibbons, A. (2014), 'Fictionality and Ontology', in P. Stockwell and S. Whiteley
    (eds), *The Cambridge Handbook of Stylistics*, Cambridge: Cambridge University
    Press: 410–25.
Gibbons, A. (unpublished), Online Responses to a Questionnaire about Audience
    Experience of *Sleep No More*, 25 Participants, Collected March 2014.
Herman, D. (1994), 'Textual "You" and Double Deixis in Edna O'Brien's *The Pagan
    Place*', *Style*, 28.3: 378–410.
Herman, D. (2002), *Story Logic: Problems and Possibilities of Narrative*, Lincoln and
    London, NE: University of Nebraska Press.
Iser, W. (1974), *The Implied Reader: Patterns in Communication in Prose Fiction from
    Bunyan to Beckett*, Baltimore, MD: John Hopkins University Press.
Machon, J. (2009), *(Syn)aesthetics: Redefining Visceral Performance*, Basingstoke:
    Palgrave Macmillan.
Machon, J. (2013), *Immersive Theatres: Intimacy and Immediacy in Contemporary
    Performance*, Basingstoke: Palgrave Macmillan.
McConachie, B. (2008), *Engaging Audiences: A Critical Approach to Spectating in the
    Theatre*, Basingstoke: Palgrave Macmillan.
McConachie, B. and Hart, E. (2006), 'Introduction', in B. McConachie and E. Hart
    (eds), *Performance and Cognition: Theatre Studies After the Cognitive Turn*,
    Oxford: Taylor and Francis: 1–25.
Papaioannou, S. (2014), 'Immersion, "Smooth" Spaces and Critical Voyeurism in the
    Work of Punchdrunk', *Studies in Theatre and Performance*, 34.2: 160–74.
Punchdrunk (2013–14), 'Mr Stanford Welcome Speech' from *The Drowned Man*,
    Temple Studies. Script shared with author through personal correspondence
    with Jennie Hoy (general manager of Punchdrunk) [Email communication],
    20 November 2013.
Shaughnessy, N. (2013), 'General Introduction: Operating in Science Theatres', in
    N. Shaughnessy (ed.), *Affective Performance and Cognitive Science: Body, Brain and
    Being*, London: Bloomsbury: 1–24.
Time Out (2013), 'Punchdrunk: The Drowned Man', *Time Out London*, online
    comment by Dewi <http://www.timeout.com/london/theatre/punchdrunk-the-
    drowned-man> [accessed 7 July 2014].

Vincs, K. (2013), 'Structure and Aesthetics in Audience Response to Dance', in
  J. Radbourne, H. Glow and K. Johanson (eds), *The Audience Experience: A Critical
  Analysis of Audience in the Performing Arts*, Bristol: Intellect: 129–42.
White, G. (2013), *Audience Participation in Theatre: Aesthetics of the Invitation*,
  Basingstoke: Palgrave Macmillan.
Whiteley, S. (2011), 'Text World Theory, Real Readers and Emotional Responses to *The
  Remains of the Day*', *Language and Literature*, 21.3: 23–42.
Worthen, W.B. (2012), '"The Written Troubles of the Brain": *Sleep No More* and the
  Space of Character', *Theatre Journal*, 64.1: 79–97.

Speaker Enactors in Oral Narrative

Isabelle van der Bom

6.1   Text World Theory and oral narrative

Since its conception, Text World Theory has been applied extensively to a range of discourse genres including, among others, narrative prose (e.g. Gavins 2003, 2010; Hidalgo Downing 2000; Werth 1999; Whiteley 2011), poetry (e.g. Giovanelli 2013; Lahey 2006; Nahajec 2009) and drama (Cruickshank and Lahey 2010). Face-to-face discourse has received relatively little attention from text-world theorists to date. This chapter offers a text-worlds approach to the study of linguistic identity in discursive interaction. Taking Werth's (1999) and Gavins's (2007) seminal publications on Text World Theory as a starting point, in this chapter I analyse face-to-face interview discourse. Specifically, I focus here on excerpts of an interview I held with a British-born Chinese female called Yàn, which features her experiences of growing up and how this impacted on her sense of self. My analysis suggests that the text-worlds framework offers a means of systematically exploring linguistic self-representation, and is able to account for how identity can be achieved and negotiated in interactional discourse. My aim in this chapter is to demonstrate how Text World Theory can be usefully extended to face-to-face discourse, and how the theory can contribute to fields of discourse studies and identity studies. Before proceeding with a text-world analysis, however, it is important first to discuss the ethnographic context in which the interview should be placed, and the view of 'identity' on which the analysis in this chapter rests.

6.2   Researching identity

The approach to identity I take in this chapter is a cognitive-discursive one. Starting from the idea of 'self' as constructed in interaction, I investigate those discursive practices through which Hong Kong migrants and British-Chinese people linguistically represent themselves in their interviews with me. Discursive approaches to identity tend to focus on identity as being *constructed*, rather than being *represented* in discourse (e.g. Benwell and Stokoe 2006; Bucholtz and Hall 2005; De Fina, Schiffrin and Bamberg 2006). Whereas the term 'represented' suggests that identity is pre-existing, identity 'construction' carries a sense of identity as something which is continuously created afresh. Analysts taking a discursive approach to identity argue that the represented view of identity characterizes identity as fixed and stable, and a creation of 'mind, cognition, the psyche, or socialization practices' (Benwell and Stokoe 2006: 9). They react against this approach by claiming that identity is relational (Hall 2004: 51), socially situated, fluid, fragmented and constructed in discourse (Bucholtz and Hall 2005), although they do typically accept that there is an overlapping continuance of identity from 'situation to situation as well as across the lifespan' (Bamberg, De Fina and Schiffrin 2011: 179).

I agree that it is important to show how 'identity' is on the one hand created in discursive interaction, while on the other hand emphasizing the continuity of identity beyond discourse, and across time and space. For this reason I adopt both approaches in this chapter. The main tenet underlying Text World Theory, namely that language shapes the kind of conceptual world a reader or hearer creates, directly affecting the conceptual processes used in the comprehension of meaning, is compatible with the ideas of identity as both discursively *constructed*, and conceptually *represented* in text-worlds. These text-worlds can furthermore be fleeting representations, or they can be fully detailed (cf. Whiteley 2011: 24; see also Werth 1999: 72; see also Gibbs 2005).

Bamberg, De Fina and Schiffrin (2011) discuss the dual directions that all theorists using discursive approaches to identity should follow: namely, combining the participant constructing the world (as in the discursive approaches to identity outlined above) with the world constructing the participant (as in alternative, representational approaches) (Bamberg, De Fina and Schiffrin 2011: 189). Text World Theory is well-suited to this type of dual-focused analysis, because it combines multiple discourse levels in its approach, incorporating larger macro-level ideological discourses and (world-)knowledge that participants bring to the discourse, with the kinds of worlds and identity positions that originate from the discursive level of the interaction. In this way Text World Theory accounts for both the more stable aspects of knowledge and experience that inform discourse as well as the dynamic, 'online' aspects of identity that may arise in and through it.

This chapter contributes to research on language and identity specifically by examining linguistic self-representation of a British-born Chinese female. An investigation of how Chinese migrants and their families linguistically represent themselves and talk about their life experiences is particularly relevant at a time when the Chinese community in the United Kingdom is undergoing change. Although immigration from Hong Kong to the United Kingdom has declined steadily since the 1990s, immigration from mainland China has grown exponentially, and is still growing (Office for National Statistics, 2011 Census). The new influx of Chinese immigrants with different backgrounds, who have migrated from other areas of China from Hong Kong, affects the experiences of those longer-settled Chinese migrants, and thus is also likely to affect identity formation and representation. The identity of settled Chinese migrants and their families is also likely to be affected by a number of other linguistic, socioeconomic and historical circumstances, such as the transfer of sovereignty over Hong Kong from the United Kingdom to China in 1997, and migration to the United Kingdom.

The ways in which people linguistically represent themselves is important. Rather than existing as a tool for simply conveying ideas, language has increasingly been recognized as being at the centre of who we are, how we see ourselves, where and how we belong, and the ways in which we relate to other people (cf. Joseph 2010: 9). Examining linguistic identity construction using Text World Theory helps to gain further insight into narrated life-experiences of migrant families and British-born Chinese people in Sheffield.

6.3   The ethnographic context of Yàn's interview

People of Chinese ethnicity are one of the fastest-growing ethnic groups in the United Kingdom according to recent census data (Office for National Statistics, 2011 Census). Whereas traditionally, Chinese migrants predominantly came from Hong Kong and the New Territories, most of the recent movements of Chinese people migrating to the United Kingdom stem from Mainland China. Such migratory movements, as well as other sociohistoric and economic changes, are likely to affect the experiences of longer-settled Chinese migrants and British-Chinese people in Britain, which makes them an interesting group of study. The data discussed in this chapter are drawn from a wider ethnographic research project exploring belonging, migration and identity among staff and students at a Chinese community school in Sheffield and focusing on longer-settled Chinese migrants (van der Bom 2015).

Yàn, whose interview I analyse in detail here, is part of the voluntary management staff of the school, in which I undertook ethnographic fieldwork for approximately two years. Yàn was born in Sheffield to immigrants from Hong Kong, but moved to Hong Kong upon birth, and lived there until she was three. Before the start of primary school, she moved back to Sheffield, and consequently she received almost all of her education in England. In college, she studied fashion and design, and in her early twenties, unable to find a job in Sheffield, she returned to Hong Kong. There, she established a family and built up a career as a fashion merchandiser. After fifteen years, she decided to give up her career in Hong Kong and return to Sheffield with her two children. Yàn described the main reason for her move back to Sheffield as family-related, explaining that she had done all of her travelling and career, and that it was 'family time now' (Interview with Yàn, February 2012). Upon her return to Sheffield in the early 2000s, Yàn took up part-time employment in a retail company, as well as voluntary work at the Dancing Dragon, the Chinese community school in which the research on which this chapter is based was carried out. She first worked in an assistant position, but when the person Yàn was assisting resigned and no replacement could be found, she took on all the responsibilities associated with her previous supervisor's role. Yàn found it important to improve her skills but was not always confident in her abilities. She told me several times that she found her new responsibilities difficult, but that she hoped it would improve her chances on the job market. Similarly, although she was fluent in English and Cantonese, she commented in the interview and on several separate occasions that she was not good at Chinese, and would like to be more fluent in Mandarin. Furthermore, although Yàn was most fluent and most confident in English, she was also enrolled in evening classes at a local college, because she wanted to improve her English and maths skills. It is relevant to mention this here, because Yàn's positioning towards the languages she spoke and her confidence in her own abilities might have impacted on how she related to me as another volunteer and researcher in the school and how she described herself in her narrative.

6.4   The discourse-world of Yàn's narrative

Despite its status as the 'prototypical' discourse type, face-to-face discourse presents an immediate and important challenge to Text World Theory because of its ontological complexity. The initial discourse-world created during the interview I held with Yàn included both of us as discourse participants, together with all the knowledge and ideologies we brought with us, and the elements perceivable to us at the time (Werth 1995: 52). The content of the stories Yàn was telling me in the interview discourse-world were conceptualized by us in the form of text-worlds which we both built at the time of the interaction in response to the discourse. At the time I analysed the transcript of the interview, which was much later, another discourse-world was created. This discourse-world included myself as an analyst, in a separate communicative situation with the 'authors' of the text – Yàn and an earlier version of myself as co-participant in the original discourse situation (I will refer to this earlier version of myself as 'Isabelle', for reasons of clarity). Logically speaking, during the analysis phase I was communicating with this earlier version of myself; however, this communication was indirect communication. In the discourse-world of my analysis of the interview, I was just an eavesdropper on a separate discourse situation (Goffman 1981; Werth 1999: 17–18). Although this is not normally explicitly acknowledged in sociolinguistics and discourse analysis, it is important to mention it because it has significant consequences for how we view transcripts and data. By presenting, selecting and analysing a particular piece of data, such as an interview or an excerpt of an interview, we take it out of its 'original' context and modify it. In doing so, we automatically construe a particular ontological domain in relation to the data and the participants in the data, as well as their social reality. Using a theory that is properly sensitive to this, such as Text World Theory, is an improvement, in this respect, on preceding approaches to the analysis of face-to face discourse. The transcript of the opening of the interview with Yàn (Excerpt 6.1) is provided below.

Excerpt 6.1

Isabelle	now it should now it should now it's working right
Yàn	ways <x> isn't it @@
Isabelle	yeah
Yàn	yeah
Isabelle	but I also had once that the battery @@ during the interview
Yàn	oh okay
Isabelle	but I just have put new batteries so it should not
Yàn	oh okay cause it runs out yeah it should last

As is clear from this excerpt, Yàn and Isabelle initially speak in the present-tense in this part of their conversation. This is logical in a face-to-face interview situation since participants normally share the same spatio-temporal context. The present-tense creates an initial text-world that is situated at that temporal moment and occupied by enactors of Isabelle and Yàn (Text-World 1). As the entire text consists of interview, this present time-zone underlies the entire discourse. It is the 'here-and-now' level of interaction, and concurrent to the discourse-world for the discourse participants Isabelle and Yàn at the time of the interview. Isabelle and Yàn refer into their own discourse situation in Text-World 1, through the use of present tense, first-person reference and specific definite reference to the shared perceptual item of the recording device.

6.5 The text-worlds of Yàn's narrative

In Excerpt 6.2, Yàn describes that she had a traditional Chinese upbringing. She explains that even though she was mainly exposed to English culture while growing up, her parents found it important that their children knew the Chinese language and culture, and were 'quite traditional Chinese really' (line 22).

Excerpt 6.2

1. Isabelle	okay erm so erm how did you experience growing up in Sheffield, or
2.	did you not grow up [in]
3. Yàn	[erm] I think for me it was a little bit easier because I I didn't know you know
4.	the culture in
5. Isabelle	[yeah]
6. Yàn	[China] or Hong Kong at the time so it was like being born here but then I was
7.	taken back to Hong Kong at a very very early age
8. Isabelle	oh you were oh
9. Yàn	so I did study I did study for a while in Hong Kong but i-it was mainly like erm
10.	nursery school
11. Isabelle	yeah
12. Yàn	and then it was a- a bit of travelling back and forth and my mum and dad had to
13.	go back and come back and you know so it there wa- there was a lot of <x>
14.	back and forth, so I did get a bit of the culture the Chinese culture but not a great
15.	deal because I was too young at the time
16. Isabelle	hmhm
17. Yàn	erm so a- it was mainly the Chin- the English culture that I knew growing up
18.	but being very traditional both my parents had to make sure that the

19.   children..(0.7) knew that we had to speak the language, know the culture erm
20.   [erm]
21. Isabelle [*yeah*]
22. Yàn   basically being quite traditional Chinese really

A past-tense text-world (Text-World 2) is cued in this fragment by Isabelle's use of the past tense in 'okay erm so erm how did you experience growing up in Sheffield?' (line 1). This world contains Yàn as enactor. Yàn's presence is indicated by the personal pronoun 'you', which most listeners will interpret as directly referring to Yàn. Yàn starts her reply to Isabelle with the words 'I think for me' (line 3), which creates a world-switch to an epistemic modal-world (the use of 'I think' clearly indicates that Yàn is emphasizing her own thought processes) through which Yàn briefly refers into the present time-zone, before continuing in the past tense. Text-World 2 continues to develop with a past-tense time signature, as Yàn describes a past situation, namely her childhood.

Following the statement 'it was a little bit easier' in line 3 of Excerpt 6.2, Yàn continues with a negation, 'I didn't know' (line 3). This creates a shift from the epistemic modal-world cued at the start of the line by 'I think' to a second epistemic modal-world (cued by the verb 'know'). In this world Yàn's knowledge of the culture in China and Hong Kong is conceptualized and then negated ('I *didn't* know you know the culture in China or Hong Kong at the time': lines 3–6). As she is talking about her childhood experiences of growing up, the negated meaning of the utterance feeds back into the first epistemic modal-world of Yàn's experiences, cued by 'I think', and contributes to the characterization of Yàn during her early childhood. Figure 6.1 illustrates the different worlds created diagrammatically.

Text-World 2 is represented on the left side of the figure and the epistemic modal-world of Yàn's early childhood is shown emerging from this in the top-right corner of the figure. The negated epistemic modal-world is represented diagrammatically in the bottom left-hand corner of the figure. As Yàn continues her narration detailed in Excerpt 6.2, further worlds are created that capture Yàn's childhood experiences. The enactor of Yàn in Text-World 2 further develops through enrichment of these worlds.

Yàn's narrative in Excerpt 6.2 is interspersed with discourse markers, including 'you know', 'like' and 'really'. In Section 6.5.1 I examine the functions of 'you know', focusing on how this discourse marker positions Yàn within the 'here-and-now' level of interaction.

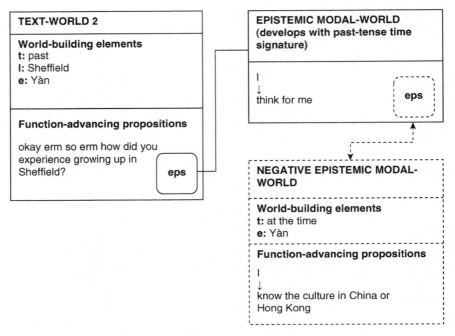

Figure 6.1 Text-world patterns in Yàn's narrative, lines 1–6

6.5.1   The here and now of face-to-face discourse

The negated utterance in lines 3 to 6 of Excerpt 6.2 ('I I didn't know you know the culture in China or Hong Kong at the time') includes the discourse marker 'you know'. The functions of 'you know' have been discussed extensively in academic research over the past decades (e.g. Holmes 1986, 1995; Lakoff 1973; Müller 2005; Schiffrin 1987). Although traditionally 'you know' was considered a filler (c.f. Müller 2005), more recently the term has been recognized as having a variety of different textual and interpersonal functions (Müller 2005: 147; Schiffrin 2001: 139).

The scholarship on discourse markers such as 'you know' demonstrates that it is difficult to interpret the exact function of these features, because often a marker can be interpreted in multiple ways. From a text-world perspective, the verb 'know' is usually treated as modalized, and is therefore treated as addressing an interactant's knowledge, thus creating an epistemic modal-world in which the utterance is conceptualized. However, speakers and listeners in face-to-face discourse will be familiar with the pragmatic norms of discourse markers and so are likely to treat 'you know' as fulfilling a more interpersonal function. This shows how important it is for text-world analysts to examine the

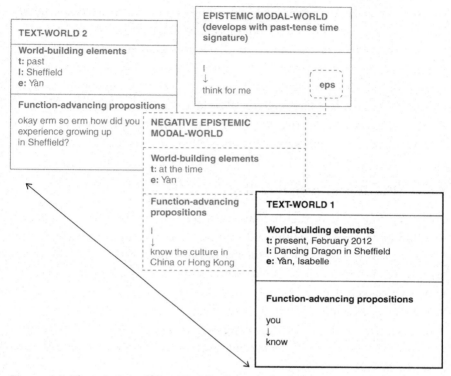

Figure 6.2 The priming of Text-World 1 through the discourse marker 'you know'

specific context in which language is used; in this case, the assumed pragmatic norms associated with face-to-face encounters have implications for how the clause 'you know' may be interpreted: although 'you know' can hold multiple possible meanings in a discourse-world of spoken interaction, as a discourse marker 'you know' points to the interactive level of the discourse, or the 'here and now' present-tense time zone of the interview. In this specific discourse context, 'you know' can function either as a filler or as a more intersubjective strategy. In the case of Yàn's interview, I would argue that 'you know' acts to prime Text-World 1, the present-tense text-world underlying the entire interaction. As such, it briefly brings Text-World 1 into attention, as is represented diagrammatically in Figure 6.2.

The concept of priming stems from Contextual Frame Theory (Emmott 1997: 123), and happens when one contextual frame (a mental representation broadly equivalent to a text-world) becomes the main focus of attention for the reader. This most commonly occurs when the action in a narrative shifts from one frame, or text-world, to another. In the way I use priming here, however, it can also occur when no shift takes place, but features of the narration never-theless point to worlds distinct from those in which the main action develops. Because the main action continues to develop in another text-world than the one primed, the shift of attention to the primed text-world is only temporary in such cases. The text-world that is primed is only a fleeting representation. In the case of Yàn's narrative, although Text-World 1 is primed frequently, the text-worlds and modal-worlds that are likely to continue to be the main focus for listeners or readers in this part of the interaction are those of Yàn's childhood.

6.5.2   The discourse marker 'like'

Following Yàn's use of the discourse marker 'you know' and the negation 'I I didn't know you know the culture in China or Hong Kong at the time' (lines 3–6), Yàn returns back to the main embedded epistemic modal-world, represented in Figure 6.1, with the words 'so it was like being born here but then I was taken back to Hong Kong at a very very early age' (lines 6–7). This utterance contains another interesting discursive feature, namely the discourse-marker 'like'. It is interesting to pay more attention to this linguis-tic feature in the interview transcript, because the function of 'like' is not always clear-cut.

Linguists have studied the different functions of 'like' for several decades (e.g. Andersen 1997, 2001; Miller and Weinert 1995; Romaine and Lange 1991; Schourup 1985; Tagliamonte 2004; Underhill 1988). Although the discourse marker has a great array of possible pragmatic and non-pragmatic meanings, including its potential to fulfil a number of different pragmatic functions at the same time (D'Arcy 2005: 16), the literature has mostly focused on three functions of 'like'. First, 'like' may be used as a quotative, a use which has been widely investigated (e.g. Romaine and Lange 1991; Tagliamonte 2004, 2005, 2012). Quotative uses of 'like' occur when 'like' is used to introduce reported speech and thought. Second, 'like' has been recognized as a focuser, or, in other words, as a marker of new information or focus (e.g. Andersen 2001; D'Arcy 2005; Miller and Weinert 1995; Underhill 1988). Third, 'like' has been described as a feature denoting 'approximation' or 'non-equivalence' (e.g. Andersen 2001; Jucker and Smith 1998; Schourup 1985). In this case, 'like' is used to indicate a disjunction between what is said and what is thought, thereby marking psy-chological distance towards the linguistic expression that follows (cf. Andersen 2001: 219). Although not as widely acknowledged, 'like' is also seen as a stance strategy by some linguists (e.g. Helt and Foster-Cohen 1996: 316). In such cases, it is used by speakers to indicate for the listener the significance of upcoming information.

Similar to the linguistic feature 'you know', it is interesting to examine the possible function(s) of 'like' in Yàn's utterance, as it allows further exploration of how pragmatic meaning is incorporated into the Text World Theory model. Readers or listeners might interpret Yàn's 'like' in lines 6–7 ('so it was like being born here but then I was taken back to Hong Kong at a very very early age') as an indication of approximation, or in other words, as indicating that growing up in Sheffield can be equated with being born in Sheffield, but then being taken back to Hong Kong at an early age. This interpretation however, even if taken non-literally, only seems to capture a few years of Yàn's childhood rather than her entire upbringing. Readers or hearers are likely to understand that this interpretation does not comprise the full extent of Yàn's experiences of growing up, and that there may be alternative, more fitting interpretations. It is also possible that Yàn's utterance 'it was like' will be interpreted by listeners as a marker that new information is to follow, information that further exemplifies Yàn's experiences of childhood. It is worth mentioning that Yàn narrates these experiences following the discourse marker 'like' in the passive voice, which suggests that she had no control over being taken back to Hong Kong.

In short, 'like' as it is employed in lines 6–7 of Excerpt 6.2 has a textual function (marking new information), but, like 'you know' discussed above, it can also be seen as serving an interpersonal function (marking the significance of the new information to the listener, or signalling to the listener that the expression captures growing up only loosely). Because Text World Theory is flexible enough to account for the complexities of human syntax as well as the nuances of language in context (Werth 1999: 31), it is able to incorporate all the readers' or listeners' possible interpretations of 'like' into its framework. If 'like' is interpreted as signalling the loose approximation between growing up and 'being born here but then taken back to Hong Kong' (lines 6–7), readers might use this linguistic information to enrich the text-world of Yàn's childhood, Text-World 2. They will also enrich Text-World 2 with their imaginations of what else growing up was like for Yàn. If 'like' is interpreted by readers as marking the importance of the information following, this would foreground the experience of being born in Sheffield but being taken back to Hong-Kong in the Text-World 2. Simultaneously, this would prime Text-World 1 for listeners or readers, because they could interpret the use of this discourse feature as especially emphasizing the importance of the information following 'like' to both the interviewee Isabelle and to themselves as readers of the transcript.

6.5.3 The discourse marker 'really'

Yàn describes her upbringing in Excerpt 6.2 as 'basically being quite traditional Chinese really' (line 22). Note Yàn's use of the discourse marker 'really' in this utterance. 'Really' has syntactic flexibility, but is more common in medial-position than in utterance-final position as it is found here (Gray 2012: 153). Surprisingly, only limited research has been conducted into the function of 'really' in final position, but it has been argued that it functions as an afterthought (Paradis 2003: 205). Biber, Conrad and Leech describe the adverb 'really' as a stance marker because it overtly marks a speaker's attitude to a clause (2002: 385). They see the use of 'really' in clause-final position as bearing the 'epistemic stance meaning of "in reality" or "in truth"' (Biber, Conrad and Leech 2002: 385). 'Really' additionally can be seen to function as a mitigating strategy that lessens the force of the preceding statement; specifically, it can be seen to indicate approximation or 'looseness', placing emphasis on the speaker's presence in the interaction, and hence, his or her subjectivity. In my reading, Yàn's use of 'really' fulfils this last function, emphasizing her own presence in the interaction, and therefore highlighting the truth-value of the preceding utterance concerning her upbringing ('basically being quite traditional') and signalling that this represents her own beliefs or point of view, rather than an unmitigated assertion.

So far, I have discussed the text-world patterns Yàn creates when talking about her childhood experiences and identity. I have described the text-worlds of Yàn's childhood experiences, and shown how these worlds contribute to the characterization of Yàn during her early childhood. I have also focused on Yàn's positioning within the 'here-and-now' level of interaction. Through an analysis of the discourse markers 'you know', 'like' and 'really', I have provided insight into how Yàn constantly primes the text-world of the interview. I would argue that by priming Text-World 1 frequently, Yàn indicates her awareness of Isabelle in the interaction, highlighting the negotiated nature of the reality Yàn represents to Isabelle in the interview. I now focus my Text World Theory analysis on how Yàn brings together the enactors of Text-World 1 and Text-World 2 in a subsequent excerpt of the interview.

6.5.4 Generalized experience

Excerpt 6.3 below is a continuation of the conversation begun in Excerpt 6.2:

Excerpt 6.3

23. Yàn   err which was a bit you know at that age you think oh do I know myself as
24.   English or do I know myself as Chinese but you look at yourself and you say

25.   that yes I am Chinese but just being brought up in a different country
           really so

Here Yàn explains that being exposed to both the English and Chinese cultures made her question her identity at a certain age, but that she resolved this by seeing herself as Chinese, 'but being brought up in a different country' (line 25). Interestingly, in this excerpt there is a switch in tense through Yàn's use of 'you think' (line 22), which causes a world-switch to an epistemic modal-world situated in a present time-zone. Note that the 'you' in the example 'you think' is generalized (Fludernik 1993, 2002; Herman 1994), and also the specific age Yàn is referring to is unclear. This suggests a world in which a generalized enactor at an unspecified age thinks, looks at him or herself and says something. However, listeners or readers are in fact likely to interpret the 'you' in this fragment as including Yàn at least, especially as the direct thoughts and speech described are much more specific, and only directly applicable to Yàn in the context of the interview. Listeners might furthermore feel included themselves by the 'you', because they might experience Yàn's words here as a form of personal address (cf. Fludernik 1993, 1994; Margolin 1990).

The doubly deictic (Herman 1994) effect of this is that a 'multiple version' of the enactor 'you' is created, in which all the different functions of 'you' are brought together. Herman (1994, 2002) has incorporated a multifunctional form of the second-person pronoun in his typology of 'you' in relation to literary narrative. This doubly-deictic 'you' is an ambiguous amalgam between different functions. It occurs when the pronoun 'you' can be seen to both address a fictional entity and readers of a text. As Herman's explains, such a form of 'you' in is a doubly deictic one because the second personal pronoun can be seen to address two types of entities at the same time: virtual (e.g. referring into the fictional world) and actual entities.

In the case of Yàn's oral narrative, because the interview took place in a face-to-face discourse situation, it is likely that the potential for ambiguity around double situatedness would be lessened, since the discourse participants in that situation could have easily clarified indefinite uses of 'you' by reference to their immediate environment. Having said that, the ontological boundaries between different conceptual levels nevertheless allow for a double deixis, or multiple functioning of the personal pronoun 'you', which is open to multiple interpretations by the discourse participants. In summary, 'you' as it is used here can be seen to represent a generalized experience in the text-world, but it simultaneously indexes Yàn, and might also imply some form of address to listeners.

The enactor that Yàn creates of herself in Text-World 3 represents an interesting coming together of Yàn's younger self and her current self. Although Yàn in this text-world is talking about her younger self, which is clear from her reference to 'that age', suggesting a time in the past, the description of what she was thinking and saying to herself is narrated in the present tense, which separates the mental processes of Yàn's younger self from her other childhood description of self, which she encapsulated in a past time-zone in Text-World 2. The present-tense discourse makes her conclusive statement about her identity as Chinese in the final lines of the excerpt relevant to the enactor in Text-World 1, because it suggests this description of self still applies to Yàn in the present time-zone. The enactor of Yàn in Text-World 3 contains elements of enactor 1 (Yàn's current self) and enactor 2 (Yàn's younger self), and can therefore be characterized as a conceptual blend (e.g. Fauconnier and Turner 2002) of enactor 1 and 2.

Yàn's narrative exemplifies the continuity of identity on the one hand and the constructed fluidity of identity on the other hand. In Text-World 3 she connects her younger self to their discursive self-representations in the 'here-and-now' of the discourse, thereby achieving a continuity of identity. Meanwhile, the discursive negotiation of these older selves simultaneously point to a *discursively* constructed notion of identity that is fluid and bound to the moment of interaction. The use of the second-person pronoun 'you' adds to this sense of timelessness and continuity, because it generalizes the represented experience considerably, thereby giving it a more universal impression.

6.6   Conclusion

The aim of this chapter has been to provide a text-worlds approach to the study of linguistic identity in discursive interaction, and to demonstrate how Text World Theory can be extended to face-to-face discourse and contribute to the field of discourse- and identity studies. I have examined linguistic identity by tracing Yàn's discourse through a text-world which holds her childhood experiences (Text-World 2), and through a second text-world in which Yàn's positioning is in the 'here-and-now' level of interaction. I have shown how Yàn frequently primed Text-World 1 with the use of the discourse markers 'you know', 'like' and 'really'. I have argued that this demonstrates the negotiated nature of the reality Yàn represents to Isabelle in the interview. Finally, I have shown how Yàn is able to merge elements from two distinct enactors in order to create a third text-world enactor which represents a coming together of Yàn's younger self and her current self. In doing so, I have demonstrated how Text World Theory is a useful framework for uncovering the multiple identities people create in multiple layers of the discourse.

My analysis shows that Text World Theory can offer a means of systematically exploring linguistic self-representation, because it allows for an understanding of how people frame their lived experiences and position themselves on several conceptual layers within in their own discursive worlds. The pattern of worlds and enactor positions that is uncovered in this narrative points to the multiplicity of identity, and allows for further exploration of research participants' more deeply embedded layers of self. I hope to have shown that Text World Theory is an ideal framework to analyse the interplay between different factors that involve the production and comprehension of a discourse, specifically because it makes the distinction between the different conceptual levels of the discourse-world, the text-world and modal worlds. It is also hoped the analysis in this chapter has shown that further development of Text World Theory into face-to-face interaction holds great promise for future research.

Transcription conventions

Italics	backchannelling
[]	overlap
<x>	inaudible
?	rising intonation
,	continuing intonation
@	laughter
-	truncated utterance

References

Andersen, G. (1997), ' "They like wanna see like how we talk and all that": The Use of "Like" as a Discourse Marker in London Teenage Speech', in M. Ljung (ed.), *Corpus-based Studies in English: Papers from the 17th International Conference on English Language Research on Computerized Corpora*, Amsterdam: Rodopi: 37–48.

Andersen, G. (2001), *Pragmatic Markers and Sociolinguistic Variation*, Amsterdam: John Benjamins.

Bamberg, M., De Fina, A. and Schiffrin, D. (2011), 'Discourse and Identity Construction', in S. J. Schwartz, K. Luyckx and V. L. Vignoles (eds), *Handbook of Identity Theory and Research*, London: Soringer: 177–200.

Benwell, B. and Stokoe, E. (2006), *Discourse and Identity*, Edinburgh: Edinburgh University Press.

Biber, D., Conrad, S. and Leech, G. (2002), *Longman Student Grammar of Spoken and Written English*, Harlow: Pearson Education Limited.

Bucholtz, M. and Hall, K. (2005), 'Identity and Interaction: A Sociolinguistic Cultural Approach', *Discourse Studies*, 7 (4–5): 585–614.

Cruickshank, T. and Lahey, E. (2010), 'Building the Stages of Drama: Towards a Text World Theory Account of Dramatic Play-Texts', *Journal of Literary Semantics*, 39.1: 67–91.

D'Arcy, A. F. (2005), *Like: Syntax and Development*, Unpublished PhD Thesis, University of Toronto.

De Fina, A., Schiffrin, D. and Bamberg, M. (2006), *Discourse and Identity*, Cambridge: Cambridge University Press.

Emmott, C. (1997), *Narrative Comprehension: A Discourse Perspective*, Oxford: Clarendon Press.

Fauconnier, G. and Turner, M. (2002), *The Way We Think: Conceptual Blending and the Mind's Hidden Complexities*, New York: Basic Books.

Fludernik, M. (1993), 'Second-Person Fiction: Narrative "You" as Addressee and/or Protagonist', *Arbeiten aus Anglistik und Amerikanistik (AAA)*, 18.2: 217–47.

Fludernik, M. (1994), 'Introduction: Second-Person Narrative and Related Issues', *Style*, 28.3: 281–311.

Fludernik, M. (2002), *Towards a 'Natural' Narratology*, 2nd ed., London: Routledge.

Gavins, J. (2003), ' "Too Much Blague?": an Exploration of the Text Worlds of Donald Barthelme's *Snow White*', in J. Gavins and G. Steen (eds), *Cognitive Poetics in Practice*, London: Routledge: 129–42.

Gavins, J. (2007), *Text World Theory: An Introduction*, Edinburgh: Edinburgh University Press.

Gavins, J. (2010), ' "Appeased by the Certitude": The Quiet Disintegration of the Paranoid Mind in "The Moustache" ', in B. Büsse and D. McIntyre (eds), *Language and Style*, Basingstoke: Palgrave Macmillan: 402–18.

Gibbs, R. W. Jr. (2005), *Embodiment and Cognitive Science*, Cambridge: Cambridge University Press.

Giovanelli, M. (2013), *Text World Theory and Keats' Poetry: The Cognitive Poetics of Desire, Dreams and Nightmares*, London: Bloomsbury Academic.

Goffman, E. (1981), *Forms of Talk*, Philadelphia, PA: University of Pennsylvania Press.

Gray, M. (2012), 'On the Interchangeability of "Actually" and "Really" in Spoken English: Quantitative and Qualitative Evidence from Corpora', *English Language and Linguistics*, 16.1: 151–70.

Hall, D. E. (2004), *Subjectivity*, London: Routledge.

Helt, M. E. and Foster-Cohen, S. H. (1996), 'A Relevance Theoretic Approach to Older Children's Use of Discourse Markers', in A. Stringfellow, D. Cahana-Amitay, E. Hughes and A. Zukowski (eds), *Proceedings of the 20th Annual Boston University Conference on Language Development*, Somerville, MA: Cascadilla Press: 308–17.

Herman, D. (1994), 'Textual "You" and Double Deixis in Edna O'Brien's *A Pagan Place*', *Style*, 28.3: 378–410.

Herman, D. (2002), *Story Logic: Problems and Possibilities of Narrative*, Lincoln, NE: University of Nebraska Press.

Hidalgo Downing, L. (2000), *Negation, Text Worlds and Discourse: The Pragmatics of Catch-22*, Stamford, CT: Ablex.

Holmes, J. (1986), 'The Functions of "You Know" in Women's and Men's Speech', *Language in Society*, 15: 1–22.

Holmes, J. (1995), *Women, Men and Politeness*, Harlow: Longman.

Joseph, J. E. (2010), 'Identity', in C. Llamas and D. Watt (eds), *Language and Identities*, Edinburgh: Edinburgh University Press: 9–17.

Jucker, A. and Smith, S. (1998), 'And People Just You Know Like "Wow": Discourse Markers as Negotiating Strategies', in A. H. Jucker and Y. Ziv (eds), *Discourse Markers: Theory and Descriptions*, Amsterdam: Benjamins: 171–201.

Lahey, E. (2006), '(Re)thinking World-Building: Locating the Text-Worlds of Canadian Lyric Poetry', *Journal of Literary Semantics*, 35: 145–62.

Lakoff, R. (1973), 'Language and Women's Place', *Language in Society*, 2.1: 45–80.

Margolin, U. (1990), 'Narrative "You" Revisited', *Language and Style*, 23.4: 425–46.

Miller, J. and Weinert, R. (1995), 'The Function of "Like" in Dialogue', *Journal of Pragmatics*, 23.4: 365–93.

Müller, S. (2005), *Discourse Markers in Native and Non-Native English Discourse*, Amsterdam: John Benjamins.

Nahajec, L. (2009), 'Negation and the Creation of Implicit Meaning in Poetry', *Language and Literature*, 18.2: 109–27.

Office for National Statistics (2011), '2011 Census: Aggregate Data (England and Wales)', *UK Data Service Census Support* <http://infuse.mimas.ac.uk> [accessed 17 September 2014]. This information is licensed under the terms of the Open Government Licence <http://www.nationalarchives.gov.uk/doc/open-government-licence/version/2>.

Paradis, C. (2003), 'Between Epistemic Modality and Degree: the Case of "Really"', in R. Facchinetti, M. G. Krug and F. R. Palmer (eds), *Modality in Contemporary English*, The Hague: Mouton de Gruyter: 191–220.

Romaine, S. and Lange, D. (1991), 'The Use of "Like" as a Marker of Reported Speech and Thought: a Case of Grammaticalization in Progress', *American Speech*, 66.3: 227–79.

Schiffrin, D. (1987), *Discourse Markers*, Cambridge: Cambridge University Press.

Schiffrin, D. (2001), 'Discourse Markers: Language Meaning and Context', in
D. Schiffrin, D. Tannen and H. Hamilton (eds), *Handbook of Discourse Analysis*,
Oxford: Blackwell: 54–75.

Schourup, L. (1985), *Common Discourse Particles in English Conversation: "Like",
"Well", "Y'know"*, New York: Garland.

Tagliamonte, S. A. (2004), ' "It's Just Like So Cool!" English in the 20th Century',
Paper presented at the International Association of University Professors of
English (IAUPE), Vancouver, British Columbia, 8–14 August.

Tagliamonte, S. A. (2005), 'So Who? Like How? Just What? Discourse Markers in the
Conversations of Young Canadians', *Journal of Pragmatics*, 37.1: 1896–915.

Tagliamonte, S. A. (2012), *Variationist Sociolinguistics: Change, Observation,
Interpretation*, Oxford: Wiley-Blackwell.

Underhill, R. (1988), 'Like is, Like, Focus', *American Speech*, 63.3: 234–46.

van der Bom, Isabelle (2015), *Text World Theory and Stories of Self: A Cognitive
Discursive Approach to Identity*, Unpublished PhD Thesis, University of Sheffield.

Werth, P. (1995), 'How to Build a World (in a Lot Less Than Six Days and Using
Only What's in Your Head)', in K. Green (ed.), *New Essays on Deixis: Discourse,
Narrative, Literature*, Amsterdam: Rodopi: 48–80.

Werth, P. (1999), *Text Worlds: Representing Conceptual Space in Discourse*, Harlow:
Longman.

Whiteley, S. (2011), 'Text World Theory, Real Readers and Emotional Responses to *The
Remains of the Day*', *Language and Literature*, 20.1: 23–43.

Text World Theory as *Cognitive Grammatics*: A Pedagogical Application in the Secondary Classroom

Marcello Giovanelli

7.1   Introduction

In this chapter I explore how teachers can use Text World Theory as a ped-agogical tool. Drawing on Halliday's (2002) notion of 'grammatics' as a way of using knowledge about language 'to think with', I argue that teachers can exploit Text World Theory's position as a cognitive discourse grammar to design meaningful tasks and activities that are mindful of the discourse strate-gies and resources that students use when reading. Since Text World Theory is fundamentally a reader-response theory, I argue that it ought to sit comfortably within secondary teachers' own philosophical and pedagogical belief systems, and has the potential to provide a richer, more nuanced perspective on how students engage in the process of reading texts. I exemplify my argument with detailed reference to a case study involving a secondary English teacher in a UK school, Laura, using Text World Theory to inform her teaching of the William Carlos Williams's poem 'The Red Wheelbarrow'.

7.2   Text World Theory, cognitive linguistics and pedagogy

Text World Theory has predominantly been used as an analytical framework within the field of cognitive poetics, where researchers have exploited its poten-tial to account for a range of literary and non-literary discourse (see Giovanelli 2013: 5 for a recent summary of work in this area). However, some emergent work has suggested that Text World Theory can offer much to the classroom teacher. For example, researchers have demonstrated its versatility to support the teaching of different genres and text types, in a variety of different learning contexts (de Obregón, Garcia and Diaz 2009; Giovanelli 2010; Scott 2013). These approaches are similar in that they are student-oriented, promoting the value for the learner in using aspects of the theory – usually involving the notions of world-building and world-switching – to develop analyses of texts, and to support the planning and drafting of writing. The value of Text World Theory as *teacher-oriented*, as a resource for the teacher, has to my knowledge received no direct attention. In the rest of this chapter, I explore how Text World Theory can facilitate teachers' knowledge of what happens in classroom contexts, and help them to make decisions about how they might best support students' learning.

Giovanelli and Mason (2015) highlight how an understanding of the cognitive linguistic notions of figure-ground and narrative schemas can provide a foundation from which decisions about learning and teaching can be taken. In a discussion of the perils of imposing certain ways of interpreting and responding to texts, we argue that teachers can promote more authentic reading experiences by avoiding privileging their own knowledge of a text over that of their students. We emphasize the need for practitioners to significantly reconfigure their role from transmitters of linguistic knowledge to informed users of that knowledge to support their classroom practice. In doing so we highlight what Carter (1982: 8) defines as the difference between 'teaching linguistics' and 'having linguistics as a foundation for classroom language teaching' for the teacher. In the latter, ideas about language and communication become tools to inform a range of teacher practices including the planning and delivery of activities, assessment and the analysis of and reflection on classroom practice.

The rich history of debates in the twentieth- and early twenty-first centuries on the value of grammar teaching in schools (see Locke 2010 for an overview) offers a striking example of why a teacher-oriented linguistics has much to offer. The wealth of evidence that exists against a certain kind of explicit grammar teaching in UK schools (see e.g. Andrews et al. 2006) is essentially evidence against a certain kind of language pedagogy, namely a deficit model of language that emphasizes prescription and correction with, as Carter describes:

> Teachers fulfilling the role of a kind of linguistic dentist, polishing here and there, straightening out, removing decay, filling gaps and occasionally undertaking a necessary extraction. (Carter 1990: 105–6)

In contrast, recent research has highlighted the value of a rhetorically-driven and contextually-sensitive model of language, underpinned by secure and confident teacher knowledge in developing students' writing (Myhill et al. 2012).

Such work has stressed the potential for a teacher-oriented linguistics to act as a springboard for practitioners to develop their own knowledge through research, reading and other forms of continuous professional development.

However, there has been no consensus regarding the model of linguistic knowledge that might be useful for teachers. In UK schools, a functional model of language established in the late 1960s through the work of Michael Halliday (see e.g. Doughty, Pearce and Thornton 1971) became the backdrop for official government policy documents from the 1970s to the 1990s. This included the *Language in the National Curriculum* (*LINC*) project, which the government of the time initially funded but then refused publication on ideological rather than pedagogical grounds (see Carter 1996a for discussion). In recent years, and in the face of a return to explicit testing of the grammatical knowledge of primary school children, there has been a concomitant return to a 'name the parts pedagogy' (see Giovanelli 2014: 12–19 for discussion). Overseas, a resilient systemic functional linguistics still provides the conceptual template for language work in education in parts of Australia, particularly in genre-based literacy programmes (e.g. Rose and Martin 2012), and in the United States (e.g. Hancock 2005).

I have argued elsewhere (Giovanelli 2014) that some fundamental principles of cognitive science and linguistics that draw together the mental, the experiential and the social can provide a radical and welcome way for teachers to think about teaching aspects of structure and meaning to students. Indeed in the field of second-language acquisition, there is a significant and growing body of research centred on learning and teaching informed by cognitive linguistics (Holme 2009, 2012; Littlemore 2009), with empirical evidence that such pedagogies have greater impact on student learning than those based on generative and functional models of grammar (Tyler 2012).

It seems to me that cognitive linguistics, and for the purposes of this discussion, specifically Text World Theory, is valuable in offering to the teacher a usable framework to reflect on learning and teaching. Current work focusing on real readers in non-educational contexts (e.g. Gavins 2013; Whiteley 2011) clearly has the potential to be replicated through considering the ways that students interact and position themselves in classroom activities, and project themselves into fictional worlds. Additionally, as Giovanelli and Mason (2015) demonstrate, Text World Theory has the potential to be a powerful tool for teachers to think about reading practices in their classrooms, in engaging in classroom interaction and the setting up of classroom activities.

I have discussed elsewhere (Giovanelli 2014: 36–7) that these potential uses represent a cognitively oriented example of Halliday's term 'grammatics'

(Halliday 2002: 386). Halliday makes the distinction between the grammar of a language, and the study of that phenomenon, 'grammatics'. The relationship between the two, Halliday argues, is the same as that between a similar pair of terms: language (the phenomenon); and linguistics (the study of the phenomenon). While students acquire and are able to work within the parameters of their native language's grammar unconsciously as part of their general linguistic development, grammatics is an explicit type of meta-reflection that becomes foregrounded and explored in educational contexts. In a teacher-oriented grammatics, a practitioner uses the best and most valuable insights from linguistics not simply to teach rules and notions of correctness (a deficit model) or descriptions of form, structure and meaning (a descriptive model), but rather, as Halliday (2002: 416) suggests, 'to think with' (a pedagogical model).

The most detailed and developed application of Halliday's concept has unsurprisingly been within the systemic functional tradition. For example, Macken-Horarik (2009) explores how knowledge of the ideational, interpersonal and textual metafunctions of language can facilitate a more sensitive appreciation of children's writing and support the giving of constructive feedback. Here, a teacher moves away from a deficit pedagogy towards a practice informed by an understanding of how linguistic choice and form shape meanings in the context of designing classroom tasks, and engaging in dialogue with students about their own writing. In the case of a functional grammatics, the emphasis is on the value of 'meaning rather than form' (Macken-Horarik 2009: 63). A *cognitive grammatics* offers the potential to draw on concerns such as the embodied nature of meaning, the activation of schematic knowledge in reading, metaphorical mapping between concrete and abstract domains, and the relationship between grammatical construal and meaning. It prioritizes exploring the 'how' as well as the 'what' and exploring interpretation, reading and writing as *process* in more expansive ways than simply as *product* (see Carter 1996b for further discussion of these terms).

As Werth argues, Text World Theory offers a more 'human' level of descriptive linguistic enquiry that acknowledges that 'language must be viewed as a phenomenon which is intimately bound up with human experience' (1999: 19). Since from a pedagogical perspective this is very attractive, here are some ways that Text World Theory consequently appears ideally placed to support a teacher's thinking in the classroom.

1. It has a focus on the contextual aspects of communication as well as the textual. In recognizing the interplay between the two, it promotes the recognition of both and the downplaying of neither.

2. It can account for textual elements and the ways in which readers engage with these in the process of reading. The experience that arises from such an enterprise provides opportunities for discussing a fully formed 'texture' (Stockwell 2009) of reading.

3. Its emphases on the dynamic nature of context as an interpersonal construct, and on the situational and social dimensions of reading sit comfortably with the theoretical and educational concerns of participatory theories of learning (Rogoff 2003). As a cognitive discourse grammar, Text World Theory is well placed to be mindful of the wider factors that shape literacy practices, and how 'real-world contexts influence the production of discourse' (Gavins 2013: 7). As a model of communication, it acknowledges the importance of the vast range of psychological, social and textual resources that readers bring to literary experiences.

4. Standard Text World Theory notation presents conceptual space in a visual and concrete way, and emphasizes the visual nature of much mental operation (Werth 1999: 8). Used in learning activities, the diagrammatic aspect of Text World Theory emphasizes how meanings are primarily derived from spatial and physical imagery (Holme 2012), and is a prototypical *virtual embodied learning activity* (Giovanelli 2014). Text World Theory's diagrams can support the teaching of the complexity that results from spatial, temporal and point-of-view world-switches in texts (Giovanelli 2010). The emphasis on the visual can help students to make implicit learning explicit in a way that allows subsequent formative dialogue between teacher and student (Ainsworth, Prain and Tytler 2011).

5. Finally, its emphases on textuality, context and negotiated meanings mean that Text World Theory is ideally placed to develop students' own process-driven thinking. The principled relationship that exists between the text and students' own schematic knowledge in the act of making meaning means that Text World Theory has the potential to develop students' metalinguistic skills and metacognition (Flavell 1976) in relation to the reading process more generally.

7.3   Poetry and reader response

Surveys of beginning and in-service English teachers have frequently high-lighted that they value a personal response to literature, and subscribe to a 'personal growth model' (DESWO 1989: 60) emphasizing the imaginative and aesthetic nature of the literary experience (Goodwyn 1992, 2011; Goodwyn and Findlay 1999). Free from the pressures of GCSE and A-level examinations, where assessment and accountability can promote a mutual dislike of poetry among teachers and students (Xerri 2013), poetry teaching to lower age secondary students in the United Kingdom (Years 7–9) tends to allow teachers the freedom to be more creative and less transmissive in their approaches (Atherton, Green and Snapper 2013).

However, curriculum reform and the shifting emphasis on the theory of literature at A-level has filtered down to practice with younger students so that practitioners understand that the teaching of literature requires more than just an unqualified passion for reading books, or what Beavis (1997) terms 'the discourse of charismatic pedagogy'. Theoretical concerns particularly around the reception of literature have promoted specification requirements to focus on alternative interpretations of texts by different groups of readers, highlighting the co-constructed nature of meaning and the importance of readers' backgrounds and experiences. However, official documentation still ensures that students' responses need to be accountable to the text itself. For example, the most recent National Curriculum programme of study for Key Stage 3 English states that students should be able to explore and articulate 'how language, including figurative language, vocabulary choice, grammar, text structure and organizational features, presents meaning' (DfE 2013: 4). With this in mind, I would like to briefly draw attention to the way that Text World Theory complements Rosenblatt's 'transactional theory' (Rosenblatt 1970, 1978), a reader-response theory that rests easily with the kinds of dynamic and personal models of meaning-making that English teachers value.

Rosenblatt utilizes a principle of transactional psychology that proposes that individuals make sense of incoming stimuli through past experiences. Mapped into a model of reading, she explains the reading process as a reciprocal 'coming together' (1978: 12) where the reader creates the text and simultaneously responds to it in a specific spatio-temporal context. The model rejects both at one extreme a formalist reification of the text at the expense of discussion of the situational aspect of reading, and at the other, recourse to personality-driven theories of the reader that pay little attention to the text itself. As Rosenblatt explains:

> Through the medium of words, the text brings into the reader's consciousness certain concepts, certain sensuous experiences, certain images of things, people, actions, scenes. The special meanings and, more particularly, the

submerged associations that these words and images have for the individual
reader will largely determine what the work communicates to him. (Rosenblatt
1970: 30–1)

There is a clear relationship between the communicative models proposed by
Rosenblatt and Werth. They both draw attention to the importance of readers' background knowledge and life experiences, the 'personality traits, memories of past events, present needs and pre-occupations, a particular mood of
the moment, and a particular physical condition' (Rosenblatt 1970: 30), and
'frames … whole chunks of experience and situations, codified and stored
in memory' (Werth 1999: 20). And, they stress the way that the text acts as
'stimulus' (Rosenblatt 1978: 11) or provides 'referential information' (Werth
1999: 52) that activates idiosyncratic schematic knowledge and applies con-
straints on the degree of knowledge that is deemed to be useful and appropriate; in other words the text 'helps to regulate' (Rosenblatt 1978: 11) *what*
and *how much* through the principle of 'text-drivenness' (Werth 1999: 151).
Werth's concept of a text-world as a dynamic conceptual scenario reconfigures
Rosenblatt's notion of reading 'as an event in the life of a reader, as embodied in
a process resulting from the confluence of reader and the text' (1978: 16) from
a cognitive perspective. As such, it can add a rich cognitive dimension to an
established way that teachers think about the reading processes.

7.4   Teaching 'The Red Wheelbarrow'

The case study detailed below involves an English teacher, Laura, in her third
year of teaching at a comprehensive secondary school in the south of England.
Laura had completed an undergraduate degree in English Literature but had
taken a linguistics elective in her final year, and was interested in developing
her subject knowledge and expertise in language work. Although the school
she worked at had a large sixth form with healthy numbers of students taking
English Language at A-level, Laura had not yet taught any post-16 classes herself. She was thus hopeful that developing her linguistic knowledge would be
good preparation for A-level teaching in the future.

Over the course of six months, Laura had completed some general reading in
linguistics, and had read Gavins's *Text World Theory: An Introduction* (Gavins
2007). In meetings and e-mail exchanges that formed part of a larger research
project, we discussed how the book and Text World Theory might be useful

for a teacher in the classroom. We planned a sequence of activities on 'The Red Wheelbarrow' for a Key Stage 3 Year 7 class (11–12-year olds) before Laura took ownership of the activities and resources, mediating them to best fit the needs of her students. She undertook all the teaching with the class. My approach was broadly ethnographic and interpretative, and my following discussion of her teaching is based on field notes, interviews and informal conversations, and observing students at work.

Laura decided to use William Carlos Williams's 'The Red Wheelbarrow' since it was a short and accessible poem that evoked a rich scene in a striking way. The poem itself has minimal world-building detail; there are no specific spatial or temporal locators, and referential world-building is limited to the noun phrase 'a red wheelbarrow', post-modified by the adjectival phrase, 'glazed with rain water', and the prepositional phrase 'beside the white chickens'. However, the object-attribute-location pattern compensates to some extent for the lack of initial world-builders, and guides readers to construct a fictional world. These features made it ideal for some of the work that Laura wanted to do on knowledge activation and student reflection on that process. Originally published in Williams's collection *Spring and All* in 1923 under its original title *XXII* (poems were numbered sequentially using Roman numerals), 'The Red Wheelbarrow' has since been a staple of poetry anthologies (see Rizzo 2005 for discussion of the production and reception of the poem) and had been used with Key Stage 3 students in Laura's school before.

The Red Wheelbarrow
so much depends
upon
a red wheel
barrow
glazed with rain
water
beside the white
chickens.

      (Williams 1923)

Laura's learning and teaching objectives and outcomes centred around two separate strands: an exploration of the role of knowledge in the reading process (the focus of this chapter); and developing complexity and layers in point of view when writing. A summary of Laura's plan for the first two lessons is below.

- Allow students to read poem individually for two minutes.
- Students identify three key words in the poem that they feel are the most striking.
- Students draw the scene depicted in the poem: this should be as detailed as possible, capturing as many of the senses as possible.
- In pairs, students compare each other's pictures and explain why they have constructed the world of the poem, thinking about similarities, differences and what might have influenced them to draw the scene as they have.

Teacher differentiation: teacher can intervene as necessary with questions, additional material (visuals, descriptions of a farm etc.)

- Show students authorial detail on PowerPoint. Explain who William Carlos Williams was.
- Show William Carlos Williams's description of how he came to write the poem.
- Ask students to reflect on what they have just read/seen and heard. Does this affect their reading of the poem? In what ways would they now update their imagined world?
- Ask students to think about what they have learnt about themselves as readers and how we read literature.

7.4.1   The use of drawings

Laura had decided to use drawings as a way of making students' initial implicit responses to the poem explicit in a way and to allow them to think about the kinds of resources and knowledge they brought to the reading experience. Two examples are shown in Figure 7.1 (James) and Figure 7.2 (Simon).

Although the drawings are crude, they are evidence of high-level participation, and present a genuine way of promoting discussion about the world-building process in explicit terms. The drawings offer a way for the students to represent conceptual space in a concrete way, analogous to the process of working with a 'blank space which gradually gets filled in and defined as one reads through it' (Werth 1999: 53). Although the drawings clearly do not offer direct evidence of students' mental operations, nonetheless they are an example of what Suhor (1984: 250) terms 'transmediation', a process by which

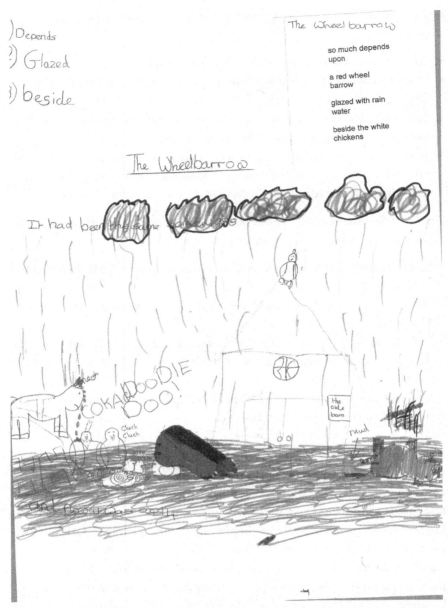

Figure 7.1 James's drawing

one symbolic code (here the written language of the poem) becomes encoded in another (here the multimodal nature of drawing). Crucially, the shifting across media involves a process of generating meaning from the initial code. In other words, it offers an upfront act of meta-reflection on the process of reading itself.

Figure 7.2 Simon's drawing

James's drawing is arguably much richer than Simon's in its amount of detail. In his comments he remarked that he had spent a great deal of time on a farm when he was younger, and that this had informed his vision of the poem. In comparison, Simon's drawing focuses on a central image of the red wheelbarrow. Commenting on his vivid foregrounded image of the wheelbarrow, he was able to offer evidence of a more specific frame that must have been activated in the act of reading.

> *I drew a wheelbarrow like that as I saw a wheelbarrow when I was little and my uncle was a builder.* (Simon)

In both instances Laura was able to ask questions to the students to probe them and get them thinking about their own knowledge activation in more detail. For example, when Simon read his reasons for his drawing out to the class, Laura encouraged him to build on his response as follows, finding out in the process that Simon's uncle as well as being a builder had also painted farm landscapes, and Simon had retained vivid memories of these.

Laura: *what exactly did your uncle do?*
Simon: *well he was a builder but he used to draw stuff as well and that's how he drew it (the wheelbarrow)*
Laura: *so you must have seen your uncle draw one as well?*
Simon: *yeh.*

7.4.2   Knowledge

For Laura, asking the students to think about those aspects of frame knowledge that were both general and idiosyncratic became an important stage in the students' understanding of the relationship that exists between readers as active makers of meaning and the text as a stimulus and constraint on the kinds of knowledge that can be drawn on. The activity also allowed Laura herself to reflect carefully about the types of frame knowledge her students brought to the classroom. The students were largely drawing on autobiographical memories to make sense of the scene depicted in the poem. For example, other students were able to recount vividly and enthusiastically stories of visits to farms with their families or while at primary school. One student, Ali, was able to talk in great detail about how his grandfather's farm in Pakistan had influenced his reading of the poem; his drawing included a landscape that was distinctly Asian with carefully drawn indigenous trees and plants. Another girl, Sarah, remembered reading the novel *Charlotte's Web* (White 1952) at primary school, and explained how this had impacted on her reading and imaginative construction of the scene. When they expanded on these memories in their groups, they were able to explain in rich detail the sights, sounds and smells associated with the places that they had remembered. It was evident that the students were paying attention not only to referents of words but to emotions, memories and experiences associated with them; that is, their knowledge was clearly embodied.

Of course, there are problems inherent in trying to capture any sense of student response through introspective recall, and in particular, difficulties in students being able gain access to and account for in any accurate way the vast amount of cognitive processing that occurs during the reading process (Gibbs 2006). However, I would argue that the students' drawings represent a starting point, and a concrete mark for them to engage in some inwards-looking reflection in an attempt to explore the strategic resources that they bring to the reading experience. In turn Laura was able to monitor, assess and strategically steer the direction of the lesson through a series of inferences based on what the students had completed. The drawings and subsequent discussion represented in this instance 'visible surfaces ... to "fix" moments of learning' (Franks 2014: 201).

7.4.3   Incrementation and world-replacement

In the act of reading the poem, the students and Williams share a split discourse-world since they are separated both spatially and temporally. Of course, Laura too was a discourse-world participant, although her position as a teacher and a figure of authority and academic knowledge meant that she had a privileged role. Indeed this privilege, which includes knowledge of biographical, historical, and literary-critical matters relating to the poem, meant that the text-world that Laura had herself built was likely to be much richer than those of her students. There is a danger that this kind of knowledge can in itself be used to downplay or over-ride students' initial responses to a poem so that these responses are marginalized in favour of the stronger teacher reading (Giovanelli and Mason 2015).

To avoid this, Laura initially kept contextual information, including the title of the poem, from the students. In the second part of the lesson, she began by giving them some brief information about the poet. This included some biographical detail, a summary of the conventions of imagist poetry, and the following extract from 'Seventy Years Deep', an article that Williams had written for *Holiday* magazine (Williams 1954), in which he had provided a context for the writing of 'The Red Wheelbarrow'. In the version given to the students, the word 'negro' was replaced with 'man'.

> 'The Red Wheelbarrow' sprang from affection for an old negro named Marshall. He had been a fisherman, caught porgies off Gloucester. He used to tell me how he had to work in the cold in freezing weather, standing ankle deep in cracked ice packing down the fish. He said he didn't feel cold. He never felt cold in his life until just recently. I liked that man, and his son Milton almost as much. In his back yard I saw the red wheelbarrow surrounded by the white chickens. I suppose my affection for the old man somehow got into the writing. (Williams 1954: 78)

In Text World Theory, the passing of private knowledge into the common ground is known as the process of incrementation (Werth 1999: 95). When Laura revealed this information to the students and got them to reflect on how they now imagined the scene, the results were striking. The majority of the students drew on various AMERICA frames, and reshaped their response by utilizing the biographical detail about Williams, considering how their drawing/text-world might be updated on the basis of this information. Some students had specifically picked up on the American English lexis 'back yard' in the 'Seventy Years Deep' extract. These students used knowledge gained from either visiting America, or more commonly, from television shows set in the United States. For other students, the updating of the common ground resulted in a more radical 'world-replacement' (Gavins 2007: 142). For example, Kevin, who had originally drawn a picture that depicted a late summer quintessentially English farm scene, spoke enthusiastically about how he now imagined the poem within the cramped space of a run-down ghetto in an American city.

7.4.4   Perspectives

The added information about 'The Red Wheelbarrow' provided by the 'Seventy Years Deep' extract also allowed Laura and her students to begin a more detailed exploration of point of view in the poem. The extract led most students to believe that the 'voice' in the poem was either Williams himself or Marshall, the old man, whose voice and perspective were filtered through Williams's verse. In this way they began to position themselves as either an implied reader and/or implied narratee in relationship to an implied author (Williams) and an implied narrator (Williams/Marshall). Laura and I had previously discussed how the heavily attitudinal nature of the clause 'so much depends' suggested that a reader would enter the poem at a level below that of the normally expected text-world since the language to describe the scene, whether perceived as direct speech or not, is clearly from a particular perspective. We therefore acknowledged that in Text World Theory terms, there was an 'empty' text-world, defined by Lahey (2004: 26) as a minimal deictic space built from inference and containing only basic knowledge about enactors and their relationships. Consequently, we reconfigured the entire poem as an enactor-accessible epistemic modal focalized-world since the entry point for the reader is the deictic centre of the speaking voice. Although Laura did not want to introduce students to unnecessarily complex terminology, she was keen nonetheless to exploit the potential for students to understand that the poem might represent one perspective on a scene. This offered Laura an important teaching point and avenue for future work. As their discussions of the poem in groups became more developed, students were clearly able to think about how and why they were engaged in various types of perspective-taking projection (Whiteley 2014: 398), fleshing out enactors and exploring their various connections with them.

The direction of the lesson, and of the learning, had moved on from students reflecting on the transactional nature of the reading process to exploring the encoding of point of view. In the process of considering focalization in Williams's poem, Laura was able to lead the students onto a discussion of the perspectival nature of language drawing on simple interventionist activities (Pope 1995) to ask students to think about re-centring the events of the poem through different perceptual, spatial and temporal lenses. Here Laura made use of Text World Theory's standard diagrammatic notation as a template for supporting students' writing. Although there is not the space here to discuss the students' reactions to this and the work that followed, this opened up a vast number of possibilities that students were able to enthusiastically explore in their own writing.

7.5   Conclusion

In this chapter, I have explained how one teacher used her reading about and of Text World Theory to support teaching and learning in the classroom and consequently I hope to have demonstrated the value of Text World Theory as a teacher-oriented 'tool for thinking with'. Text World Theory offers a psychologically plausible and pedagogically sensitive way of promoting an understanding of the transactional nature of reading, and of viewing the types of cultural, personal social knowledge that students bring to reading as a valuable set of resources. As such, it offers an enabling and research-informed approach to teaching. I have also shown how for students, such an approach opens up their capacity for metacognitive and metalinguistic awareness in providing opportunities for an exploration of linguistic, contextual and embodied knowledge in generating meaning. Such an approach offers an opportunity to explore the process of reading poetry as one of personal projection and response rather than as a simple decoding of linguistic form, or an appeal to some authorial or teacher's interpretation.

In the course of her journey with Text World Theory, Laura of course understood this. In an interview with me after the sequence of lessons, she said that the experience had been informative, enabling and enjoyable, and had opened up a range of possibilities that she wanted to explore further.

> I think they [the students] found a huge amount of value in it. If finely-tuned enough that would help them with literature and the understanding of context, and eventually, or probably before, it would help them with seeing different viewpoints, where they are as readers and where they are as writers. I know it's not completely there yet, but that's where I see it as being valuable.
> (Laura)

The students also found the activities stimulating and revealing. The lessons facilitated extended periods of debate about the nature of poetic form, representation, point of view and the relationship between reader and text in the shaping of meaning, and opened up a space for genuine metacognitive reflection, evident in the students' comments afterwards. Indeed, one student, Paul, when asked by me what he thought the lessons had taught him, paused for a moment and then simply replied 'well, they were lessons about thinking weren't they?'

References

Ainsworth, S., Prain, V. and Tytler, R. (2011), 'Drawing to Learn in Science', *Science*, 333: 1096–97.

Andrews, R., Torgerson, S., Beverton, A., Freeman, T., Lock, G., Low, G., Robinson, A. and Zhu, D. (2006), 'The Effect of Grammar Teaching on Writing Development', *British Education Research Journal*, 32.1: 39–55.

Atherton, C., Green, A. and Snapper, G. (2013), *Teaching English Literature 16–19: An Essential Guide*, London: Routledge.

Beavis, C. (1997), ' "Lovely Literature": Teacher Subjectivity and Curriculum Change', paper presented at the AARE annual conference, Brisbane, <http://www.aare.edu.au/data/publications/1997/beavc245.pdf> [accessed 16 October 2014].

Carter, R. (1982), *Linguistics and the Teacher*, London: Routledge.

Carter, R. (1990), 'Introduction', in R. Carter (ed.), *Knowledge about Language and the Curriculum: The LINC Reader*, London: Hodder and Stoughton: 1–20.

Carter, R. (1996a), 'Politics and Knowledge about Language: The LINC project', in G. Williams and R. Hasan (eds), *Literacy in Society*, Harlow: Longman: 1–28.

Carter, R. (1996b), 'Look Both Ways Before Crossing: Developments in the Language and Literature Classroom', in R. Carter and J. McRae (eds), *Language, Literature and the Learner: Creative Classroom Practice*, Harlow: Longman: 1–15.

de Obregón, P., Garcia, R. and Diaz, A. (2009), 'Text World Theory in the EFL Reading Comprehension Classroom', *Memorias Del V Foro De Estudios En Lenguas Internacional*, 243–54.

DESWO (1989), *English for Ages 5 to 16*, London: HMSO.

DfE (2013), *English Programmes of Study: Key Stage 3: National Curriculum in England*, London: HMSO.

Doughty, P., Pearce, J. and Thornton, G. (1971), *Language in Use*, London: Edward Arnold.

Flavell, J. (1976), 'Metacognitive Aspects of Problem Solving', in L. B. Resnick (ed.), *The Nature of Intelligence*, Hillsdale, NJ: Erlbaum: 231–6.

Franks, A. (2014), 'Drama and the Representation of Affect – Structures of Feeling and Signs of Learning', *Research in Drama Education: The Journal of Applied Theatre and Performance*, 19.2: 195–207.

Gavins, J. (2007), *Text World Theory: An Introduction*, Edinburgh: Edinburgh University Press.

Gavins, J. (2013), *Reading the Absurd*, Edinburgh: Edinburgh University Press.

Gibbs, R. (2006), 'Introspection and Cognitive Linguistics: Should We Trust Our Own Intuitions?', *Annual Review of Cognitive Linguistics*, 4.1: 135–51.

Giovanelli, M. (2010), 'Pedagogical Stylistics: A Text World Theory Approach to the Teaching of Poetry', *English in Education*, 44.3: 214–31.

Giovanelli, M. (2013), *Text World Theory and Keats' Poetry: The Cognitive Poetics of Desire, Dreams and Nightmares*, London: Bloomsbury.

Giovanelli, M. (2014), *Teaching Grammar, Structure and Meaning: Exploring Theory and Practice for Post 16 English Language Teachers*, London: Routledge.

Giovanelli, M. and Mason, J. (2015), ' "Well I Don't Feel That": Schemas, Worlds and Authentic Reading in the Classroom', *English in Education*, 49.1: 41–55.

Goodwyn, A. (1992) 'Theoretical Models of English Teaching', *English in Education*, 26.3: 4–10.

Goodwyn, A. (2011), *The Expert Teacher of English*, London: Routledge.

Goodwyn, A. and Findlay, K. (1999), 'The Cox Models Revisited: English Teachers' Views of Their Subject and the National Curriculum', *English in Education*, 33.2: 19–31.

Halliday, M. (2002), 'On Grammar and Grammatics', in J. Webster (ed.), *On Grammar: Vol 1 of the Collected Works of M.A.K. Halliday*, London: Continuum: 384–417.

Hancock, C. (2005), *Meaning-Centered Grammar: An Introductory Text*, London: Equinox.

Holme, R. (2009), *Cognitive Linguistics and Language Teaching*, Basingstoke: Palgrave Macmillan.

Holme, R. (2012), 'Cognitive Linguistics and the Second Language Classroom', *TESOL Quarterly*, 46.1: 6–29.

Lahey, E. (2004), 'All the World's a Sub-World: Direct Speech and Sub-World Creation in "After" by Norman Craig', *Nottingham Linguistic Circular*, 18: 21–8.

Littlemore, J. (2009), *Applying Cognitive Linguistics to Second Language Teaching and Learning*, Basingstoke: Palgrave Macmillan.

Locke, T. (ed.) (2010), *Beyond the Grammar Wars: A Resource for Teachers and Students on Developing Language Knowledge in the English/Literacy Classroom*, London: Routledge.

Macken-Horarik, M. (2009), 'Navigational Metalanguages for New Territory in English: The Potential of Grammatics', *English Teaching: Practice and Critique*, 8.3: 55–69.

Myhill, D., Jones, S., Lines, H. and Watson, A. (2012), 'Re-Thinking Grammar: The Impact of Embedded Grammar Teaching on Students' Writing and Students' Metalinguistic Understanding', *Research Papers in Education*, 27.2: 139–66.

Pope, R. (1995), *Textual Intervention: Critical and Creative Strategies for Literary Studies*, London: Routledge.

Rizzo, S. (2005), 'Remembering Race: Extra-Poetical Contexts and the Racial Other in "The Red Wheelbarrow"', *Journal of Modern Literature*, 29.1: 34–54.

Rogoff, B. (2003), *The Cultural Nature of Human Development*, Oxford: Oxford University Press.

Rose, D. and Martin, J. (2012), *Learning to Write, Reading to Learn: Genre, Knowledge and Pedagogy in the Sydney School*, London: Equinox.

Rosenblatt, L. (1970), *Literature as Exploration*, London: Heinemann.

Rosenblatt, L. (1978), *The Reader, The Text, The Poem: The Transactional Theory of the Literary Work*, Carbondale and Edwardsville, IL: Southern Illinois University Press.

Scott, J. (2013), *Creative Writing and Stylistics: Creative and Critical Approaches*, Basingstoke: Palgrave Macmillan.

Stockwell, P. (2009), *Texture: A Cognitive Aesthetics of Reading*, Edinburgh: Edinburgh University Press.

Suhor, C. (1984), 'Towards a Semiotics-Based Curriculum', *Journal of Curriculum Studies*, 16.3: 247–57.

Tyler, A. (2012), *Cognitive Linguistics and Second Language Learning: Theoretical Basics and Experimental Evidence*, London: Routledge.

Werth, P. (1999), *Text Worlds: Representing Conceptual Space in Discourse*, Harlow: Longman.

White, E. B. (1952), *Charlotte's Web*, London: Hamish Hamilton.

Whiteley, S. (2011), 'Text World Theory, Real Readers and Emotional Responses to *The Remains of the Day*', *Language and Literature*, 20.1: 23–42.

Whiteley, S. (2014), 'Ethics', in P. Stockwell and S. Whiteley (eds), *The Cambridge Handbook of Stylistics*, Cambridge: Cambridge University Press: 393–407.

Williams, W. C. (1923), *Spring and All*, Paris: Contact Publishing.

Williams, W. C. (1954), 'Seventy Years Deep', *Holiday*, 16.5: 54–5, 78.

Xerri, D. (2013), 'Colluding in the "Torture" of Poetry: Shared Beliefs and Assessment', *English in Education*, 47.2: 134–46.

Worlds from Words: Theories of World-building as Creative Writing Toolbox

Jeremy Scott

8.1   Writing and reading: Creative practice and research

Creative writing has been looking at itself quite hard recently. This introspection has been prompted by its increasing popularity as an academic discipline within a higher education context and its need to justify a position in that research-led context as an object of rigorous scholarly activity (see Kroll and Harper 2012; Leavy 2009; Sigesmund and Cahnmann-Taylor 2008; Smith and Dean 2009). In short, creative writing is arguably in need of a sound and principled theoretical infrastructure. Previous practioners in this area have suggested poetics, broadly, and narratology, more specifically, as possible candidates for this infrastructure (see e.g. Rodriguez 2008).

The field of poetics has concerned itself with the categorization of types of literary discourse; indeed, Aristotle's collected writings on the subject were for centuries viewed as a rulebook for dramatic and poetic composition. Subsequently, much later literary and linguistic theory, particularly genre theory, narrative theory and the work of Mikhail Bakhtin and György Lukás (Leitch 2001: 88), performed a similar role, exploring the mechanics of narrative fiction from the perspective of its use of language. However, as I have suggested previously (Scott 2014), a more worthy contender for the role of theoretical underpinning for creative writing might be stylistics. To develop this argument in more detail, I wish to suggest here that cognitive poetics and that discipline's focus on processes of linguistic world-building and the mechanics of 'actualizing' readings provide the creative writing with invaluable insights into what happens when readers read.

It is hoped, then, that this chapter will be pioneering, and a survey of potentialities and directions for future exploration rather than in any sense definitive. It considers the implications of linguistic approaches to textual analysis from, as it were, the other end of the telescope: explicitly *for the creative writer* and his or her creative practice. The central (and simple) proposal for the chapter is this: there is a remarkable facility in the mind of the reader which enables her or him to be transported imaginatively to fictional worlds which may or may not bear relation to his or her actual world (AW): to modern Bangkok, ancient Greece, Victorian London, the mountains of Tolkien's Middle Earth, the surface of Mars. This process might sometimes be referred to in everyday terms as 'suspension of disbelief', but the cognitive poetics term 'world-building' is more accurate and useful. This remarkable facility of human language is something that creative writers should understand and aim to exploit – and, crucially, should also be wary of disrupting unnecessarily (or, at least, be mindful of what happens when it is disrupted). It is in advancing writerly understanding of readerly sensibilities that cognitive poetics, and linguistic theories of world-building specifically, have much to offer practitioners. The writer can gain sophisticated and nuanced appreciation of the ways in which language can be used to create and manipulate worlds that exist at different cognitive, discoursal and rhetorical 'levels' and in different relationships to one another.

There are countless themes within cognitive poetics that are ripe for exploration from the perspective of creative practice. By necessity, this chapter is selective in its scope and will consider the following as a starting point for future debate: abstract versus concrete conceptions of world and language; relationships between language and thought and imagination and creativity (Schema Theory); deixis and empathy; perceived compatabilities between worlds and discourses; and avoiding inhibition of return. Overarching all of these themes will be theoretical architecture drawing on first, Text World Theory and, second, Possible Worlds Theory. Although not associated directly with cognitive poetics, Possible Worlds Theory has interesting and relevant points to make about the relationship between fiction and truth which shed light on other issues explored in this chapter). A final qualifying point: the term 'storyworld' will be used throughout to refer in a general sense to the overarching fictional world invoked by the text in the imagination of the reader, rather than in a strictly theoretical sense (e.g. Herman 2004 and Phelan 2004).

This chapter should not be seen as suggestions towards pedagogy, although of course these ideas could and should have such impact. Rather, its principal purpose is to connect more directly to creative practice out there 'at the coal face', and to the workings and interactions between the creative and the critical. Stylistics and its sub-disciplines can aid creative writers involved in

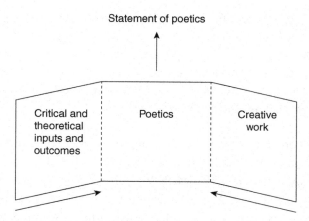

Figure 8.1 The triptych of practice-led creative writing research

practice-led research in articulating rigorously the relationship between creative output and its inputs, thus developing a principled perspective on practice. Lasky (2012: 22) represents these relationships diagrammatically (Figure 8.1).

The central component of Figure 8.1 is the hinge between the panels (the dotted line) that allows movement between them; through exploration of the connections between these processes, it should be possible for creative writers to produce a principled reflection rooted in cognitive poetics that can underpin practice-based research. There are problems inherent here, of course. To name two: overt focus on practice and lead to an excessive and inhibiting self-consciousness; and a disassociation of creative and critical attitudes and aspects can in some instances be undesirable. However, it is hoped that at the very least, the following will lay the ground for subsequent more detailed discussion and debate.

In partial resolution of the second problem, I would like to invoke a neologism coined by the cognitive linguist, Keith Oatley (2003), which allows us not only to view the role of creative practitioner and critical analysis as part and parcel of the same entity, but also to better understand the cognitive processes that are engaged during creative practice. Oatley uses the term 'writingandreading' to describe the way in which two activities, traditionally considered separate, are often intimately bound together.

> 'Writingandreading' is not an English world. It should be. We tend to think
> of the two parts as separate. Pure writing is possible. One may just write an

email, careless of syntax and spelling, then press a key, and off it goes into the ether. Pure reading is also possible: one can absorb, if that is an apt meta-phor, the information in a newspaper article with almost no thought except what the writer has supplied. More usually we writeandread ... A text is not autonomous. That is to say it does not stand alone: responsibility is distributed between writer and reader. (2003: 161)

Oatley refers here to an essential dichotomy which lies at the heart of creative writing and the worlds that it builds: between that which is autonomous and that which is heteronomous (Howarth 2012). If the former term can be used to categorize something that can be demonstrated to exist independently of perception, then the latter refers to that which is brought into existence and validated only by the presence of an observing and sentient consciousness. Dufrenne (1973), from the perspective of literary criticism, views the matter as follows:

... whoever grants the heteronomous existence of sentences (and thus of the literary work), must also accept all of its autonomous foundations and must not be content with pure acts of consciousness (which are sufficient to define the heteronomy of the intentional object). These supplementary foun-dations are, on the one hand, the subjective operations which preside over the creation of the work. On the other hand, and above all, they are 'ideal concepts' to which the sentences of the work refer and which are actualised in them. (209–10)

However, a treatment based on cognitive poetics combined with Oatley's writ-ingandreading can do better. It can highlight the essential interconnectedness of the 'sentences' and 'ideal concepts' which they create, in essence by treating the heteronomous worlds formed in the act of reading and the autonomous texts which give birth to them as equivalent and interchangeable. Creative writ-ing as artefact, as typed or printed words on a page or screen, is autonomous. It has a physical, sensory presence as we turn its pages or, indeed, scroll through it with a mouse or a fingertip. The worlds that it creates in our imaginations are – at least intuitively – heteronomous. In philosophical terms, then, this con-cept is closely related to phenomenalism: the idea that physical objects, events, properties and artefacts are reducible to mental objects, events, properties and artefacts. To put this as simply as possible, and at the risk of glibness: our thoughts do not just shape out world, they *are* our world. As cognitive poetics can demonstrate, this proposal is analogous to processes of world-building from linguistic prompts as well as the ways in which such worlds take on a powerful, resonant and affective existence in the imagination. It also raises various philosophical and ontological questions. In what sense is the felt experience of a storyworld different from the felt experience derived from the AW? How is it that storyworlds can take on an existence of their own? We have all had the experience of being truly gripped, moved, gladdened or saddened by a poem or story; if the worlds that these texts create are 'unreal', then how do they both stimulate and simulate real emotional responses? (See Oatley 1992: 18–20 and Stockwell 2002: 171–3 for further discussion of this as well as some theoretical propositions in response to the question).

Creative practice at its most invigorating should involve becoming both writer and reader at the same time, through the processes of writingandreading. The act of creative writing is characterized by the two activities being more integrated, or part and parcel of the same process: to write as we read, and to read as we write. This assertion is given further strength if we take into account the idea of reading as performance as formulated through reception theory. Any text constructed from language is not simply 'received' in a passive sense by its reader (Jauss 1982), but is interpreted according to individual cultural contexts and lived experience. Cognitive poetics also asserts this via its appropriation of Schema Theory (see Bartlett 1932; Jeffries 2001; Schank and Abelson 1977 and Semino 2001).

A schema (Bartlett 1932; Schank and Abelson 1977) is a cognitive framework that helps the participant in the discourse-world (in the case of creative writing, the reader) to sort, organize and interpret incoming linguistic information by activating pre-existing 'mental baggage', often dependent on cultural context and background. For example, British and Irish readers will have a particular 'pub' schema which will be activated when processing that noun, calling to mind mental representations of a bar area, beer taps, glasses, customers, the smell of food, the hum of conversation and so on. Schemas allow shortcuts to be taken when interpreting the, often complex, linguistic information provided by a text. It is this facility in the mind of the reader that writers exploit when providing linguistic cues from which readers subsequently build worlds; from minimal linguistic input, a rich and complex text-world can be constructed cognitively through a combination of the 'top down' information stored in the relevant schema (say, the pub schema mentioned above) with 'bottom up' linguistic information from the text itself (which might impart more specific information, building on the initial schema: the pub has a thatched roof and is next to a pond, for example). The reader's perception of the world built by a text is dependent upon the ways in which that reader's package of schemas is reinforced or challenged during the act of reading (Semino 1997: 119). I am proposing a melding of schema-based conceptions of world-building (focused on reading practice) with stylistic analysis of the discourse of the text, and placing an awareness of this combination at the forefront of creative practice. The remainder of this chapter will be devoted to exploring just a few of the many ways in which this could be done.

8.2   Words and worlds

One of the principal cognitive models for understanding what happens when a reader processes discourse is Text World Theory (Gavins 2007; Werth 1999), which can be aligned with the *reading* end of Oatley's neologism. 'Steam' stylistics/narratology (Carter 2010: 61) can be aligned to the *writing* end. To reiterate: creative writers should think of writingandreading as a synthesis of complementary and inseparable activities. However, I wish to demonstrate in this section that one or the other will be in the ascendency during different stages of the creative process, and that Text World Theory can help show how this happens and why.

To illustrate this notion more concretely, it will be useful to turn to a literary example. In Jorge Luis Borges's short story 'Tlön, Uqbar, Orbis Tertius' (2000: 72), the author posits the existence of a world, Tlön, where a language is spoken/written that does not contain nouns. Without nouns, argues the narrator, all Western thought becomes impossible. He cites the following example (the numbering is my own for ease of reference):

(1)   The moon rose above the water.

This sentence is rendered in the Tlönic language as follows:

(2)   Hlör u fang axaxaxas mlö.

To attempt a translation into English that is syntactically rather than semantically authentic, the narrator offers the following:

(3)   Upward behind the onstreaming it mooned.

This 'syntactic simulation' (3) has two prepositions (*upward* and *behind*), an article, a neologistic verb-as-noun or gerund (*onstreaming*) and a past-tense verb (*it mooned*). In keeping with the cognitive approach, we should posit that the syntactical simulation has a cognitive effect. To lend weight to this assertion, it will be useful to invoke the Generalization Commitment (Lakoff 1990; Langacker 1991 and 1999) which asserts that different levels of language share common features. Accordingly, there is no clear separation between syntax and semantics; in the cognitive view, syntactic structures are themselves inherently meaningful. Thus, the structures and systems of language have an impact on the way we create a text-world in response to a discoursal prompt. This effect should be of great interest to the creative writer.

What is the nature of the text-world produced by the linguistically deviant sentence (3)? While both sentences (1) and (3) cue the construction of text-worlds containing world-building and function-advancing elements, the text-world built by sentence (1) will be qualitatively different due to the schemas invoked, which will be drawn from previous readings, experiences and imaginings of that (relatively) commonplace scene. The text-world built by (3), with its deviant syntax, will be built with reference to sentence (1), which haunts the background of the 'literal' translation. Thus: in (3), our 'writing' of the sentence as we read it, as we build a world from it, is demonstrable, dynamic and obvious; in (1), it is less obvious, but the process is taking place nonetheless. We writeandread in both cases, but on a cline; (3) emphasizes the writing end of that cline, (2), the reading end.

8.3   Deixis and empathy

The ways in which a reader builds worlds in response to a piece of creative writing is also related to deictic function. As already mentioned, cognitive approaches to discourse are based on the idea that mind and body are inextricably connected, and that the centre of perception in cognitive terms equates more or less neatly with the deictic centre, or *origo*. Evidence for this comes from the language we use to position ourselves in relation to the world around us, giving rise to a – often inescapable – sense of subjectivity. However, deixis is not limited to spatial descriptives, but can also refer to the position of objects and entities, and to perception, time and relation. It is deictic function that allows world-building elements in a text-world to take effect.

A further important point can be drawn from this discussion of relations between language and perception, and that is how deixis helps us to identify with the characters of a text, or, more specifically, to experience empathy. Stockwell (2002: 43) refers to this process as 'deictic projection'. In everyday discourse, we are able to 'throw' our deictic centre (in a similar way to the way a ventriloquist throws his or her voice) to occupy an external position by saying, for example, 'Look behind you!' or 'It's to your right.' Put simply, it is this deictic function of language that allows readers to empathize with characters, narrators and their situations.

It is obviously desirable to shy away from making too many hard-and-fast pronouncements about what constitutes 'good' writing, but I would argue with some confidence that the creation (or simulation) of empathetic engagement is as close as we can get to one (see Keen 2010 for a principled account of the significance of empathy in the study of the novel). Readers are more likely to empathize with autonomous objects (such as fellow human beings) than with heteronomous notions or concepts. Through its proposal that readers conceptually project to the contextual locus of the speaker of deictic cues in order to comprehend them, Deictic Shift Theory (e.g. Galbraith 1995) offers a model of how the deictic references determining contextual coordinates are processed by readers, how they render the deictic centre of the text autonomous (making 'concrete' the simulated actions, perceptions, experiences etc. of the narrator of character), and how this contributes to readers' conceptualization of the world of the story.

Deictic Shift Theory accounts for the psychological and physical processes whereby our own deictic centre (both spatial and ontological) can be transposed to form an imaginative structure that we construct both conceptually and orientationally. Our deictic centre, or *origo*, is then used within this imaginative structure to orient ourselves. Merleau-Ponty (1962: 112) called this process 'a summoning of the body's freedom from immediacy'. In creative practice, the writer should be mindful of levels of engagement, or freedom from intimacy, and where on the scale of empathetic engagement the reader will situate him- or herself in relation to the text through deictic shifting. Of course, it should be mentioned too that some creative writing will deliberately alienate the reader, or attempt to defamiliarize his or her reading experience (see Section 8.5).

8.4   Compatibility: Real worlds and fictional worlds

If the previous section explored how discourse is related to or 'attached' to real-world objects, and, accordingly, how readers build worlds in response to it, then this section concerns itself with the ontological nature of worlds built from words, their status as fiction, and the ways in which exploration of these questions can be brought to bear on practice. The previous section drew on Text World Theory, a model designed to account for discourse processing. Here, Possible Worlds Theory (Bell 2010; Doležel 1998; Ronen 1994; Ryan 1991) in relation to world-building will be called into service due to its connection with truth-conditional semantics, which provides the creative writer with a way of thinking explicitly about the status as 'truth' of his or her created, imaginary world as well as the relationship between it and the context (AW) in which the creative practice takes place.

To call a spade a spade is to state that which is true and verifiable in its own terms (in other words, those of the world in which it is uttered: the AW). To call a spade a rake raises obvious questions about the relationship between signifier and signified in the sentence; in semantic terms, the truth conditions of the sentence are called into question. However, what happens if a sentence is written or uttered, but the match to AW conditions is unsuccessful? This is the case in the sentence above, rephrased as 'a spade is a rake'. Of course, we can quite easily conceive of a situation in which a rake might be used as a spade (they are similar enough in function; more on this notion shortly) – and this is precisely the point. Human language, uniquely (as far as we know), can be used to refer to worlds that are other than the world; that is, to abstract conceptions of worlds that are not based in the current 'reality' of the discourse situation. However, that reality is conceived in Possible Worlds Theory as the sum of the imaginable rather than as the sum of what exists physically. The centre of this system is known as the AW, while the conceivable worlds within it are non-actual possible worlds (APWs). Crucially, for the purposes of this section: for a world to be deemed possible, it must be linked to the AW by a relation of accessibility, which refers to the various ways in which the APWs are connected/linked to the AW. On the basis of this model, we can define a proposition as necessary if it is true in all worlds linked to the AW (including the AW itself); as possible if it is true in only some of these worlds; as impossible (e.g. contradictory) if it is false in all of them; and as true, without being necessary, if it is verified in the AW of the system but not in some other possible world.

This is the essence of how fiction works. Reality has a modal structure that is made up of a world that is actual, and then an – in principle – infinite number of possible worlds. Fiction, then, is a particular version of reality where a world treated as actual is circled by a number of other worlds which are non-actual. Fiction arises through what Ryan (1984, 1991) describes as recentring; the implied reader's frame of reference as used for locating notions of possibility and truth shifts from the AW to a possible world. Crucially, however (and I would argue that this point is of great relevance to creative writers), these worlds must be familiar enough, similar enough, to the AW (the context of the discourse situation) to be recognizable. The point is: the further we stretch the gap between the world of the story and the AW, the more difficult it becomes to maintain that essential contract between reader and writer.

Ryan (1991: 32–3) has established a typology of fictional worlds based on consideration of their possibility in relation to fictional genre. Taking as a starting point the already-outlined assumption that 'possibility' means accessibility from the world which stands at the centre of a given system, Ryan defines the characteristics of each world type in terms of accessibility relations linking the actual worlds to the worlds projected by various types of fictional text. In the following quotation, TAW is standard for 'Textual Actual World' (the world upon which the reader's frame of reference has been re-centred).

> In decreasing order of stringency, the relevant types of accessibility relations from AW involved in the construction of TAW include the following:
>
> (a) *Identity of properties:* TAW is accessible from AW if the objects common to TAW and AW have the same properties.
> (b) *Identity of inventory:* TAW is accessible from AW if TAW and AW are furnished by the same objects.
> (c) *Compatibility of inventory:* TAW is accessible from AW if TAW includes all the members of AW, as well as some native members.
> (d) *Chronological compatibility:* TAW is accessible from AW if it takes no temporal relocation for a member of AW to contemplate the entire history of TAW. (This condition means that TAW is no older than AW, i.e. that its present is not posterior in absolute time to AW's present. We can contemplate facts of the past from the viewpoint of the present, but since the future holds no facts, only projections, it takes a relocation beyond the time to regard as facts events located in the future.)
> (e) *Physical compatibility:* TAW is accessible from AW if they share natural laws.

(f) *Taxonomic compatibility*: TAW is accessible from AW if both worlds contain the same species, and the species are characterized by the same properties. Within F, it may be useful to distinguish between a narrower 'F' stipulating that TAW must contain not only the same inventory of natural species, but also the same type of manufactured objects as found in AW up to the present.

(g) *Logical compatibility*: TAW is accessible from AW if both worlds respect the principles of non-contradiction and of excluded middle.

(h) *Analytical compatibility*: TAW is accessible from AW if they share analytical truths, i.e. if objects designated by the same words share the same essential properties.

(i) *Linguistic compatibility*: TAW is accessible from AW if the language in which TAW is described can be understood in AW.

Moving from the top of the list downwards, it can be seen that the first categories describe non-fictional work (TAW is identical with AW). As we move further down the scale, the distance between AW and TAW increases. For example, science fiction novels begin to violate (c), and also (d)–(f) (they often feature different artefacts, different time frames and even different natural laws; their space ships can travel faster than light, say). Once we reach (g) and (h), worlds become logically impossible. Contradictory states of affairs would be admissible, as is the case in Robbe-Grillet's nouveau roman *La Jalousie* (1957), where the principal character is described simultaneously and without any intended irony as both dishonest and honest. He is a high-ranking employee of an old commercial company and also a customs official. The company is performing very well. The company is heading towards bankruptcy and fraud. And so it continues. It is difficult to make firm assertions about such a text's status as fiction, let alone 'truth'. Once we reach (i) on the scale, we are in the realm of nonsense verse and experimental sound poetry; the lack of any correspondence to the AW leads to a lack of any coherent and sustained process of world-building in the imagination of the reader. Sentence (2) from the Borges short story as discussed in Section 8.3 is a good example of discourse from a world occupying point (i) on the scale.

The lessons for the creative writer are twofold. First, the writer should be wary of the moment of arrest at which the world of the story (and, much less explicitly, the poem) becomes too incompatible, too at odds with, the implied reader's understanding of how the AW operates. As Ryan's scale shows, this is *not* to inhibit the creation of science fiction or fantasy worlds (these particular possible worlds have an internal coherency of their own). Rather, creative writers should look to avoid story attributes such as character actions, dialogue, imagery, narrative registers which, as far as the reader is concerned, do not accord with or follow from the premises of the fictional world created. For example, a character does something which does not chime with our understanding of her or him from the rest of the story (character actions can surprise, of course, but should not stretch credulity); a narrator uses language that does not match the reader's understanding of his or her sensibility; a metaphor is created using a source domain that comes from something outside (or not integral to) the TAW of the poem, or a narrator leaves epistemological gaps in her or his mediation of the storyworld that the reader is unable to fill due to incomplete or incompatible schema. When this moment of arrest happens, the crucial processes of world-building are interrupted and the vital contract between creative writer and reader (the will to suspension of disbelief) is broken. Ryan's typology of accessibility relations provides creative writers with a useful and principled scale with which to test the relationship between narrative or poetic discourse and the world of the story and allows us to describe rigorously the degrees of compatibility between the two. It should be useful both editorially (i.e. in terms of rereading and rewriting work after the first draft) when looking for inconsistencies, and also, I would argue, in the midst of creative practice, where deliberately invoking incompatibility might give a piece of work new energy and a new direction (Borges's 'Tlön, Uqbar, Orbis Tertius' takes this concept to a highly entertaining and thought-provoking extreme).

To attempt a summary of the notion of accessibility and its pertinence for creative practice, I would like to make use of another aspect of Ryan's work: the Principle of Minimal Departure (Ryan 1980). This principle proposes that when readers construct fictional worlds, they work from an underlying assumption that the two worlds (AW and TAW) share the same properties and attributes unless they are told explicitly otherwise. In other words, this assumption can only be overruled by the text itself; as Semino writes, 'we still assume that everything else matches the world of our experience' (1997: 64). If a poem describes a brown polar bear, then the TAW built in response will contain an animal that resembles the reader's conception of a polar bear (a 'polar bear schema' will be invoked) in every aspect apart from its colour. The statement 'polar bears have four legs and live in the Arctic' will of course remain true in the TAW but the statement 'polar bears have wings and breathe fire' will be false in both worlds, *unless it is specified as true by the text*. This is the Principle of Minimal Departure in essence: readers will default to their understanding of the AW and will only depart from this understanding if made to do so by the writer.

Second, and to reiterate: language creates possible worlds when the truth conditions surrounding an utterance are not matched in the AW. This relatively simple concept shows us how fiction 'works' and, as argued, might serve as a reasonable definition of creative writing. It is up to the creative writer to act as a guide through these worlds, however small, however complex, keeping the reader's engagement and interaction with the text in mind at all times. Herein lies the fundamental relevance of theories of world-building to the creative writer: it is in the appeal to a reader that a piece of writing stands or falls.

8.5   Avoiding inhibition of return

As already argued, creative writing requires a reader (and that reader may well be the writer), and it is in the successful activation of readers' schemas that creative writing comes to life (just as, from the perspective of the writer, it is the activity of writingandreading that characterizes the process of creativity). To invoke the famous (infamous?) creative writing dichotomy between showing and telling, or mimesis and diegesis (see Scott 2014: 16–20), it is the former process that exploits and makes use of the reader's capacity to imagine most effectively. If mimesis can be defined as an artistic representation of reality (Auerbach 1946), then language that is less overtly descriptive and proscriptive fulfils this function best by engaging the reader's imagination more actively. A simple example will demonstrate this effect. Take the following sentence:

The man sat in the armchair by the fire reading a book.

A world will be built in the imagination in response to this sentence. In this world, what age is the man? How is he dressed? What kind of material is the armchair made of? What colour is it? What time of day is it? What kind of book is he reading? Is it dark or light in the room? The answers to these questions are, for me at least, along the following lines: elderly, in a suit, leather, red, evening, old and hardback, dark. The building of the world is also to some extent cumulative, in that once I 'have' the man as old, many of the rest of the (unwritten) world-building elements fall into place. Of course, none of this information is supplied 'bottom up' from textual cues, but comes from schemas. The point is that the sentence could have been written as follows:

The old man sat in the red leather armchair by the fire one evening wearing a suit and reading an old hardback book in the dark.

However (arguably) this sentence commits the sin of being 'over-written', and is overtly diegetic and descriptive. Too much information is given, and the reader's own capacity for imaginative engagement is mistrusted. Put simply: this is why the creative writer should aim to rely on mimesis over diegesis – sufficient 'space' is left for the reader's imagination to respond to the text. The mimetic function of literary discourse leaves enervating space for the reader's imagination to respond to those foregrounded features of the text by invoking schemas to build worlds (bearing in mind the strictures discussed in Section 8.4). If the language of the text is mostly diegetic in orientation, that process is to some extent already complete. The writer has done all of the imagining on the reader's behalf. There is less (although never no) need for readerly schema to be activated, disrupted, reinforced or preserved, and thus less space for vibrant and invigorating engagement with the text. The text is positioning itself too far towards the reading end of the writingandreading cline. To put this another way: given that in Carter and Nash's (1990) assertion we 'see' though language into the storyworld beyond, it is important for the writer to decide whether or not she or he wishes that language to be foregrounded (the reader 'looks at' the discourse) or whether it is the storyworld beyond that should be the focus (the reader 'sees through' the discourse). Of course, many narratives will move backwards and forwards along the writingandreading cline. James Joyce's *Ulysses* (1922) is a good example of a novel that, arguably, moves at some point through every possible position along that cline. In addition, it is perfectly possible to conceive of a situation where the writer might wish to emphasize diegetic effect (as in the second example above) for artistic purposes.

In addition, emphasizing the mimetic orientations of narrative discourse during creative practice can help to avoid *inhibition of return,* a concept drawn from cognitive science:

> A literary text uses stylistic patterns to focus attention on a particular feature, within the textual space. The precise nature of those patterns will vary according to circumstances, but attention will only be maintained by constant renewal of the stylistic interest, by a constant process of renewing the figure and ground relationship. This is because attention is typically caught by movement (in the visual field); in fact, elements in view that remain static are swiftly lost to attention: literature is literally a *distraction* that pulls attention away from one element onto the newly presented element. (Stockwell 2002: 18)

The 'movement' we look for in a piece of creative writing is a movement of the readerly imagination, a dynamism that is the result of schemas being activated, reinforced, disrupted and changed. It should be noted too that schema disruption, in the terms of Possible Worlds Theory, comes about as a result of some degree of incompatibility between the AW and the TAW. If mimetic orientations are at the forefront, then a common problem of beginning creative writers will be avoided: overwriting, or overwrought descriptive language. Resisting the temptation to *tell too much,* to set the stage too meticulously, is essential if the reader's imagination is to remain engaged and wanting more.

8.6   Summary: Suggestions and speculations

It is hoped that this chapter might point the way towards a principled and rigorous reflection on creative practice based on linguistic conceptions of world-building. Given the myriad ways in which cognitive poetics has shed stark and revealing light on the mysterious imaginative processes involved in reading, it would be an insular writer indeed who refused to engage with a body of critical theory that has so much to say about the target of her or his work. The summary and suggestions that follow are intended to prompt further research, exploration and debate in this direction. It is suggested that creative writers would benefit from:

A. Generally, and as an overarching ambition: setting the notion of writingandreading at the centre of the creative process (indeed, as a definition of *creative* writing), with a focus on the ways in which the autonomous features of language can transform into the heteronomous storyworlds that inhabit readers' imaginations and the fact that the acts of writing and reading can be viewed as interchangeable. Awareness of what happens when readers read should be a prominent factor in creative practice.

B. Being mindful of the insights of Schema Theory, and the ways in which creative writing can reinforce, disrupt or modify schemas.

C. Considering the extent to which Deictic Shift Theory and deictic projection (Stockwell 2002: 43) account for and enhance the extent to which a reader empathizes with characters and their situations. The appropriateness of the term 'empathy' in this context is also in need of more detailed consideration.

D. Using Text World Theory to interrogate and itemize the internal coherence of individual text-worlds; e.g. ensuring a consistency and acceptability of point of view, checking how much a character knows or does not know about another character or situation, or tracking the progression and consistency of narratives with complex structures. Text World Theory might also be put to service in revealing how multiple text-worlds interact with one another and how this interaction can be used, for example, to enhance themes or emphasize dramatic irony. It should also help creative writers understand the complex but fundamental relationship between discourse, imagination and the worlds that are built in the interaction between the two.

E. Using Possible Worlds Theory to monitor narrative momentum (minimal departure), accessibility and to avoid inhibition of return. Possible Worlds Theory also accounts for the relationship between fictional worlds (TAW) and the actual world (AW) in strict linguistic terms, allowing rigorous reflection on the relationships between fiction and truth. It is not sufficient to dismiss narrative fiction as simply stories that are not 'true'. Possible Worlds Theory poses challenging questions about, and offers constructive ways of exploring, the complex relations between the worlds of fiction and the 'real' world.

F. Using Schema Theory to monitor the merits and contextual appropriateness of diegetically- versus mimetically oriented narrative discourse, bearing in mind that the disruption and modification of schemas is one of the key processes that lends dynamism and momentum to narrative fiction. This is also relatable to Possible Worlds Theory in that schema modification comes about through a mismatch between AW and TAW.

This chapter has been an extended appeal to creative writers, particularly those who work in an academic context, to consider engaging with these principled critical approaches to linguistic world-building and the relationship between writing and reading. Even if the relevance of this framework is rejected, then it is hoped that some energy can be found in the disagreement. To summarize the notion as far as possible, I would like to turn to Bertrand Russell:

> We have a number of experiences which we call 'seeing the sun'; there is also, according to astronomy, a large lump of hot matter which is the sun. What is the relation of this lump to one of the occurrences called 'seeing the sun'? (2011: 117)

The 'lump of hot matter' is the artefact; 'seeing the sun' is its writingandreading. Both, I would argue, should sit firmly at the heart of the practice and meta-discourses of creative writing.

References

Auerbach, E. (1946), *Mimesis: The Representation of Reality in Western Literature*, Princeton, NJ: Princeton University Press.

Bartlett, F. C. (1932), *Remembering: A Study in Experimental and Social Psychology*, Cambridge: Cambridge University Press.

Bell, A. (2010), *The Possible Worlds of Hypertext Fiction*, Basingstoke: Palgrave Macmillan.

Borges, J. L. (2000), *Labyrinths: Selected Stories and Other Writings*, London: Penguin.

Carter, R. (2010), 'Methodologies for Stylistic Analysis: Practices and Pedagogies', in D. McIntyre and B. Büsse (eds), *Language and Style*, Basingstoke: Palgrave MacMillan: 55–70.

Carter, R. and W. Nash (1990), *Seeing Through Language: A Guide to Styles of English Writing*, Oxford: Wiley-Blackwell.

Doležel, L. (1998), *Heterocosmica: Fiction and Possible Worlds*, Baltimore, MD: John Hopkins University Press.

Dufrenne, M. (1973), *The Phenomenology of Aesthetic Experience*, Evanston, IL: Northwestern University Press.

Galbraith, J. (1995), 'Deictic Shift Theory and the Poetics of Involvement in Narrative', in J. F. Duchan, G. A. Bruder and L. E. Hewitt (eds), *Deixis in Narrative: A Cognitive Science Perspective*, Hillsdale, NJ: Lawrence Erlbaum: 19–59.

Gavins, J. (2007), *Text World Theory: An Introduction*, Edinburgh: Edinburgh University Press.

Herman, D. (2004), *Story Logic: Problems and Possibilities of Narrative*, Lincoln, NE: University of Nebraska Press.

Howarth, P. (2012), 'Autonomous and Heteronomous in Modernist Form: From Romantic Image to the New Modernist Studies', *Critical Quarterly*, 54.1: 71–80.

Jauss, H.-R. (1982), *Towards an Aesthetic of Literary Reception*, Upper Saddle River, NJ: Prentice Hall.

Jeffries, L. (2001), 'Schema Affirmation and White Asparagus: Cultural Multilingualism among Readers of Texts', *Language and Literature*, 10.4: 325–43.

Joyce, J. (1922), *Ulysses*, Oxford: Oxford University Press.

Keen, S. (2010), *Empathy and the Novel*, New York: Oxford University Press USA.

Kroll, J. and G. Harper (eds) (2012), *Research Methods in Creative Writing*, Basingstoke: Palgrave Macmillan.

Lakoff, G. (1990), 'The Invariance Hypothesis: Is Abstract Reason Based on Image-Schemas?', *Cognitive Linguistics*, 1.1: 39–74.

Langacker, R. (1991), *Concept, Image, Symbol: The Cognitive Basis of Grammar*, Berlin: Mouton de Gruyter.

Langacker, R. (1999), *Grammar and Conceptualization*, Berlin: Mouton de Gruyter.

Lasky, K. (2012), 'Poetics and Creative Writing Research', in J. Kroll and G. Harper (eds), *Research Methods in Creative Writing*, Basingstoke: Palgrave MacMillan: 14–33.

Leavy, P. (2009), *Method Meets Art: Arts-Based Research Practice*, London: The Guildford Press.

Leitch, V. B. (2001), *The Norton Anthology of Theory and Criticism*, New York: W.W. Norton and Company.

Merleau-Ponty, M. (1962), *Phenomenology of Perception*, London: Routledge.

Oatley, K. (1992), *Best Laid Schemes: The Psychology of Emotions*, Cambridge: Cambridge University Press.

Oatley, K. (2003), 'Writing and reading: The Future of Cognitive Poetics', in J. Gavins and G. Steen (eds), *Cognitive Poetics in Practice*, London: Routledge: 161–73.

Phelan, J. (2004), *Living to Tell About It: A Rhetoric and Ethics of Character Narration*, Ithaca, NY: Cornell University Press.

Robbe-Grillet, A. (1957), *La Jalousie*, Paris: Les Éditions de Minuit.

Rodriguez, A. (2008) 'The "Problem" of Creative Writing: Using Grading Rubrics Based on Narrative Theory as Solution', *New Writing*, 5.3: 167–77.

Ronen, R. (1994), *Possible Worlds in Literary Theory*, Cambridge: Cambridge University Press.

Russell, B. (2011), *The Problems of Philosophy*, New York: Simon and Brown.

Ryan, M. L. (1980), 'Fiction, Non-factuals and the Principle of Minimal Departure', *Poetics*, 9.4: 403–22.

Ryan, M. L. (1984), 'Fiction as a Logical, Ontological and Illocutionary Issue: Review of *Fictive Discourse and the Structures of Literature* by Felix Martínex-Boanti', *Style*, 18.2: 121–39.

Ryan, M. L. (1991), *Possible Worlds, Artificial Intelligence and Narrative Theory*, Bloomington, IN: Indiana University Press.

Schank, R. C and R. P. Abelson (1977), *Scripts, Plans, Goals, and Understanding*, Hillsdale, NJ: Lawrence Erlbaum Associates, Inc.

Scott, J. (2014), *Creative Writing and Stylistics*, Basingstoke: Palgrave Macmillan.

Semino, E. (1997), *Language and World Creation in Poems and Other Texts*, Harlow: Longman.

Semino, E. (2001), 'On Readings, Literariness and Schema Theory: A Reply to Jeffries', *Language and Literature*, 10.4: 345–55.

Sigesmund, R. and M. Cahnmann-Taylor (2008), 'The Tensions of Arts-Based Research in Education Reconsidered: The Promise for Practice', in

M. Cahnmann-Taylor and R. Sigesmund (eds), *Arts-Based Research in Education: Foundations for Practice*, London: Routledge: 230–8.

Smith, H. and Dean, R. T. (eds) (2009), *Practice-Led Research, Research-Led Practice in the Creative Arts*, Edinburgh: Edinburgh University Press.

Stockwell, P. (2002), *Cognitive Poetics: an Introduction*, London: Routledge.

Werth, P. (1999), *Text Worlds: Representing Conceptual Space in Discourse*, Harlow: Longman.

The Texture of Authorial Intention

Peter Stockwell

9.1   Authorial intention as mind-modelling

The human prototype for communication is face-to-face verbal conversation. Writing and reading literature are communicative acts, but the experience differs from the prototypical situation primarily in that the discourse-world is split: reader and author are usually not present in the same time frame or space, and the direction of the conversation is one-way. Apart from a few special cases of living authors in contemporary discussion, authors affect what happens in readers' minds, but the reverse is not directly the case.

Discussions of literature since antiquity have made assumptions and connections between the content of a literary work and its author's life. At its most straightforward, this has resulted in a form of biographical criticism that regards the literary work unproblematically as an utterance of the author, without any sense that a text-world boundary has been crossed or a separate text-world co-created by author and reader within the discourse-world. Such accounts of literature were common and unquestioned in the nineteenth and early twentieth centuries; astonishingly, they still feature in the pages of the arts press and many academic journals of literary criticism even today. Speculations and telepathic claims to insights into authorial thinking and motivation can be found readily even in the pages of scholarly journals in literary studies. Although typically framed within a New Historicist materialism, modern biographical criticism continues to be a significant part of literary historiography. By contrast, reacting to earlier, even more simplistic treatments of the assumed accessibility of authorial intention, the New Critics set a prohibition on such discussions (Wimsatt and Beardsley 1954a) as an 'intentional fallacy': 'The design or intention of the author is neither available nor desirable as a standard for judging either the meaning or the value of a work of literary art' (Wimsatt 1976: 136). The same impulse in different guise came from modernism with its effacement of the author and from deconstruction with its favouring of read-erly and social freeplay of meaning. In all of these cases, a strong intentional-ism and biographical criticism were regarded as irredeemably Romantic, with a flawed privileging of imagination, inspiration, creative genius and the trans-mission of these through a literary work.

For all these reasons, many critical theorists have developed ever more com-plex accounts of the relevance of authorial intention in literary reading, but have generally been hampered by their ignorance of modern linguistics and cognitive science. Instead, debate has focused on the extent to which different critical approaches presume different definitions of intention, and whether the ideological consequences of these definitions serve to impose a set of authori-tarian values or not (see Dutton 1987). For example, everyone accepts that a set of intentions as motivations to speak/write underlie every text, but there is a question as to how far those intentions are recoverable from the text, and whether that recovery is even desirable. Very few people think that a writer's intentions absolutely delimit and close off the meaning of a text, but perhaps the strongest complex position in this direction is that of E. D. Hirsch. Hirsch (1967, 1976) differentiates *meaning* (the socially coded use of language shared by author and reader) from *significance* (which he sees as a more critical evalu-ation). There is an apparent intention in the former, which can be analysed for precision, but not in the latter, which is a sort of intuitive guess. However, Hirsch argues that a critic's sense of significance has then to be put to a test of *validation*: once a significance has been perceived, the 'logic of validation' dic-tates that the critic must demonstrate the scientific basis of their guess (Hirsch 1967: 207, and see García Landa 1991 for a criticism). This position generally aims to make any critical assertion objectively falsifiable or verifiable. In this view, there is a possibility of arriving not so much at a correct meaning but at a verifiably objective one.

By contrast, towards the contrary extreme, Derrida (1980) argues for an emphasis and constant awareness of the 'free-play' of meaning, by which he meant a foregrounding of the potential for textual meaning to undermine itself. Although Norris (1990: 171) points out that this is not a free-for-all in which a text can mean anything at all, in practice many deconstructionist critics have indeed taken this more open attitude. Ironically, the effect for the notion of authorial intention is similar to that of Hirsch: authorial meaning for Derrida is not recoverable because stable meaning itself is not recoverable from anything.

Irvin (2006) similarly distinguishes intentionalism (the author's psychology at the moment of composition) from conventionalism (the linguistic rules of a

culture at a historical moment). She finds fault with both as mutually exclud-
ing aspects of the other, and presents a *hypothetical intentionalism* as a possible
solution to both. Here, a competent reader imagines an idealized author, on the
basis of textual evidence and any other information that a reader might possess. The notion that authorial intention can be located as a model within the
reader is a phenomenological position that was adopted by the Geneva School
linguists, and most notably George Poulet (1969). For him, the critic's task
involves establishing a sense of the authorial consciousness, on the basis not
only of the literary work in hand, but also on any other available textual and
cultural knowledge.

Across all of these approaches, almost all of the critical theory seems to have
been primarily interested in validating a meta-theoretical position. Statements
about what should or should not be available to literary critics are not only
founded on a prescriptive sense, but are concerned solely with scholarly criticism rather than accounting descriptively for what natural readers do. When
'readers' are discussed, they tend to be idealized and schematized, rather than
treated, for example, as sociolinguistic communities of actual people. When
authors are invoked it is either as actual historical persons, who are inaccessible, or as historical artefacts that can be objectified and recovered, or also as
idealizations of 'authorness'. All the various categories of ideal author, perfect
author, ideal reader, implied author, implied reader and so on are idealizations
of either authorness or readerliness (see Searle 1994).

Taking a more descriptive approach – drawn from its roots in applied linguistics – the field of stylistics has in the past abided by the prohibition on
both authorial intention and readerly psychology (see also the 'affective fallacy' of Wimsatt and Beardsley 1954b). The focus was traditionally on the text
itself. However, in recent years stylistics has shifted to include an interest in
pragmatic context and interpretation (see the developments across Carter and
Stockwell 2008), and a cognitive poetics has emerged that has seen the 'affective
fallacy' largely abandoned (Brône and Vandaele 2009; Gavins and Steen 2003;
Stockwell 2002; Tsur 2008). By contrast, stylisticians still generally eschew any
suggestion of authorial presumption or biographical criticism. This has meant
that stylistics has not directly addressed issues of creative intention, other than
phenomenologically as stylistic 'choice'.

However, the stylistician is faced with a challenge here. Not only have literary critics continued to discuss intention with a variety of degrees of rigour,
but – perhaps more importantly – non-academic, 'civilian' readers commonly
treat literary works as having some sort of access to authorial lives. Civilian

readers tend overwhelmingly to read contemporary fiction by living authors (Amazon's bestsellers in September 2014 featured only living authors until we get to John Steinbeck at number 54, followed by F. Scott Fitzgerald and Harper Lee; Waterstones similarly has Steinbeck at 55 (in a study edition), with Charles Dickens at 62 and Robert Louis Stevenson at 87 – all preceded by the likes of Donna Tartt, Ian McEwan, George R. R. Martin, Haruki Murakami, John Grisham and so on). These living authors are accessible not only through their fiction but also through magazine, television and online interviews: they are visible and fully realized people, so it is not surprising that an easy connection is made between their artistic outputs and their imagined interior lives. If this is the familiar author-reader situation, it is furthermore not surprising when readers impute intentions easily to dead authors from history as well.

We can understand this process more precisely as a form of mind-modelling (Stockwell 2009a; Stockwell and Mahlberg 2015). Just as we mind-model a fictional mind as a character in a text-world, and just as we mind-model actual people either in our face-to-face lives or in the discourse-world at large, so we mind-model authors. In this respect, authors and authorial intention are products of readerly creativity – not in the Poulet (1969) sense of an abstract awareness of consciousness but as an actual psychological process. Just as we cannot claim a truly telepathic accuracy either for real-life people or fictional minds, so we cannot be certain of the truth of our imaginary constructions of authors' minds. This does not stop most people from being very vehement and assertive about their own models of authorial minds.

Text World Theory models the rich world of a literary reading as a mental representation that is co-produced in the mind of the reader by an author's choices in providing textual patterns. A key problem for the account of readerly engagement has been explaining how texts that always inevitably underdetermine their worlds can nevertheless produce worlds in the minds of readers that go way beyond the textual denotation. The experience of the world (its *texture*) is greater than the text which initiates it. Even if you widen the world-building capacity of the semantics of a text to include entailment, presupposed situations, connotations, associations, inferences and implications, different readers will still flesh out their mental representations with material that is far richer than the text can possibly be cueing up directly. This key problem for literary reading is neatly handled in Text World Theory by recasting the determining notion of textuality. In this view, the text is not a sort of software code that generates a world in a computational reading mind (indeed, this naive model of language seems to underpin most critical theoretical arguments about meaning and intention). Instead, any notion of textual fixity is replaced by the concept of *text-drivenness*. The reader brings their accumulated life and consciousness and the text shapes but does not absolutely determine each reader's mental representation. Because readers exist socially and culturally, it is not surprising that there is often broad agreement on the effects that a particular text generates; but idiosyncratic connections, memories and delicate associations can be made by all individual readers. At this end of individuation, Text World Theory sets a constraint between genuine socially valid reading and eccentricity on the basis that any statement about a literary world has to have a textual correlate that is articulable and comprehensible to other readers. Text World Theory thus explains how readers can generate worlds that are richer than their textual origins, and the same exponential effect must also hold for the mental creation of character and author.

Just as we do not build a world from scratch, neither do we build our mental representations of other people from nothing. It seems most plausibly to be the case that we start off with a rough template of person-ness, and then the patterns of the text drive that model into the specific form of the character who is being drawn in the reading. Our default sense of person-ness must be the most schematic sense of our own consciousness, because that is the best prototypical model of a person that we possess (see Stockwell and Mahlberg 2015). In this sense, everyone else we encounter in our lives is fundamentally like us, apart from the ways in which various texts have differentiated them in various ways. So whenever I encounter a reference to another person (whether real or fictional), I make assumptions about their embodied human condition and I impute consciousness, perception, memory and experience to them – all based on my own experience and self-consciousness, to start with. The process of holding an understanding of other people in our heads is *mind-modelling*.

In the cognitive poetic approach, there is no difference in our relationships between actual and fictional minds at the level of aesthetics and meaning. We find ourselves able to become angry, upset, filled with grief or joy at fictional characters equally as well as at the range of actual people we know from close friends to distant acquaintances and unmet strangers. The principal effective difference between real and fictional people is an ethical one: whatever it feels like, the experiences of fictional relationships do not have the same ethical value as actual relationships.

It is a principle of cognitive science that there is no special mental module that handles literature or fiction. Instead, literary art simply exploits the continuities of our cognitive faculties. We impute a consciousness to others (we run our *theory of mind* for them: see Zunshine 2006), and we are able to do this regardless of whether they are actually real or not. In this respect, person-ness is not an absolute but a prototypical scale. You are in the centre of the scale as your best example of person-ness; close friends and people you have a richly textured relationship with are scaled next, right out past other people whom you do not know so well; all the way to faceless people you have never met. Beyond that are animals, cartoon characters and even places and objects that you have an affectionate or hostile feeling for – these are not so much non-persons as simply very poor examples of persons, for you. Note that these minimal persons can be made more person-like by stylistic techniques of personification, just as actual people can be depersonified. Whether any particular person on this scale is real or fictional is relatively unimportant.

The process of mind-modelling is creative and active (which is why I prefer the term to the more passive and receptive 'mind-reading'). It begins with a default Theory of Mind assumption about the person-ness of the other entity invoked by the text, but quickly attracts traits, properties, aspects and other textural features that start to fill out a rich personality. This personality is built as an enactor within the text-world that is also under construction. Some fictional characters achieve a very high degree of *impersonation* (Stockwell 2009a), to the point at which they are almost indistinguishable from actual people. Other characters remain at a mechanical, flat, tokenistic or undeveloped level, falling far short of person-hood. The degree to which characters are modelled richly or not is, of course, partly a matter of writerly skill and the textual richness, and partly a matter of the creative disposition of the reader.

Mind-modelling accounts are usually focused on fictional characters (Keen 2010; Vermeule 2010; Zunshine 2006); however, the fractal scaling that is a main design feature of Text World Theory reminds us of the continuities of cognition between fictional and actual people in our experience. As people in the world we are constantly within a discourse-world shared with other interlocutors, building text-world structures as a means of orientating ourselves and making sense of our lives. Text World Theory accounts for face-to-face interaction in exactly the same way as literary and other forms of interaction in which interlocutors are split temporally and spatially across a discourse-world. This means that the account of mind-modelling that has been developed to understand the creative reading of fictional characters is in practice and on theoretical principles no different from its application to real-world relationships. The real-world relationship that lies between actuality and fictionality is, of course, the author-reader relationship, and this brings us back to a resolution of the key issue within authorial intention: in both fictional and actual encounters, we assume intentionality and can then model a hypothetical intention on the basis of that presumption.

9.2 Experiencing a preferred and empathetic world

In previous work (Stockwell 2011, 2013), I have traced the different readerly positioning involved in emotional connections with fictional characters. A distinction can be made between sympathy (a feeling for someone) and empathy (a feeling with someone), the latter being closer and usually more deeply affecting. In both cases, the closeness of the emotion can be understood also diagramatically as a closeness of text-worlds, with fewer text-world boundaries between reader and character for empathy compared with sympathy. In other words, Text World Theory models empathy as being a more direct relationship between reader and character, whereas sympathy is often further removed or deflected via another character or narrator.

In both cases, though, the emotional engagement of the reader is created along what we might imagine as a *deictic braid* that connects the reader's mind with the fictional mind inside the text-worlds (see Stockwell 2009a). This connection is formed from the deictic patterns provided stylistically by the text. Every entity (enactors, characters, narrator and author) involved in the modelling constitutes a deictic centre that is linguistically constructed by the reader. So reading involves not only keeping track of embedded enactors, characters and narrator at the levels of personal, temporal and spatial egocentric deixis, but it also involves keeping track of the interpersonal relations between these people usually encoded in social deixis. Of course, all of this patterning is understood not as face-to-face reality but as part of an imagined world created in the mind of the author: all authorial traces contribute to a textual and compositional deixis that readers use to model authorial intention.

Modelling authorial intention involves imagining authorial motivation and preference as well. We assume an intended thought behind every utterance, and it is implausible to suggest that readers do not make educated and text-driven guesses about authorial motivation on the basis of the whole literary work as well. This is not the same as asserting that those creative mind-models of the author are true and correct. The readerliness of authorial intention modelling is key. Different readers will disagree about authors' minds, and readers will alter their models of authorial intentions over time. However, since authorial intention in this sense is text-driven, and since readers exist socially in cultures and communities, there is in general a consensus for the most part on what a particular text 'actually means'. There is, in other words, a *preferred reading* that is derivable from the mind-modelling that similar communities of readers create from authors. (See Stockwell 2009b, 2013 for more on the sociolinguistic origins and workings of preferred and dispreferred readings).

It should be emphasized that a preferred reading is not my notion of a correct reading. A preferred reading is a descriptive account of what actual readers actually tend to do with any given text. For the vast majority of literary works throughout history, most readers agree roughly on what the author was trying to communicate. Even where texts appear ambivalent, ambiguous, contestable or difficult, that very instability is modelled as an intended authorial preference.

To illustrate some of these arguments, here is one of the most famous literary works from the Great War of exactly one century ago.

Break of Day in the Trenches

The darkness crumbles away.
It is the same old druid Time as ever,
Only a live thing leaps my hand,
A queer sardonic rat,
As I pull the parapet's poppy
To stick behind my ear.
Droll rat, they would shoot you if they knew
Your cosmopolitan sympathies.
Now you have touched this English hand
You will do the same to a German
Soon, no doubt, if it be your pleasure
To cross the sleeping green between.
It seems you inwardly grin as you pass
Strong eyes, fine limbs, haughty athletes,
Less chanced than you for life,
Bonds to the whims of murder,
Sprawled in the bowels of the earth,
The torn fields of France.
What do you see in our eyes
At the shrieking iron and flame
Hurled through still heavens?
What quaver—what heart aghast?

Poppies whose roots are in men's veins
Drop, and are ever dropping;
But mine in my ear is safe—
Just a little white with the dust.
            Isaac Rosenberg

I have chosen this poem here because it is extremely well-known: there are dozens of scholarly analyses and commentaries on it, including notes for students and schools, and hundreds of other online instances and readings. Like other celebrated First World War poems, the writer is characterized as 'a war poet' and the poem as a testimony of reality. It is a poem that is generally not treated as a fiction or dramatic monologue: that is, there is a collapsing of the narratorial persona and the named author Isaac Rosenberg. In Text World Theory terms, there is a very strong counterpart connection between the discourse-world Rosenberg and the narrating enactor Rosenberg within the matrix text-world. Since the reader is also within the (split) discourse-world with the authorial Rosenberg, the text-world that the reader is building has a particularly strong discourse-world force. This in itself encourages a closely empathic reading – how sympathetic or involvingly empathetic this is will depend on readerly disposition of course.

The personal, temporal and spatial deictic aspects of the poem all work consistently to allow a reader to model an observing poetic persona in this way. The poem maintains first-person perspective, with 'my hand', 'my ear' and 'this English hand' throughout. There is even a second-person deictic address. However, where this might be more poetically oriented to a lover, or a patron, or a fellow artist (and the conventional metaphorical poeticism of the first two lines also sets this echo up), in fact the poem is addressed to a rat. Many online readers note the undercutting irony of this, and the ironic address is sustained by the even-handedness of the rat who treats the English and German soldiers equally.

The rat itself is a character in the constructed text-world of the trench – here, in fact, within a metaphorical world switch in which the rat is personified with humour ('Droll rat'), emotion ('sympathies' and 'pleasure') and an ethical evaluative faculty ('inwardly grin'). So distracting is the focus of attention on the rat that in fact it is the rat's perspective that we follow, rather than Rosenberg's. Perhaps there is always a residual readerly address whenever a second-person deictic appears (though in this poem it is not the full *double-deixis* of a 'you' address to a narratee and reader: Herman 1994, 2004). So it is the rat, not Rosenberg, who crosses 'the sleeping green' of no-man's land between the trenches, regards both enemies as the same 'haughty athletes', renders them equal in its sight. The projection of deictic perspective is completed in the orientation of the question 'What do you see in our eyes' – this is the rat looking in to the poetic mind. From that point onwards, though, the perspective moves back to the poetic persona. The value-systems, culture and lexical choices of 'shrieking iron and flame' and 'still heavens' are those of the poet. The obvious personification of 'shrieking iron' and the alliteration of 'hurled through ... heavens' is poetic, and the last few lines are self-consciously poetic in the reflexive questions, in the lexical choice, in the mythological allusions of poppies stained red with blood, and in the metaphorical transference that blends poppies and men 'dropping'. There is even an echo of the opening Rosenberg perspective in the repetition of 'ever ... ever', 'druid ... drop', 'same ... safe', and the continuity of the dawn and life as 'darkness crumbles' to white dust.

All of this deictic shifting is achieved subtly, however. The transitions from Rosenberg to rat and back again, from the day to a lifetime, from dawn to death, from the poetic to the demotic and back again, from one trench to the other are all combined delicately rather than disjunctively. It is possible to read this as the vast majority of readers seem to read it – as Rosenberg's equanimity and resignation to the situation, even though that situation is murderous and horrific. In other words, the egocentric deictic elements (person, time and place) are folded into the textual and compositional deictic elements (poetic techniques and patterning) to close up the identification of the poetic persona as Rosenberg.

There is a very strong preferred response in evidence across all the readings – both scholarly and civilian – of this poem. There is an 'anti-war' assumption, a perception of calm stoicism in the author's mind, a sense of wry humour and an understanding that war is horrific and murderous rather than heroic, glorious, picturesque or stirring. No one reads this poem (or other 'war poems' like it) in these latter terms. The mind-modelling of Isaac Rosenberg as the author-narrator is very strong, it seems, for almost all readers of the poem.

In fact, this is not Rosenberg's poem at all. This version – the most widely anthologized and popularly known – is the one which appeared in a 1922 edition of Rosenberg's poems, edited by poet and art collector Gordon Bottomley. It is not clear whether Bottomley's alterations were based on notes or revisions by Rosenberg himself (fragments now lost), or whether Bottomley himself simply 'improved' the text as an editor. Rosenberg's original text as published in the Chicago magazine *Poetry* in December 1916 is as follows:

BREAK OF DAY IN THE TRENCHES

The darkness crumbles away—
It is the same old Druid Time as ever.
Only a live thing leaps my hand—
A queer sardonic rat—
As I pull the parapet's poppy
To stick behind my ear.
Droll rat, they would shoot you if they knew
Your cosmopolitan sympathies
(And God knows what antipathies),
Now you have touched this English hand
You will do the same to a German—
Soon, no doubt, if it be your pleasure
To cross the sleeping green between.
It seems you inwardly grin as you pass:
Strong eyes, fine limbs, haughty athletes,
Less chanced than you for life;
Bonds to the whims of murder,
Sprawled in the bowels of the earth,
The torn fields of France.
What do you see in our eyes
At the boom, the hiss, the swiftness,
The irrevocable earth buffet—
A shell's haphazard fury.
What rootless poppies dropping? . . . . .
But mine in my ear is safe—
Just a little white with the dust.

    Isaac Rosenberg (original 1916 version)

The main variations are in the punctuation throughout, the excised exclamation tion '(And God knows . . .)', and the last six or seven lines. I have not found any published literary criticism that suggests that this earlier draft is better; my own opinion is that the well-known 1922 version is more intense and striking. Less subjectively, we can see in this version a much less artful effect. The very brief text-world and deictic account of the 1922 version given above draws a very subtle, transitory shift from Rosenberg to the rat's roaming perception, and back again to the poetic authorial voice. By contrast, the transitions in this original 1916 version might be impressionistically characterized as being much more fragmentary and clunky. Instead of an incremental and subtle shift into the text-world and shift into the rat's perceptive world-switch and final shift outwards again, in the 1916 version the transitions are punctuated by em-dashes. These seem to draw attention to the compositional deictic level much less subtly than the later revision of simple stops and commas. In the 1922 version, the shift into the rat's perspective is effected delicately until we are in the rat's mind and its 'cosmopolitan sympathies'. In that version, our rat projection is sustained. Instead in the 1916 version, it is disjunctively interrupted by a return to the authorial text-world level with the exclamation '(And God knows what antipathies)'. The parentheses only make the apparent jarring worse.

Towards the end of the poem, instead of the subtle transitional shift back to the poetic deictic centre, we get in the 1916 version a continued rat-like demotic lexical choice: 'the boom, the hiss, the swiftness', then the poetic 'irrevocable', followed by the rat-view 'earth buffet' and a disjunctive em-dash. The 'rootless poppies dropping' place us firmly back in a poetic sensibility, but the phonetic patterns in the phrase are overly clumsy compared with the more artfully subtle phonetic echoes of the previous text. My argument is that Bottomley's revisions, wherever they came from, have made a better poem.

But where does that leave 'Rosenberg' – the authorial mind that I and many thousands of readers of the poem over the last century have modelled as an authentic war voice? Do we have to create a disjunction in the strong counterpart link between Rosenberg in the discourse-world and the enactor of Rosenberg in the text-world? Is DW-Rosenberg actually a composite mind with Bottomley, and TW-Rosenberg is a poetic persona? Perhaps this matters for historical truth, but I do not think it matters much in purely literary terms. 'Break of day in the trenches' is a literary work co-created by readers, and Rosenberg is a readerly creation too.

Rosenberg, and indeed 'Rosenberg', has been created and transformed by readers over the years. The actual Isaac Rosenberg was killed returning to the front in 1918, and like his contemporary Wilfrid Owen, all of his work takes on a tragic texture as a result of his death. Readers are authorially predisposed to be sympathetic to the preferences of his texts. Stylistic patterns in the work are interpreted in a way that is consistent with this mind-modelled authorial view. Hardly anyone suggests that the poems glorify war, or are jingoistic, so whether the real Rosenberg was a closet militarist or was insensitive to his fellow-soldiers would not matter even if it were true. Sometimes the common mind-modelled version of an author is historically accurate, and sometimes it is not.

The view of 'the war poets' writing a personal view of 'the pity of war' (in Owen's phrase) is a modelling of these authors very much shaped by post-war history. Poetry that was far more nationalistic, aggressive and stirring was most celebrated at the time. Jingoism was popular until a revised version of the First World War and the war poets emerged in the 1960s. Clark's (1961) influential version of men led by incompetent generals, and Joan Littlewood's Theatre Workshop production of *Oh What A Lovely War!* in 1963, both contributed to a refocusing of attention on writers such as Wilfrid Owen, Siegfried Sassoon and Isaac Rosenberg. Sheffield (2001) and Todman (2005) describe how these revisions to history became highly influential, and the cultural framing of the war has certainly become part of the inescapable discourse-world predisposition of most contemporary readers.

This is not to say that text-driven preferred (and dispreferred) responses can suddenly shift with the cultural wind. There is no revisionary re-reading of Rosenberg, Owen or Sassoon: each text comes to us with its textually traced preferences of apparent intentions intact – essentially part of its discourse grammar. Instead, cultural shifts move attention to other writers, or emphasize other poems, such as those earlier by Sassoon which are more patriotic (see Bond 2002; Wohl 1979). Or this most famous 1914 work by Rupert Brooke, which begins:

Peace

Now, God be thanked Who has matched us with His hour,
And caught our youth, and wakened us from sleeping,
With hand made sure, clear eye, and sharpened power,
To turn, as swimmers into cleanness leaping,
Glad from a world grown old and cold and weary,
Leave the sick hearts that honour could not move,
And half-men, and their dirty songs and dreary,
And all the little emptiness of love!

Reading this now, 100 years later, with the deaths of up to 15 million from the Great War, 60 million from the Second World War, the Nazi holocaust and the 40-year Cold War between us, it is almost impossible to re-create much empathy for the clearly preferred response inherent in this text (Lehmann 1980). For me, reading the poem leaves a bad taste, but that effect is largely because I have a very clear idea of Brooke's preferred response, and it very definitely does not accord with my views. While my claim is that texts contain their own preferred readings as part of their extended textuality, including a model of authorial intention, of course it does not follow that readers must take those preferred paths. Like the Brooke poem, there are obvious political texts for which the reader is perfectly aware what the authorial intention was (still a recognition of textual preference), even if a particular reader is resistant to that set of modelled intentions.

9.3   The texture of creativity

Literary linguistic analysis has come a long way over the last century. The expansion of linguistics into pragmatic, ideological, social and discoursal contexts in the 1970s and 1980s marked a break with formalist, clause-focused accounts. The advances in computational corpus stylistics and in cognitive poetics since then have further enriched the field, to the point at which we have a great opportunity to be able to explore creativity, authorial production, literary culture and significance – and do it in a principled, systematic and scientifically rigorous manner. The development of Text World Theory has been key to this progress.

It should be evident from this and emphasized here that the stylistic return to authorial creativity is not a revolution but a recognition of where we have been in the intervening years. I am certainly not advocating a stylistically inflected continuation of the naive biographical criticism that remains prevalent in arts scholarship. Much cultural criticism is little more than literary tourism. Where literary scholars are less interested in authors, they are more interested in themselves as readers, and in their own critical practices. This reflexivity is of little wider interest. The description of readerly mind-modelling is a description primarily of 'civilian' readers, and only secondarily of literary critics as readers. Equally, a cognitive poetics of mind-modelling is not intended to arbitrate in the debate between Barthes's (1977) dismissal of the author as anything other than a 'scriptor' and Burke's (2010) reinstatement of biography. Burke (2002) asserts over and over again that there cannot be a general theory of biography, but in a far more sophisticated form, that is exactly what Text World Theory offers. It is offered, though, not in the prescriptive spirit of critical theory but in the descriptive spirit of applied linguistics.

Authorial intention is a cognitive model, built and enriched by the reader. Authorial intention is part of a reader's experience. It begins not at the moment of reading the text, but in the reader's culture: we are predisposed by culture and by experience to begin modelling an author's mind in particular ways. But those cultural and experiential predispositions cannot fly in the face of the text-driven conceptual and aesthetic structure of the literary work in front of you. Mind-modelling is a discourse-world feature, though of course the realization of the text-worlds and switched worlds within the text are also taken generally by readers as material for making inferences about authorial intentions and preferences.

An author is a mind like any other. An author is no more nor less than an actual person, and no more nor less than a fictional mind. When readers model the authorial intentions behind their readings, this too is part of the texture of literature.

References

Barthes, R. (1977 [1967]), 'The Death of the Author', in S. Heath (ed. and trans.), *Image – Music – Text*, New York: Hill and Wang: 142–8.

Bond, B. (2002), *The Unquiet Western Front: Britain's Role in Literature and History*, Cambridge: Cambridge University Press.

Brône, G. and Vandaele, J. (eds) (2009), *Cognitive Poetics. Goals, Gains and Gaps*, Berlin: Mouton de Gruyter.

Brooke, R. (1915), 'Peace', *1914 and Other Poems*, London: Sidgwick & Jackson: 11.

Burke, S. (2002), 'The Biographical Imperative', *Essays in Criticism*, 52.3: 191–208.

Burke, S. (2010), *The Death and Return of the Author: Criticism and Subjectivity in Barthes, Foucault, and Derrida*, Edinburgh: Edinburgh University Press.

Carter, R. and Stockwell, P. (eds) (2008), *The Language and Literature Reader*, London: Routledge.

Clark, A. (1961), *The Donkeys: A History of the British Expeditionary Force in 1915*, London: Hutchinson.

Derrida, J. (1980), *Writing and Difference*, trans. A. Bass, Chicago, IL: University of Chicago Press.

Dutton, D. (1987) , 'Why Intentionalism Won't Go Away', in A. J. Cascardi (ed.), *Literature and the Question of Philosophy*, Baltimore, MD: Johns Hopkins University Press: 192–209.

García Landa, J. Á. (1991), 'Authorial Intention in Literary Hermeneutics: On Two American Theories', *Miscelanea*, 12: 61–92.

Gavins, J. and Steen, G. (eds) (2003), *Cognitive Poetics in Practice*, London: Routledge.

Herman, D. (1994), 'Textual "You" and Double Deixis in Edna O'Brien's *A Pagan Place*', *Style*, 28.3: 378–411.

Herman, D. (2004), *Story Logic: Problems and Possibilities of Narrative*, Lincoln, NE: University of Nebraska Press.

Hirsch, E. D. (1967), *Validity in Interpretation*, New Haven, CT: Yale University Press.

Hirsch, E. D. (1976), *The Aims of Interpretation*, Chicago, IL: University of Chicago Press.

Irvin, S. (2006), 'Authors, Intentions and Literary Meaning', *Philosophy Compass*, 1/2: 114–28.

Keen, S. (2010), *Empathy and the Novel*, New York: Oxford University Press.

Lehmann, J. (1980), *Rupert Brooke: His Life and His Legend*, London: Weidenfeld & Nicolson.

Norris, C. (1990), *What's Wrong with Postmodernism?: Critical Theory and the Ends of Philosophy*, Baltimore, MD: Johns Hopkins University Press.

Poulet, G. (1969), 'Phenomenology of Reading', *New Literary History*, 1.1: 53–68.

Rosenberg, I. (1916), 'Break of Day in the Trenches', *Poetry: A Magazine of Verse*, IX (111): 128–9.

Rosenberg, I. (1922), 'Break of Day in the Trenches', in G. Bottomley (ed.), *Poems*, London: William Heinemann.

Searle, J. (1994), 'Literary Theory and its Discontents', *New Literary History*, 25.3: 637–67.

Sheffield, G. (2001), *Forgotten Victory: The First World War, Myths and Realities*, London: Headline.

Stockwell, P. (2002), *Cognitive Poetics: An Introduction*, London: Routledge.

Stockwell, P. (2009a), *Texture: A Cognitive Aesthetics of Reading*, Edinburgh: Edinburgh University Press.

Stockwell, P. (2009b), 'The Sociolinguistics of Identity', *La Clé des Langues*. Delivered at Université Lyon III on 24th March 2009, <http://cle.ens-lsh.fr/1238505597236/0/fiche___article/ [posted 9th October 2009].

Stockwell, P. (2011), 'Authenticity and Creativity in Reading Lamentation', in J. Swann, R. Pope and R. Carter (eds), *Creativity in Language*, Basingstoke: Palgrave MacMillan: 203–16.

Stockwell, P. (2013), 'The Positioned Reader', *Language and Literature*, 22.3: 263–77.

Stockwell, P. and Mahlberg, M. (2015), 'Mind-Modelling with Corpus Stylistics in *David Copperfield*', *Language and Literature*, 24.2: 129–47.

Todman, D. (2005), *The Great War: Myth and Memory*, London: Hambledon and London.

Tsur, R. (2008), *Toward a Theory of Cognitive Poetics*, 2nd ed., Brighton: Sussex Academic Press.

Vermeule, B. (2010), *Why Do We Care About Literary Characters?* Baltimore, MD: John Hopkins University Press.

Wimsatt, W. K. (1976), 'Genesis: A Fallacy Revisited', in D. Newton-de Molina (ed.), *On Literary Intention*, Edinburgh: Edinburgh University Press: 116–38 [originally in P. Demetz, T. Greene and L. Nelson, Jr (eds) (1968), *The Disciplines of Criticism: Essays in Literary Theory, Interpretation and History*, New Haven, CT: Yale University Press: 193–225].

Wimsatt, W. K. and Beardsley, M. C. (1954a), 'The Intentional Fallacy', in W. K. Wimsatt (ed.), *The Verbal Icon: Studies in the Meaning of Poetry*, Lexington: University of Kentucky Press: 3–18 [originally in *Sewanee Review* 54 (1946): 468–88].

Wimsatt, W. K. and Beardsley, M. C. (1954b), 'The Affective Fallacy', in W. K. Wimsatt (ed.), *The Verbal Icon: Studies in the Meaning of Poetry*, Lexington, KY: University of Kentucky Press: 21–39 [originally in *Sewanee Review*, 57.1 (1949): 31–55].

Wohl, R. (1979), *The Generation of 1914*, Cambridge, MA: Harvard University Press.

Zunshine, L. (2006), *Why We Read Fiction: Theory of Mind and the Novel*, Columbus, OH: Ohio State University Press.

Building Resonant Worlds: Experiencing the Text-Worlds of *The Unconsoled*

Sara Whiteley

10.1 Introduction

Some literary texts seem to have lasting effects, creating a felt influence immediately after their pages are closed and remaining in memory long after they are finished. Stockwell (2009) identifies such effects as a feeling of 'resonance', and describes resonance as: 'a tone [or] atmosphere in the mind that seems to persist long after the pages [of the literary work] have been put down' (Stockwell 2009: 17). Although resonance is a subjective notion which tends to appear in non-scholarly or impressionistic descriptions of the experience of reading, it is one of a range of experiential phenomenon currently receiving attention within cognitive poetics and the study of literary worlds. This chapter examines a novel which some readers describe as having a resonant effect: *The Unconsoled* by Kazuo Ishiguro, which was described upon publication as 'one of the strangest books in memory' (Iyer 1995). The aim of this chapter is to investigate some of the cognitive stylistic aspects of this text's strangeness and memorability.

Text World Theory (Gavins 2007; Werth 1999) will be used as the basis for an analysis of the conceptual spaces cued by this novel. As my focus is on an experiential aspect of reading, Text World Theory is an ideal framework to apply because it incorporates a principled awareness of the reader and their context of reading (the discourse-world) into close textual analysis. The central premise of Text World Theory is that readers construct mental representations known as 'text-worlds' as they read, formed from the combination of linguistic cues in a text and inferencing processes. In order to discuss literary resonance, I combine this text-world approach with Stockwell's (2009) 'attention-resonance' model, which was developed to facilitate the analytical discussion of resonance in cognitive terms. Stockwell's model integrates well with Text World Theory because it links resonant experiences to the conceptual spaces created during reading and their interaction with readers' attention, disposition and reading intensity. In Section 10.2, evidence of *The Unconsoled*'s resonant effects is presented in the form of readers' comments taken from online discussion forums about the book. Section 10.3 sets out the attention-resonance model and its combination with Text World Theory in more detail. Finally, Section 10.4 examines the ways in which an excerpt from *The Unconsoled* manipulates reader attention and interacts with reader expectations in a manner which makes it potentially highly resonant.

10.2   Readers' responses to *The Unconsoled*

The Unconsoled is narrated by a character named Ryder, who is a famous concert pianist. At the opening of the novel, Ryder checks in to a hotel in an unnamed city and is uncertain as to why he is there. The use of European names, reference to European languages and mention of cafes, squares and an Old Town suggests a Central European location, but the city described resembles several European cities rather than a single one (see Robinson 2006). As Ryder makes his way through various meetings and functions he discovers that the purpose of his visit is to perform an important concert that he cannot remember agreeing to give. Neatly summarizing the novel's plot is difficult because the text-worlds the novel creates depart in several ways from the physical laws and behavioural norms of the real world: time and space are often distorted; emotions occur out of proportion with events; characters who at first appear to be new acquaintances turn out to be close family members; and Ryder often inexplicably encounters people and places from his past.

Upon its publication in 1995, *The Unconsoled* received markedly mixed reviews. Some declared it a remarkable achievement (e.g. Brookner 1995), while in the *London Review of Books*, Chaudhuri (1995) declared the novel 'a failure' and, in *The Guardian* newspaper, Wood (1995) claimed that the novel 'invents its own category of badness'. Over time, the novel has received increasing acclaim and is now often featured in 'best novels' lists in the British press (e.g. Clark, Stokes and Goodman 2007; McCrum 2006). *The Unconsoled* appears to polarize opinion among readers as well as critics, as demonstrated by the fact that in online literary discussion forums such as Library Thing, Goodreads and Palimpsest the book features in threads about both 'most loved' and 'most hated' or 'top ten unfinished' reads. Ishiguro, speaking in 2008, notes that: 'I get asked about it more than anything else. When I'm touring with a book, I know that a section of the evening has to be devoted to *The Unconsoled*' (Hunnewell 2008). This sense that the novel has a powerful and lasting effect on readers makes it interesting to analyse in terms of literary resonance.

Specific reader comments about *The Unconsoled* also suggest that the novel has resonant properties. As part of an investigation into readers' emotional responses to the novel I collected readers' comments from publicly accessible internet sources identified via a UK search engine. In online comments readers are often concerned with describing and evaluating their experience of reading the text and while some reported feeling bewildered, frustrated, disoriented and stressed by the style of *The Unconsoled*, others regarded it as funny and enjoyable because of its strangeness. Among the comments I surveyed I noticed that several readers commented on how resonant and affecting they found their reading experience. The comments cited below exemplify this trend. These responses are taken from posts made on the discussion boards of several internet sites: the exchange in (a) is taken from a discussion forum focused on highbrow cultural chat and debate; comments (b), (c), (d) and (i) are from a British broadsheet newspaper's online reading group; comments (e), (f), (g) and (h) are from an online book club and cataloguing site, and comment (j) is from a freelance writer's weblog. Posts are anonymized as my focus is on their content rather than the authors' identities.

(a) *(A discussion between three participants: A1, A2 and A3)*

    A1: I'm just embarking on The Unconsoled and finding it incredibly dreamlike, to the extent that after putting it down for half an hour I still felt in a slightly surreal mood, as though the atmosphere of it had stayed with me. It's really struck me how immediately I've become immersed in it.

    A2: It snagged me in exactly the same way. Even two weeks later (a long time for me) I'm still awed by the experience. I will probably upgrade this to a [five star symbols] as it sticks with me like a bizarre dream

    A3: ... I had the same experience, in that the atmosphere of the book pervaded real life. I was reading it by the pool on hols and when I got up to do something else, I invariably felt rather peculiar! Having said that ... I eventually gave up around [*sic*] 350 pages in which is very unusual for me. It just became so repetitive and, well, dull and I just couldn't take any more ...

    A1: This is going to sound really odd, but I'm finding the repetitive and frustrating nature of it peculiarly addictive. I'm almost certain I'll be sticking with it ...

(b) I recall reading it every day on the way to work when it came out, a couple
    dozen pages at a time, arriving at work completely shaken and struggling
    to re-adapt after the weird dream-world I'd just inhabited.
(c) I'm kind of stuck in a dreamlike state of my own, simultaneously rushing
    to finish it while lingering over parts that (damn them!) are too interesting
    not to linger over.
(d) For me it was very affecting, I felt part of the dream world as I was
    reading it.

These comments highlight the immersive and dreamlike properties of the
novel, as readers describe feeling 'immersed', 'snagged' or 'part of' the world it
creates. The comments also describe the novel's atmosphere or tone as influenc-
ing readers' moods and perceptions after reading. In (a), A1 describes feeling
'in a slightly surreal mood' and A3 describes feeling 'rather peculiar' after putting the book down. Similarly, (b) describes feeling 'shaken and struggling to
re-adapt' to real life after reading sessions. As well as noting its immersive and
affecting properties, readers also report thinking about *The Unconsoled* long
after they have finished or abandoned reading it:

(e) A horrible, haunting, work of genius, this book isn't right, isn't normal,
    and I'm sure it will stay with me forever.
(f) ... the tense, intriguing mood and skewed, shadowy universe it created are
    still tangible to me days after closing the covers.
(g) I read this book nearly two years ago, but, in memory, it still exerts the
    resonant power that I felt from the second page of the text on to the final
    [page].
(h) I found it truly transporting. I sometimes wonder if I ever actually
    finished reading it, or if I've just entered it.
(i) It's really thought provoking. I'll be walking through the maze of its
    themes for a long time yet.
(j) I hated reading it, yet think about it more than any other book I've
    ever read.

Across all the comments cited above (a–j) readers report being at different
stages in reading the novel, yet their descriptions share a sense of the novel's
resonant effect. Some are mid-way through the text (A1 in (a), (c)), others have
abandoned it (A3 in (a)), others finished it days (f), weeks (A2 in (a)) or even years
ago (b, g). This suggests that the effects they are describing have something to
do with the quality of the novel throughout its development, rather than solely

being related to plot resolution, for example. As well as portraying its resonant effect, the readers also evaluate the novel differently. For example, (j) declares that they 'hated it' and in (a), A1 says it is both frustrating and 'addictive' and A3 found it 'dull'. The resonant effects described do not seem to be dependent upon a positive evaluation of the novel. The similarities between these online comments are interesting from a cognitive poetic perspective because they suggest that some readers associate the novel with particular psychological effects.

Online reader responses are useful for providing a broad picture of the kinds of experiences readers associate with particular works. However in online fora readers tend to discuss the novel in overarching terms rather than pinpointing the effects of specific stretches of text. In order to conduct a cognitive poetic analysis that speaks to the effects discussed by readers, it is necessary for the analyst to select and analyse a short, exemplary section of text. Section 10.4 focuses on the opening of the final scene of this lengthy novel, chosen because it comes from a part of the text where readers may expect narrative resolution and is therefore likely to be read with intensity: a feature which Stockwell (2009) suggests contributes to resonance. The cognitive poetic analysis of this short section from the novel aims to offer an account of the way stylistic features of the text might be reflected in the kinds of reading experiences which are described online.

Cognitive poetic analysis can also contribute to existing literary critical understanding of this novel. The novel's linguistic style has received relatively limited analytical attention, despite the impact which *The Unconsoled* seems to make on both reviewers and readers. Literary critics usually compare the novel's surrealism or absurdity to the work of other writers such as Kafka and Beckett (e.g. Broder 2014; Robinson 2006: 120; Shaffer 1998; Villar Flor 2000). Harris (2013) presents a more comprehensive account of the novel's narrative style, characterizing it as an example of 'oneric realism' (see also François 2004). Oneric realism attempts to render a lifelike illusion of the experience of dreaming, hence offering an explanation for the novel's spatio-temporal distortions and unusual connections. Broder (2014) offers a more cognitively informed assessment of the novel's style, describing Ryder's perspective as that of 'a distinct, non-normative amnesic consciousness' (2014: 235) which deviates from expected patterns of 'normal attentiveness' (2014: 236). The text-world analysis in Section 10.4 considers Ryder's patterns of attentiveness and provides some support for the deviance which Broder identifies. First, Section 10.3 sets out the analytical frameworks which will be used in this analysis.

10.3   A cognitive poetic approach to resonance

During reading, readers create dynamic conceptual spaces which represent the scenes and events portrayed in a text. These text-worlds are formed from the interaction between readers' existing knowledge (including memories, experiences and attitudes) and linguistic cues in the text. The linguistic cues which inform text-world creation are divided into two types: world-builders and function-advancers (Gavins 2007: 35–52; Werth 1999: 180–90). World-builders nominate the spatio-temporal location of a text-world and the entities and objects it contains, and are usually noun phrases or locative propositions. Function-advancers advance the development of a text-world and in narrative texts are typically verb phrases.

Stockwell's (2009) account of resonance proceeds from the notion that elements in conceptual space – here, the world-building and function-advancing elements of text-worlds – present an array of cognitive perceptual stimuli for readers in a similar way to the visual field. When a person with functional vision perceives the world, some things stand out as perceptually prominent and attract attention, while others remain backgrounded or neglected. Furthermore, a person's dispositions or goals can affect the things which appear perceptually prominent and to which they pay attention. Stockwell argues that the direction of readerly attention during literary reading operates in a similar way. He suggests that particular objects or entities in a text-world will attract a reader's attention more than others; these text-world elements are known as 'attractors' (Stockwell 2009: 20). Viewing world-building as an activity which is bound up with readerly attention emphasizes the potential depth and texture of our mental representations, which, Stockwell argues, provides insights into the 'experiential nature of literary space' (2009: 20–1). He presents resonance as a feeling which arises from the interaction between the configuration of attractors in a text and a reader's disposition and reading intensity.

Drawing upon psychological work on attention and the principles of cognitive grammar, Stockwell modifies cognitive norms of attention from the visual and experiential fields for application to a written, literary context. This culminates in a list of the typical features of good textual attractors, which are:

- **newness** (currency: the present moment of reading is more attractive than the previous moment)
- **agency** (noun phrases in active position are better attractors than in passive position)

- **topicality** (subject position confers attraction over object position)
- **empathetic recognizability** (which operates on a scale from more to less attractive: human speaker > human hearer > animal > object > abstraction)
- **definiteness** (definite ('the man') > specific indefinite ('a certain man') > non-specific indefinite ('any man'))
- **activeness** (verbs denoting action, violence, passion, wilfulness, motivation or strength)
- **brightness** (lightness or vivid colours being denoted over dimness or drabness)
- **fullness** (richness, density, intensity or nutrition being denoted)
- **largeness** (large objects being denoted, or a very long elaborate noun phrase used to denote)
- **height** (objects that are above others, are higher than the perceiver, or which dominate)
- **noisiness** (denoted phenomena which are audibly voluminous)
- **aesthetic distance from the norm** (beautiful or ugly referents, dangerous references, alien objects denoted, dissonance)

(From Stockwell 2009: 25)

This list incorporates traditional grammatical categories relating to phrase and clause structure (agency, topicality, definiteness) alongside experiential cognitive categories relating to the moment of reading (newness) and the properties of world-builders (e.g. brightness, noisiness), recognizing that in cognitive approaches, grammar and experience are not separable categories (see Stockwell 2009: 26). During reading, textual features can work to confer reader attention on particular attractors, sustain this attention or distract reader attention to other newly attractive elements. Elements in the conceptual space which are not or are no longer the focus of attention are described as being 'neglected' and will eventually 'decay' from conceptual prominence. Rather than attraction and neglect being polar categories, the attention-resonance model regards textual elements as existing on a scalar cline of prominence (Stockwell 2009: 22). Literary reading, and therefore text-world formation, involves the continual attraction (and sustenance) or neglect (and decay) of attention in relation to objects and entities in conceptual space. Stockwell argues that resonant effects (such as the establishment of a lasting tone or atmosphere) correlate with the level of intensity with which a particular passage or text is read, and that reading intensity is influenced by the interaction between both the organization of textual attractors and readerly disposition:

> [Resonant] effects are configured specifically by the selection of features for attention (a matter of particular textual style), the sustenance of attention both within the world at hand and across any world switches (a matter of textual organisation at a more discourse level also involving readerly decisions), and the control of the field of attention (by a reader with particular preoccupations or expectations). (2009: 54)

Stockwell's application of the attention-resonance model focuses predominantly on poetic texts; however, he does apply the model to one example of prose fiction in an analysis of the opening chapter of Hardy's *The Return of the Native* (Stockwell 2009: 47–53). This novel opens with a descriptive narrative about Egdon Heath, the rural setting of the fictional world. Stockwell notes that 'many readers in discussion report being able to recall this opening, not in specific detail but in the lasting impression of tone and the forceful impact of this setting for the novel that follows' (2009: 49). He attributes the chapter's resonance to the way stylistic features of the text focus attention on the landscape of Egdon Heath, continually resisting 'what might otherwise be normal cognitive distractions towards people, lightness or a change of scene' (2009: 53). This extended and persistent focus of attention on the landscape also confounds readerly expectations about narrative openings: although some description of the setting might be expected in a nineteenth-century novel, the text 'dwells on the scene at some length' (Stockwell 2009: 26). Furthermore, Stockwell notes that at this narrative opening, readers are more likely to read with heightened awareness and enthusiastic intensity (2009: 49) which will amplify the potentially resonant effects.

Stockwell does not supply specific evidence for the reader responses which he attributes to the text in this analysis, and instead his selection of resonant prose appears to be based upon a more general sense that the novel's opening is something which people remember. As shown in Section 10.2, the present discussion is motivated by readers' reports of resonant experiences relating to *The Unconsoled* in online fora. The present application of the attention-resonance model also differs from Stockwell's in terms of the type of text which will be analysed. Stockwell discusses a descriptive scene at the opening of a novel which features a third-person omniscient narrator. The analysis of *The Unconsoled* below applies Stockwell's ideas about resonance to the representation of a scene which is full of character-related action, located in the closing

chapters of the novel, and which is narrated in the first-person by the protagonist, Ryder. In Stockwell's example, readers' expectations about narrative openings are significant in the creation of resonance, but in the present discussion
readers' expectations about narrative closure and their knowledge of the characters and their relationships, which has been built up throughout prior reading, are important in the passage's effects. As such, it is profitable to combine
Stockwell's attention-resonance model with a discussion of the text-worlds of
the scene in order to facilitate a discussion of world-building and reader inference at this point in the novel.

Text-world construction involves many layers of inferencing, but in cognitive work on literary narrative, inferences that readers make about the minds
of literary characters have received particular attention (e.g. Palmer 2004;
Stockwell 2009; Whiteley 2011; Zunshine 2006). Stockwell (2009) refers to these
inferences as 'mind-modelling', which occurs as readers imagine the knowledge, beliefs and feelings of fictional entities in a narrative. Gavins (2007: 42–3)
notes that readers tend to treat text-world entities as 'real' life-like people who
have thoughts, emotions and reactions in the same way as discourse-world
participants, and this ability to imagine literary characters using the cognitive
processes which are analogous to those used in interaction with real people
is thought to be a crucial factor in readers' emotional engagement with text-
worlds. For instance, Oatley (1994, 1999) argues that readers identify the goals
of characters and simulate those goals on their own planning processes during
reading, and as such can experience real emotions as those characters' plans
meet vicissitudes. Mind-modelling is an integral part of text-world construction and, I argue in Section 10.4, mind-modelling inferences can interact with
the configuration of textual attractors in a scene and a reader's discourse-world
desires in order to create a resonant effect.

10.4   Resonance in *The Unconsoled*

The excerpt under analysis comes from the opening of the final chapter of *The
Unconsoled*, immediately after Ryder has finished performing the concert he
has travelled to the city to give. The scene it describes features three central
characters: Ryder, his partner Sophie, and their son or stepson (this is not made
clear in the text), Boris. The family have a strained relationship because of
Ryder's obsession with his work. During the concert, Sophie's father – Gustav,
a hotel porter whom Ryder meets when he first arrives in the city – falls ill and

passes away. After the concert is over, in the early hours of the morning, Ryder
finds out about Gustav's death and then catches sight of Sophie and Boris walking away from the concert hall:

Excerpt 10.1

[1] Sophie and Boris had already covered a surprising amount of ground, and
although I walked as fast as I could, after a few minutes I had hardly reduced
the distance between us. [...] [2] By the time I reached the gate myself, my
breath was coming in gasps and I was obliged to pause. [...] [3] I then saw, over
to my left, a queue in the process of boarding a tram, and Sophie and Boris
bringing up its rear. [4] I broke out again into a trot, but the tram must have
been further away than I had thought [...] [5] Only by waving frantically did
I manage to stall the driver and struggle aboard myself.

[6] The tram lurched forward as I staggered down the central aisle. [7] I was so
out of breath I only vaguely registered that the carriage was half full, and only
when I collapsed into a seat near the rear did it occur to me I must have walked
past Sophie and Boris. [8] Still panting, I leaned to one side and looked back
up the aisle.

[9] The carriage was divided into two distinct sections separated by an exit
area in the middle. [10] In the front portion, the seating was arranged as two
long rows facing one another, and I could see Sophie and Boris sitting together
on the sunny side of the tram not far from the driver's cabin. [11] My view of
them was obscured by some passengers standing in the exit area hanging onto
straps, and I leaned further over into the aisle. [12] As I did so, the man sitting
opposite me – in our half of the carriage, the seats were arranged in pairs facing one another – slapped his thigh and said:

[13] 'Another sunny day by the look of things.'

[14] He was dressed neatly, if modestly, in a short zip-up jacket, and I supposed
he was some sort of skilled workman – an electrician perhaps. [15] I smiled
at him quickly, upon which he began to tell me something about a building
he and his colleagues had been working on for the past several days. [16] I listened to him vaguely, occasionally smiling or making an assenting noise. [17]
Meanwhile my view of Sophie and Boris became further obscured as more and
more people rose to their feet and crowded around the exit doors.

                    (Ishiguro 2005 [1995]: 528–9, sentence numbers added)

This excerpt is a good example of the kind of strange scenes which occur in
The Unconsoled. Ryder boards a tram, apparently in hot pursuit of his family,

but then inexplicably seems to abandon the chase. As it is narrated in the first-person, all world-building and function-advancing features in the novel are focalized through the perspective of Ryder. Crudely speaking, the reader 'sees' what Ryder 'sees' and therefore our access to the fictional world is determined by Ryder's perceptions and attentional processes. I wish to argue that the selection of features for attention in this excerpt and their interaction with the reader's preoccupations and expectations at this point in the novel combine to produce a potentially resonant effect. This is likely to be heightened by an increased intensity of reading as the novel nears its close.

According to Stockwell's typology of textual attractors, in the first sentence of the excerpt Sophie and Boris are established as world-building elements and good attractors: they appear in the subject position in the first clause of the sentence and are high on the empathic recognizability scale because they are human and also members of Ryder's close family. Sophie and Boris immediately begin to fall into neglect, however, as Ryder appears in the subject position in the second clause of the first sentence ('and although I walked as fast as I could …'). Sentences [2] ('By the time I reached the gate myself …') and [3] maintain the attractiveness of Ryder through sustained reference. In the final clause of sentence [3], Sophie and Boris reappear as attractors through their topicality (they are the subjects of the verb phrase 'bringing up its rear'), before the attractiveness of Ryder's actions in sentences [4] and [5] comes to dominate again.

In sentences [1–5] of the excerpt, Sophie, Boris and Ryder are the most prominent attractors because they appear in the subject positions and are active. Their attractiveness is maintained by non-shift devices (Stockwell 2009: 33), such the way other objects and humans in the text-world are described in indefinite and non-individuated terms: 'a tram' [3] and 'a queue' [3]. The conceptual prominence of the characters facilitates readers' mind-modelling inferences by providing information about their physical and (by inference) emotional relation to each other.

Ryder's behaviour suggests that he strongly and urgently wants to catch up with Sophie and Boris: he begins following them and aims to 'reduce the distance' [1] between them and himself. Ryder's physical pursuit of Sophie and Boris is further justified by readers' discourse-world knowledge of the characters' relationship which has been built up during prior reading and the inferences they can make about the situational context at this moment in the text. Sophie and Boris are Ryder's close family and are recently bereaved (indeed, in the previous chapter Ryder recognizes that they must be experiencing 'distress'

(Ishiguro 2005: 527)). A reader's broader, cultural discourse-world knowledge about people's behaviour at times of family bereavement, in which people commonly gather together to offer mutual support and consolation, accords with Ryder's behaviour and explains the urgency of his chase. These mind-modelling inferences about Ryder's intentions mean that his reunion with Sophie and Boris (and desire to offer consolation) appears to be a clear goal motivating his actions. As Oatley (1994, 1999) suggests, upon identifying a characters' goal a reader may also become invested in this goal and become emotionally engaged with events in the text.

It is not possible to know whether the internet forum users cited above experienced this feeling of engagement with the story as described by Oatley. However, in my reading of this scene, I certainly wanted Ryder to catch up with Sophie and Boris: Ryder's goal aligned with my own desires about the outcome of the narrative. This scene occurs tantalizingly near the end of this long and complex novel, and the tensions between the central characters at this point in the novel still remain unresolved. As stories often end with resolution and reconciliation, I expected that the interaction of these characters at this stage in the narrative would help to resolve the plot. As a result, I read this section of the novel with heightened awareness and enthusiastic intensity (Stockwell 2009: 49). The focus on the human characters in the text-world at the beginning of this excerpt facilitates the mind-modelling inferences described above and the development of readers' investment in the resolution of Ryder's chase.

From the sixth sentence of Excerpt 10.1, however, once Ryder boards the tram, a number of textual features work to promote the neglect of Sophie and Boris for longer periods and strengthen the attractiveness of other objects and entities in the text-world. In sentence [6] ('The tram lurched forward ...') the tram is established as an attractor as it is given agency and topicality. It is also personified through the use of the verb 'lurched' which shifts it up the empathic recognizability scale increasing its attractiveness. Although the attraction of the tram is sustained in sentences [7] and [8] through referents such as 'seat' and 'carriage', Ryder becomes the most attractive element in the text-world from the second half of sentence [6] ('I staggered down the central aisle ...') to the end of sentence 8. This is because Ryder is presented as the most active entity in the text-world (he 'staggered', 'collapsed', 'leaned', 'looked' and is 'panting') and he is given topicality by repeated presence in the subject position. Ryder's attractiveness is maintained by non-shift devices such as the way the other people on the tram are represented as an attribute of the tram itself ('the carriage was half-full') rather than as empathically recognizable entities.

Although Sophie and Boris are mentioned in sentence [7], 'only then did it occur to me that I must have walked past Sophie and Boris', they are not presented as particularly strong attractors, because they appear in the object position of the final clause of a lengthy complex sentence. They are also represented as being static, as the more active Ryder 'walked past' them. Furthermore, they are represented as enactors within an epistemic modal-world representing Ryder's thoughts ('I *must* have …'), meaning that they exist in a text-world which is more conceptually remote than those created for the rest of this stretch of narrative. Ryder, the protagonist and focalizer, is maintained as the most attractive entity throughout the clauses of sentences [6–8], while Sophie and Boris fall into relative neglect.

One effect of this neglect of Sophie and Boris is the creation of suspense. Gerrig (1993: 71–99) describes suspense as a 'participatory response' which occurs as a result of readers' active participation in a narrative discourse, and which arises from a lack of knowledge about an important aspect of the text: in this case, the outcome of Ryder's chase. Gerrig notes that suspense can be heightened if the narrative outcome or resolution is delayed. The way that this excerpt establishes Sophie and Boris as important goals for Ryder and then allows their attentional neglect contributes to this delay and increases suspense. However, I would argue that, as the excerpt progresses, this attentional neglect of Sophie and Boris begins to deviate from cognitive norms of attraction in a way which also contributes to the passage's resonance.

For instance, as Ryder leans forward to look down the tram in sentence [8], cognitive norms of attraction might dictate that his eyes would be drawn immediately to Sophie and Boris whose faces he would recognize in the crowd, particularly since he boarded the tram in order to pursue them. However, sentences [9] and [10] focus primarily on the layout of the tram. The use of passive constructions ('The carriage was divided …' [9], 'the seating was arranged' [10]) places inanimate objects in the topical position and relegates human agency. In addition to creating a delay and heightening suspense, this point in the excerpt also creates a cognitive disjunction by promoting inanimate objects as attractors where one would expect human (and emotionally salient) entities.

Sophie and Boris are not actually confirmed to be in the tram (earlier, they were only in Ryder's hypothetical thoughts) until halfway through sentence [10] ('and I could see Sophie and Boris …'). This clause reinstates Ryder as an attractor with topicality ('I could see') and Sophie and Boris as attractors through empathic recognizability. The suspense generated by the neglect of Sophie and Boris in earlier sentences is released to some extent here, although they do not catch Ryder's attention for long. Sophie and Boris are described as being sat 'on the sunny side of the tram not far from the driver's cabin' [10] and this mention of the brightness of the tram immediately distracts attention from the characters and back on to the vehicle. Throughout sentences [9] and [10], then, inanimate features of the tram are promoted as attractors and, although Sophie and Boris are nominated as existing in the text-world, they are not presented as the most attractive entities in the manner which their emotional significance for Ryder might lead one to expect.

In sentence [11] Sophie and Boris fall into further neglect via physical 'occlusion', as Ryder's view of them becomes obstructed. Stockwell (2009) uses the term occlusion to describe textual patterning which results in a shift of attention from a previously focused figure to another. Occlusion results in the neglect of the previously focused figure if it is not mentioned again for several clauses (Stockwell 2009: 22). Ryder leans forward in sentence [11], presumably to get a better view of Sophie and Boris, which accords with readers' mind-modelling inferences regarding his goal. However, across sentences [12–16] Sophie and Boris and the tram fall into neglect as Ryder becomes preoccupied with the passenger sitting near him. This man is established as an attractor through reference to his noisiness ('he slapped his thigh '[12]) and his role as a human speaker. The man's direct speech cues a world-switch into the present tense which further reinforces his attractiveness. In sentences [15] and [16], the man is sustained as an attractor through repeated pronominal reference (to 'he' and 'him') although Ryder is re-established as the strongest attractor through his topicality ('I smiled' [15],' I listened'[16]). Sophie and Boris briefly reappear as attractors in sentence [17], but they remain in the object position ('my view of Sophie and Boris') and are immediately occluded once more. The second clause of sentence [17] establishes the 'people' in the tram as better attractors, as they are both spatially higher ('rose to their feet') and more active. Aspects of the busy tram distract Ryder's attention again and as a result his reunion with Sophie and Boris is further delayed.

Throughout the latter section of this excerpt a number of textual features distract from Sophie and Boris, the established and emotionally salient characters, and instead strengthen the attractiveness of spatial, contextual information and new characters. This configuration of attractors operates in direct contrast to the apparent goals of Ryder and the interest and desires of the reader at this stage in the novel. As this passage is also likely to be read with heightened intensity due to the impending narrative closure, this scene has all the ingredients which, according to Stockwell's model, contribute to the creation of resonance (see also Burke 2011: 161–80). The tension and suspense described in the above analysis is maintained at some length during the novel: following the cited excerpt Ryder begins discussing his parents with the fellow passenger (who is mentioned in sentence [12]) and does not approach Sophie and Boris for a further two pages even though the reader would expect him to rush to them. The creation of suspense and deviation from cognitive norms of attention which I have outlined in the above discussion exemplify the kinds of textual effects which may be reflected in readers' reports of resonant experiences.

10.5   Conclusion

This chapter has investigated the resonance of *The Unconsoled* from a cognitive poetic perspective, focusing on a short excerpt taken from the final chapter of the novel. The world-building and function-advancing elements of the text were examined using Stockwell's (2009) attention-resonance model, and the configuration of attractors in the scene were situated in relation to readers' mind-modelling inferences and discourse-world desires. I have argued that the excerpt manipulates reader attention and expectations in a manner which, if read with intensity, creates a resonant effect.

It has only been possible to analyse a short section from the novel here, and there are many other scenes which would merit further cognitive poetic investigation. Nevertheless, the excerpt discussed is a good example of the kind of odd and frustrating scenes which can be found throughout the novel: odd because of Ryder's unusual perspective and behaviour, and frustrating because of the way they delay or diverge from reader desires. As such, the analysis offers some insight into why *The Unconsoled* might be described as a resonant read, and why it is so strange and memorable. The present discussion also lends support to Broder's (2014) literary critical work on the novel which identifies Ryder's perception as somehow deviant from cognitive norms of attention and mind-modelling.

This chapter has also sought to demonstrate that Text World Theory is a profitable framework within which to examine the experiential aspects of literary reading. The key principles of Text World Theory work well with other cognitive linguistic models, and here I have integrated Stockwell's attention-resonance model into my text-world analysis in order to provide deeper insights into the distraction of reader attention during world-building. Crucially, Text World Theory also conceives of readers as fully psychologized discourse participants, with variable faculties of attention and emerging expectations and desires, rather than simply as mindless text-processors. This facilitates discussion of the interaction between text and reader, shown here through detailed analysis of the tension which the excerpt from *The Unconsoled* creates. As such, I hope to have shown that cognitive poetic worlds theories provide a profitable basis for the scholarly discussion of aspects of the experience of reading which have previously been beyond analytical reach.

References

Broder, H. (2014), 'Attending to the Gesture in Experimental Modernism; or, Reading With(out) Theory of Mind', *Philosophy and Literature*, 38.1A: A230–47[A1].

Brookner, A. (1995), ' "A Superb Achievement", Review of *The Unconsoled* by Kazuo Ishiguro', *Spectator*, 24 June.

Burke, M. (2011), 'Literary Closure and Reader Epiphany', in *Literary Reading, Cognition and Emotion: An Exploration of the Oceanic Mind*, London: Routledge, pp. 161–80.

Chaudhuri, A. (1995), 'Unlike Kafka', *London Review of Books*, June 8: 30–1.

Clark, A., Stokes, E. and Goodman, T. (2007), 'How Did We Miss These?', *The Observer* <http://docs.newsbank.com/s/InfoWeb/aggdocs/UKNB/11B7790A0C763750/0E3D7BA979A6E18A> [accessed 19 March 2015].

François, P. (2004), 'The Spectral Return of Depths in Kazuo Ishiguro's *The Unconsoled*', *Commonwealth Essays and Studies*, 26.2: 77–90.

Gavins, J. (2007), *Text World Theory: An Introduction*, Edinburgh: Edinburgh University Press.

Gerrig, R. J. (1993), *Experiencing Narrative Worlds: On the Psychological Activities of Reading*, New Haven, CT: Westview Press.

Harris, F. (2013), 'Ontology and Narrative Technique in Kazuo Ishiguro's *The Unconsoled*', *Studies in the Novel*, 45.4: 603–19.

Hunnewell, S. (2008), 'Interviews: Kazuo Ishiguro, The Art of Fiction No. 196', *The Paris Review,* No. 184, <http://www.theparisreview.org/interviews/5829/the-art-of-fiction-no-196-kazuo-ishiguro> [accessed 11 March 2015].

Ishiguro, K. (2005 [1995]), *The Unconsoled*, London: Faber and Faber.

Iyer, P. (1995), 'The Butler Didn't Do It, Again', *Times Literary Supplement*, April 28: 22.

McCrum, R. (2006), 'What's the Best Novel in the Past 25 Years?', *The Observer*, October: 10–11].

Oatley, K. (1994), 'A Taxonomy of the Emotions of Literary Response and a Theory of Identification in Fictional Narrative', *Poetics*, 23.2/3: 53–74.

Oatley, K. (1999), 'Why Fiction May Be Twice as True as Fact: Fiction as Cognitive and Emotional Simulation', *Review of General Psychology*, 3.2: 101–17.

Palmer, A. (2004), *Fictional Minds*, Lincoln, NE: University of Nebraska Press.

Robinson, R. (2006). 'Nowhere, in Particular: Kazuo Ishiguro's *The Unconsoled* and Central Europe', *Critical Quarterly*, 48.4: 107–30.

Shaffer, B. (1998), *Understanding Kazuo Ishiguro*, Columbia, SC: University of South Carolina Press.

Stockwell, P. (2009), *Texture: A Cognitive Aesthetics of Reading*, Edinburgh: Edinburgh University Press.

Villar Flor, C. (2000), 'Unreliable Selves in an Unreliable World: The Multiple Projections of the Hero in Kazuo Ishiguro's *The Unconsoled*', *Journal of English Studies*, 2: 159–69.

Werth, P. (1999), *Text Worlds: Representing Conceptual Space in Discourse*, Harlow: Longman.

Whiteley, S. (2011), 'Text World Theory, Real Readers and Emotional Responses to *The Remains of the Day*', *Language and Literature*, 20.1: 23–42.

Wood, J. (1995) 'Ishiguro in the Underworld', *The Guardian* May 5: 5.

Zunshine, L. (2006), *Why We Read Fiction: Theory of Mind and the Novel*, Columbus: Ohio State University Press.

'This is not the end of the world': Situating Metaphor in the Text-Worlds of the 2008 British Financial Crisis

Sam Browse

11.1 Introduction

Since the publication of Lakoff and Johnson's (1980) *Metaphors We Live By*, researchers have stressed that metaphor is both a figure of speech and thought, and that metaphor in the language system reflects the figurative ways in which humans conceive of and reason about abstract concepts (see also Gibbs 1994). Metaphor is thus characterized as 'a cross-domain mapping in the conceptual system' (Lakoff 1993: 203) in which one concrete and tangible 'domain' of human experience – the 'source domain' – is analogically mapped onto another, more abstract or phenomenologically removed 'target domain' (see also Grady 2005 for an explanation of the experiential correlations that motivate these mappings). In an effort to provide linguistic evidence for the conventional conceptual mappings that structure the human conceptual system, cognitively oriented research on metaphor has tended to emphasize the systematic inter-relation of clusters of metaphors in discourse, clusters of metaphor that conceptually cohere with one another. For example, Lakoff (1993: 207) describes a series of metaphorical mappings that cluster around a central LOVE IS A JOURNEY conceptual metaphor:

The relationship corresponds to the vehicle.

The lovers' common goals correspond to their common destinations on the journey.

Difficulties in the relationship correspond to impediments to travel.

The single source domain of JOURNEYS allows for the inferential creation of a matrix of metaphors relating to other aspects of a relationship. One of the

central occupations of researchers in the field has been to identify, either intro-
spectively or with corpus linguistic methods, such clusters of cohering metaphors in discourse.

Given that metaphor plays a role in structuring human thought, Koller
(2005: 205) has suggested that the use of disparate metaphors in a single text
can often signify 'struggles over conceptualization'. In this chapter, I examine
the ways in which the use of disparate metaphors in op-ed articles about the
2008 financial crisis signify a struggle over how to conceptualize the British
economy and the economic remedies it required (and still, at the time of writing, requires). To do so, I offer a conceptually situated approach to metaphor. By
situated, I mean an approach that contextualizes metaphor within the broader
conceptual architectures generated by readers in response to the text. I use this
situated approach to metaphor in discourse to account for how metaphor is
used to shift between and undermine different ideological perspectives on the
economic crisis. My main framework in this analysis is Text World Theory (cf.
Gavins 2007; Werth 1999), particularly Werth's (1994) notion of megametaphor. Before moving to an account (Section 11.3) and application (Sections 11.4,
11.5 and 11.6) of the theory, however, I first provide some background to the
2008 financial crisis and the role of 'op-ed' articles in the news media.

11.2   Op-ed articles and the British financial crisis

Since 2007, the US and European economies have suffered a financial crisis
that some economists have compared to the Wall Street crash of 1929 and the
subsequent Great Depression of the 1930s. The 2007/2008 global crash began
with the United States' sub-prime mortgage crisis. The crisis led to the failure
of two large banks, Freddie Mac and Fannie Mae, forcing the US government
to authorize a bank bailout package costing $700 billion. Soon, the crisis spread
to Europe and in September 2007 it led to a run on the British bank, Northern
Rock. The collapse of that bank led to a government bailout and the bank's
later nationalization in February 2008. Across Europe, the financial turmoil led
to recession, declining tax receipts and increasing government deficits. Britain
was no exception and, in October 2008, its economy officially went into recession. After the implementation of harsh austerity policies, alongside strikes
and large demonstrations, the British economy has, at the time of writing, only
recently experienced its first two consecutive quarters of growth over six years

since the recession began. There are now signs of a very sluggish and tentative recovery.

Naturally, debate and discussion about the causes of the crisis and how best to solve it dominated the media during this time. In this chapter, I examine some of the debate about the crisis in two British 'op-eds' – newspaper articles appearing 'opposite the editorial' – published in October 2008. Like editorials, op-eds express the opinion of the author on an important issue, however they are usually written by individuals who have a particular academic, professional or journalistic expertise rather than the editor of the newspaper (Chen 2011: 694). Much of the literature about op-eds and editorials emphasizes their persuasive or argumentative function (e.g. Chen 2011; van Dijk 1989, 1992). I explore this argumentative function by examining how multiple metaphors are used as a strategy for engaging with, and – in the texts discussed – ultimately discrediting, the explanations of the economic crisis offered by rival news commentators, politicians and analysts.

As will become apparent in the analyses in Sections 11.5, 11.6 and 11.7, the metaphors appearing in the op-eds are not only used to express the opinion of the op-ed writer, but also to represent those of the other social actors involved in the public political and journalistic debate about the economy. For example, metaphors can be explicitly disregarded by op-ed writers, they can be modalized, or they can be embedded in a representation of another journalist or politician's perspective. As a consequence, it is necessary to account for the ways in which metaphor interacts with other conceptual structures to generate rhetorical and ideological effects. For this reason, I now turn to Text World Theory because it provides a framework for mapping the text-driven discourse-level conceptual structures in which metaphors are situated.

11.3   Putting metaphor into conceptual context

A central concern of Conceptual Metaphor Theory (CMT) has been to find linguistic evidence for metaphor in the conceptual system. This has often led researchers to focus on clusters of metaphors that instantiate the same underlying conceptual metaphor. Werth's (1994, 1999) framework for analysing metaphor is a response to this focus on clustering. He writes:

> It is not enough to say ... [that] metaphors simply *cluster* – they *do* cluster, and
> this gives us valuable insights into our frames of reference and our efficient use

of linguistic resources. However, the fact that metaphors can also be *sustained,*
as a kind of 'undercurrent', over an extended text allows extremely subtle conceptual effects to be achieved. (Werth 1994: 89, emphasis in original)

Werth's (1994) emphasis is not on the ways in which systematically related
clause-level metaphors provide evidence for the conceptual metaphors stored
in long-term memory (such as LOVE IS A JOURNEY), but on how these metaphors contribute towards the 'subtle conceptual effects' and 'sustained' conceptual 'undercurrent' that are produced on a specific occasion, over a single text.
Werth (1994) is therefore most interested in how multiple clause-level micro-
metaphors are combined throughout a single discourse to create a discourse-
level mega-metaphorical meaning or 'gist' (Werth 1994: 101).

Werth's (1994) focus on the conceptual effects generated by metaphor in a
specific discourse event, rather than the linguistic evidence provided by multiple discourse events for socially shared conceptual metaphors, is a good starting
point for the situated approach to metaphor I have in mind. Although Werth's
(1994) main focus is on the idea that megametaphors emerge out of the conceptual relations between clause-level metaphors, this focus can be extended. It
seems to me that if megametaphor is a text-driven conceptual phenomenon it is
also necessary to analyse it with respect to the other conceptual structures created in the minds of readers as they read. Megametaphor is embedded within
a network of text-world structures all of which have different ontological and
epistemological relations to one another: that is, (mega) metaphor is a conceptually *situated* phenomenon. This means that in addition to an analysis of the
conceptual relations between clause-level metaphors, due attention must also
be paid to the text-world contexts in which megametaphor is embedded. Such
an approach constitutes a situated analysis of megametaphor in discourse.

11.4   'This is not a zombie apocalypse': An example of situated metaphor

One way in which metaphors are embedded in a text-world context is through
negation: that is, the instances in discourse when we are told explicitly that
something is *not* like something else. In Text World Theory the negation of a
state of affairs leads to the creation of a negated text-world that represents those
affairs in the minds of discourse participants. Hidalgo Downing (2000, 2002,
2003) has built extensively on Werth's (1999) framework to provide a detailed

text-world account of negation in discourse. She notes that negation 'defeat[s] expectations which have been created in the text-world by denying the applicability of information which was previously accepted to be the case' (Hidalgo Downing 2000: 224). Negative statements refer to our background assumptions about a particular situation and defy these assumptions, whereas affirmative statements tend to introduce new, salient information into our text-world representations of the text. It is for this reason that Givón (1993: 190) suggests that affirmative and negative statements relate to figure-ground relationships.

Negation foregrounds elements of the text-world that would usually be in the background. As a consequence, it tends to be used more 'when non-events become temporarily more salient than events and are consequently more informative' (Hidalgo Downing 2000: 224). This is important for a discussion of op-ed articles because, as I suggested in Section 11.2, op-eds are used not only to express the writer's opinion, but to engage with the ideas of others. The views of other politicians and journalists form a background – a context – to the op-ed writer's own argument which they may need to dismiss. This could mean negating the metaphors used by other pundits, or using metaphor to represent (or even misrepresent) other competing points of view only to negate them. The Conservative mayor of London, Boris Johnson, writing in the British broadsheet newspaper *The Telegraph* in October 2008, provides a particularly good example of negated metaphor being used in this way:

[A]fter reading the BBC's special market crisis website, complete with its jagged red arrow pointing at the floor, and after hearing the pornographic glee with which we are told that another small country has gone up the spout, and after Mr Bean, the Deputy Governor of the Bank of England, has informed us that this could be the worst financial crisis in history, I am afraid I want to thrash my FT on the table and shout, Whoa! Come off it, folks! This isn't the Black Death. Pinch yourself. Are you still there? Got a pulse? Thought so. Look out of the window. Those aren't zombies. They are men and women engaged in the normal business of getting and spending.

This isn't some disaster movie about a virus from Mars. It's a recession, a downturn, a correction of a kind that is indispensable to any kind of human activity, and it does not require that we all go around under a special kind of credit-crunch pall. It does not mean we have to cancel all parties and talk in hushed credit-crunch tones. It doesn't mean we have to line our rooms with newspaper, get in the foetal position and live on tins: in fact, it means the opposite. (Johnson 2008)

Johnson is writing specifically about how the economic crisis is viewed by the deputy governor of the Bank of England and, by extension, all those who agree that the 2008 crash was possibly 'the worst financial crisis in history'. To represent this view, Johnson draws on a variety of negated metaphors:

(1) This isn't the Black Death.
(2) Those aren't zombies.
(3) This isn't some disaster movie about a virus from Mars.
(4) It does not require that we all go around under a special kind of credit-crunch pall.
(5) It does not mean we have to cancel all parties and talk in hushed credit-crunch tones.
(6) It does not mean we have to line our rooms with newspaper, get in the foetal position and live on tins.

All six of these negated metaphors feed into a discourse-level negated megam-etaphor that compares the economic crisis to some sort of dystopian apocalyptic event. They establish and foreground in the minds of readers a network of negated text-worlds in which the crisis is metaphorically represented as 'the Black Death' or a 'disaster movie about a virus from Mars' in which there are 'zombies', and in which people 'go around under a special credit-crunch pall', 'lin[ing] their rooms with newspaper' and 'liv[ing] on tins'. The first three of these metaphors – 'this isn't the Black Death', 'those aren't zombies' and 'this isn't some disaster movie' – create negated text-worlds on the basis of modifying the world-building parameters of the existing, actual text-world (Hidalgo Downing 2000: 230–2), whereas the metaphors in (4–6) instead relate to the action of the text-world – what the enactors in the text-world should (or rather, should not) be doing (Hidalgo Downing 2000: 227–9). I have mapped this network of text-worlds in Figure 11.1. I have used a grey box to indicate the network of worlds that pertain to the negated apocalypse megametaphor.

The six negated metaphors all draw on source domains that together give quite a fine-grained, novel text-world instantiation of what I will label an APOCALYPSE frame. I use the term 'frame' here in the same sense as Werth (1999, see also Fillmore 1982), who writes that frames are

> experiential models of (part of) human life which direct and influence human understanding of aspects of the world, as mediated through human perceptions and cultural knowledge. (107)

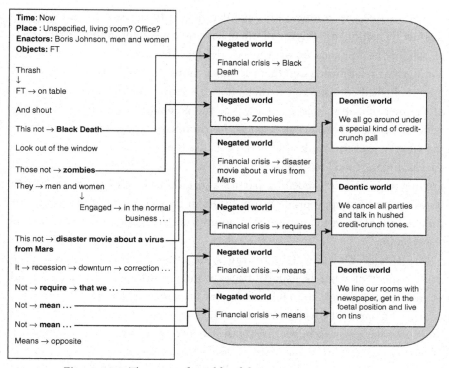

Figure 11.1 The negated worlds of the APOCALYPSE metaphor

The experiential knowledge generating this APOCALYPSE frame in the long-term memory of discourse participants is the experience of participating, or at least having a consciousness of, science fiction and dystopian film and literary culture. The different 'layers' of the megametaphor consist of a series of source-domain worlds which together constitute an instantiation of this frame, and a series of target-domain worlds representing literal happenings in the world of the economic crisis.

This layering is most clearly exemplified when Johnson writes 'those aren't zombies. They are men and women engaged in the normal business of getting and spending'. The (negated) source-world ('those aren't zombies') is created by the first sentence, and is then occluded by an explicit description of the target-world in the second ('they are men and women'). However, at times it is less clear what the counterpart relations are between source and target-world clusters. For example, the behaviours represented in the deontic modal-worlds ('going around under a special credit-crunch pall'; 'cancelling all parties'; 'talking in hushed credit-crunch tones'; 'lining our rooms with newspaper'; 'getting into the foetal position'; and 'living on tins') have no equivalent in the literal target-worlds of the financial crisis. Indeed, the fact that they have no equivalent counterpart relationship and that they are actions that only make sense within the ontological confines of the metaphorical APOCALYPSE source-world layer of the megametaphor serves to advance the polemical function of Johnson's text. The APOCALYPSE megametaphor Johnson uses satirizes the view held by the Governor of the Bank of England because the actions this view engenders ('assuming the foetal position', 'living off tins' etc.) are utterly useless remedies for the crisis. While cancelling parties and talking in hushed credit-crunch tones are perhaps appropriate responses to an impending zombie apocalypse, they do not map on to any useful or appropriate response to the crisis facing the economy.

As Hidalgo Downing (2000) argues, negation works by foregrounding some aspect of what is usually background knowledge. The background assumption made salient in Johnson's use of negation is that, in believing this crisis to be one of the worst in history, the Governor of the Bank of England must also believe it to be as threatening as the apocalypse. The negated list of behaviours related to a science-fiction APOCALYPSE frame – for example, 'assuming the foetal position', 'cancelling parties', 'living off tins' – serves to ridicule this imputed view because the use of negation implies that the Governor believes these patently absurd activities to be a worthwhile and effective response to the economic crisis. Negated metaphor is here being used to satirize the view of another politician. That the megametaphor is situated in a series of negated text-worlds makes this satirical meaning possible because Johnson uses negation to imply that these views are held by the Governor and presumably all who agree with him. This is just one example of how megametaphor is embedded in a network of text-worlds to construct an argument about the economy, an argument that engages with other politicians and journalists in the public debate over the economic crisis. The megametaphors constructed in the course of these debates are both subject to, and facilitator of, the twists and turns of narrative perspective, temporal and spatial shifts, hypotheticality, negation and modality readers encounter in the normal course of reading. I now turn to an example in which megametaphor is more subtly situated with respect to the different text-world structures of the text.

11.5   Storms and glue: Metaphor and point of view

The following is an extract from an article by Benjamin Barber which appeared in the British broadsheet newspaper, *The Guardian*, in October 2008. Barber is a political theorist and fellow of the American centre-left think-tank Demos.

> Economic remedies for the fiscal crisis continue to frustrate their political backers. On that black Monday when the US Congress refused to pass the $700bn bail-out, the market plummeted 477 points. A few days later, after Congress reversed itself and passed the $700bn bail-out, the market dropped nearly 800 points. Since then it has gyrated wildly, drawing markets in Britain, continental Europe and Asia into the maelstrom. What's going on – a crisis in economic capital or in fiscal confidence?
>
> Neither exactly. As the global hysteria makes evident, trust is at stake, but not purely fiscal or economic trust. De-leveraging banks, insuring deposit accounts, penalising CEOs and socialising risk can't do the trick because trust is ultimately political – more specifically, democratic. Trust is a crucial form of social capital, a recognition of the common ground on which we stand as citizens. It is the glue that holds rival producers and consumers together and lets them do the business that would otherwise do them in. (Barber 2008)

This extract serves as a useful example from two perspectives. First, it can be used to illustrate the ways in which megametaphors that do not rely on conventionalized cultural frames, such as the APOCALYPSE frame of the previous example, are constructed and developed across discourse. Second, it demonstrates how the use of different megametaphors corresponds with a series of world-switches to represent two different views of the crisis: the view of critics who, in Barber's eyes, are not asking the right questions of the economic crisis, and Barber's own perspective on the causes of the world economic situation. In this section, I address both these issues in turn, starting with how two distinct megametaphors are developed across the discourse. I then move on to an analysis of the text-world arrays in which these megametaphors are situated.

11.5.1   Constructing megametaphors

There are two megametaphors in this text. One uses a series of hydrodynamic spatial metaphors to represent the economic crisis as a SEA STORM. The other also uses spatial metaphors, but does so to illustrate the importance of TRUST

in dealing with the challenges posed by the crisis. I first turn to a discussion of
the SEA STORM megametaphor.

11.5.1.1 *Building a storm*

The megametaphor in Johnson's text, 'Eat Spend and be Merry', uses a variety
of negated metaphors that each in their own way elaborate a particular aspect
of an APOCALYPSE frame. Clause-level metaphors map various aspects of this
frame onto aspects of the target-world: the Black Death onto the financial crisis; zombies onto people; the general social, political and economic situation
onto a disaster movie. The result is to construct a complex negated source-
world stretching across the discourse that even includes behaviours that have
no counterpart in the target-world (adopting the foetal position, living off
tins etc.).

The process of synthesizing clause-level metaphors into an overarching
conceptual structure works slightly differently in the case of the SEA STORM
megametaphor in this extract from Barber. Whereas the various metaphors
used in the example from Boris Johnson involve *elaborating* the megametaphor
by incrementing a range of different aspects of the APOCALYPSE frame into
a network of negated source-worlds, in this example the processes are better
described as a successive *enrichment* of a range of quite abstract, schematic
spatial metaphors that at first seem unrelated. The difference between elaboration and enrichment is the difference between, on the one hand, repeatedly
incrementing conceptual material from one conceptual frame – in the example, above, knowledge of a science-fiction APOCALYPSE frame – and, on the
other, combining conceptual resources from several seemingly disparate areas
of knowledge to construct an overarching conceptual model. The SEA STORM
metaphor in Barber's article serves as an example of this latter type of process.
In this example, different schematic spatial metaphors all relate to the movement of the 'market':

> The market dropped
>
> The market plummeted
>
> [The market] has gyrated wildly, drawing markets in Britain, continental
> Europe and Asia into the maelstrom.

The market initially drops, then plummets, then gyrates. After gyrating, it
comes into contact with other markets to create a larger, more complex reified
conceptual model of the world economy. This larger, more complex conceptual

model is described as a 'maelstrom'. The process here involves using a series of seemingly unrelated schematic spatial metaphors, which are then given coherence by incrementing the additional frame knowledge of SEA STORMS or MAELSTROMS. The result is the development of a complex and dramatic description of world economic events. I use the term enrichment – rather than elaboration – to describe this process because the interrelation of apparently disparate metaphorical structures creates additional meanings beyond the scope of one frame. In what follows, I give a more detailed account of how the different spatial and hydrodynamic metaphors of Barber's piece are integrated with one another to produce these additional meanings.

In the first instance, it is important to point out that the term 'market' is itself a very complex metaphor/metonym combination (although, as Charteris-Black (2004) points out, it is nonetheless conventional). 'The market' is a metaphor insofar as its literal or 'basic' (Pragglejaz 2007) referent is not 'a public building or place where people sell goods on tables called stalls' (*Macmillan Online Dictionary*), but the New York Stock Exchange. 'The market' is also a metonym because in this instance, the 'plummeting' and 'dropping' of the market does not refer to the rapid (and quite alarming) subsidence of the physical structure of the New York Stock Exchange, but to a depreciation in the value of the commodities being exchanged. The market, then, is a metaphor for the New York Stock Exchange which itself is a metonym for the *value* of the New York Stock Exchange. In this respect, 'the market' is a linguistic manifestation of the conventional conceptual metaphor VALUE IS VERTICALITY. It is worth noting that this 'decryption' of the metaphor, so to speak, is only possible if a discourse participant has pre-existing knowledge of an ECONOMICS frame in which metaphoric and metonymic mappings such as THE STOCK EXCHANGE IS A MARKET and MARKET VALUE IS THE MARKET are conventional. Discourse participants who are unequipped with this discourse-world knowledge might struggle to comprehend exactly what is meant.

The first two instances of market movement are quite unproblematic instantiations of this VALUE IS VERTICALITY conceptual metaphor. The conceptual mapping in each case is between some negative change in market value and downward movement. This downward movement then changes to a 'gyration' in the following metaphor, 'since then, [the market] has gyrated wildly'. Vertical movement is movement along one dimension, whereas the circular movement suggested by the word 'gyrated' is two-dimensional. My prototype of this circular 'image-schema' is of a side-to-side motion (see Lakoff 1987 for a more detailed explanation of 'image-schemata'). That is, gyration does not occur

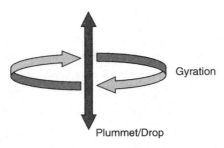

Figure 11.2 Dropping versus gyrating

along a vertical axis, but across perpendicular horizontal axes (see Figure 11.2). In the plummet/drop metaphor, a lower physical position corresponds to 'lower' values and vice versa. However, the image-schema recruited to conceptualize MARKET VALUE in this new gyration metaphor profiles a type of horizontal, circular trajectory which does not map onto the high/low, valuable/valueless scales established by the previous metaphors. This presents a coherence problem. The movement of 'the market' is at first intelligible – relating to value – and then, with the addition of horizontal movement, the mapping breaks down, becoming unintelligible. The literal meaning of the metaphor might, therefore, be summarized as follows: 'the value of the New York Stock Exchange dropped on Monday, after one course of action was taken, and then dropped again, after the opposite course of action was taken. We now have no idea what it is doing'. This is a pragmatic inference prompted by the conceptual mapping of MARKET VALUE onto two different, and clashing, image-schematic structures. The addition of the second metaphor enriches the meaning of the first by introducing new structure into the megametaphor, rather than simply elaborating an already incremented frame, as in the APOCALYPSE example from the Boris Johnson article.

The new circular path of market movement coheres with that of the maelstrom, a whirlpool-like sea storm that draws objects (in the metaphor, other markets) into its centre. The maelstrom further enriches this basic, circular structure. Moreover, it brings the value of the New York Stock Exchange into conceptual relations with other stock exchanges thus making the economic text-world more complex: markets in Britain, continental Europe and Asia are drawn into the maelstrom. I have illustrated the transition from simple vertical image-schema to the more complex and enriched SEA STORM megametaphor

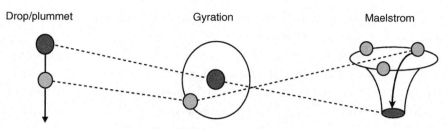

Figure 11.3 The transition from simple image-schematic metaphor to complex SEA STORM megametaphor

in Figure 11.3 (the dotted lines indicate correspondences between the different elements of each image-schema).

When markets across the world are drawn into the centre of the maelstrom, they too become subject to the chaos. The hydrodynamic logic of the maelstrom is therefore mapped against the spread of market turmoil by this mutually dependent set of spatial and oceanic metaphors.

11.5.1.2   Trust is a kind of glue and capital

In addition to the SEA STORM megametaphor, the extract contains an additional discourse-level metaphoric conceptual structure relating to the concept of TRUST:

> As the global hysteria makes evident, trust is at stake, but not purely fiscal or economic trust. De-leveraging banks, insuring deposit accounts, penalising CEOs and socialising risk can't do the trick because trust is ultimately political – more specifically, democratic. Trust is a crucial form of social capital, a recognition of the common ground on which we stand as citizens. It is the glue that holds rival producers and consumers together and lets them do the business that would otherwise do them in.

From the beginning of this passage, the word 'trust' is used as a noun instead of a verb. Following Langacker (1987: 24), 'trust' is therefore metaphorically construed as a thing or, schematically, as an OBJECT from the outset (rather than a process involving someone who trusts and someone else who is trusted). Throughout this stretch of text this abstract OBJECT image-schema is then enriched by two different metaphors: it is equated with a kind of CAPITAL and a kind of GLUE. Both conceptions are complementary, joining together to create a relatively complex conceptual model of the economy which differs quite sharply from the previous SEA STORM conception.

The first metaphor, 'social capital', is a technical term from sociology which highlights the value of social relationships and the resources they generate for individuals and groups. Like capital, social capital can be invested to yield 'higher returns' (Burt 2000: 32). This metaphor gives social relationships the same characteristics as economic relations; they have a value which can be invested. In the article, TRUST characterizes a type of social relationship which is held to be valuable, on metaphorical grounds, as 'a recognition of the common ground on which we stand as citizens'. This metaphorical conception, 'the common ground on which we stand', suggests that favourable relations between individuals are conceived in terms of proximity (SOCIAL RELATIONS ARE SPATIAL RELATIONS). The metaphor SOCIAL RELATIONS ARE SPATIAL RELATIONS paves the way for the second metaphor of TRUST, in which TRUST is conceived of as a kind of GLUE which holds people together. The structure of the complete megametaphor can be summarized as follows: 'TRUST is a kind of CAPITAL which is valuable because it acts like GLUE, bringing producers and consumers into close social proximity, therefore allowing them to do business.'

11.5.2   Situating megametaphors

The megametaphors outlined in the previous sections are very different insofar as the first represents the economy as a dynamic, chaotic place governed by dangerous tidal movements, whereas the second is a static conception and the economic actors are notably land-bound. They are two conceptually discrete models of the economy. This is mirrored in the distinct text-world structures in which the megametaphors are situated.

The SEA STORM megametaphor develops across a target-world cluster of two text-worlds. I have diagrammed this correspondence in Figure 11.4. The two target-worlds in this cluster are related temporally. Thus, the first text-world is temporally located on Monday, and the second 'a few days later'. The subsequent use of the temporal deictic marker ('since then'), and the use of present perfect tense ('it has gyrated') signal the unfolding of the action in this new text-world. The other world-builders ('location', 'objects' and 'enactors') for each text-world are listed in Figure 11.4.

Before moving onto the second, TRUST IS GLUE, megametaphor, the reader encounters a series of world-switches that have the effect of deictically repositioning the narrative voice in the text. Barber writes 'what's going on – a crisis

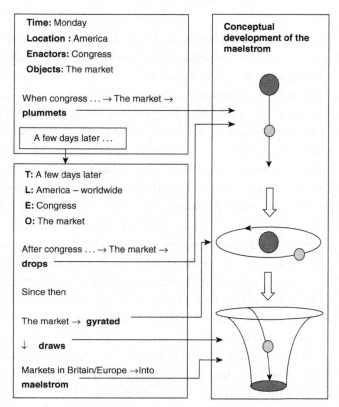

Figure 11.4 The development of the SEA STORM metaphor across text-world cluster

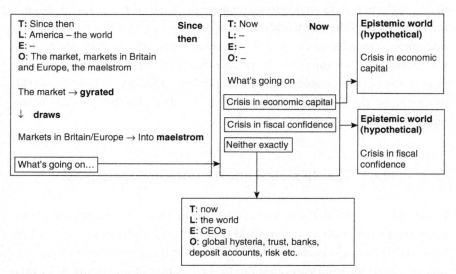

Figure 11.5 Deictic repositioning in 'Decades of Eroded Trust and Democracy Did the Damage'

in economic capital or in fiscal confidence?' This question begins the creation of a complex array of new text-worlds which re-orient the reader. I have represented this matrix of text-worlds in Figure 11.5.

The question prompts a further world-switch, although this time it is not based on a change in temporal deixis, but rather relational deixis. It triggers a movement from the third-person narration of the previous text-worlds, to an implied second-person address to the reader. It shifts us, then, to a conceptual space in which the narrator – a textual enactor of Benjamin Barber – is asking a direct question of the reader. This implied second-person narration simulates a 'face-to-face discourse-world relationship in what is actually a split discourse-world situation' (Gavins 2007: 75). The new text-world is a simulation of the discourse-world. Its 'location' and 'time' world-building elements are accordingly characterized as 'here' and 'now', and its enactors are 'Barber' and, implicitly, 'the reader'. Within this new text-world, two further worlds are created because two possible answers to Barber's rhetorical question are given. The fiscal crisis is the product of either a 'crisis in economic capital' or a 'crisis in fiscal confidence'.

In Text World Theory, epistemic modal expressions cue the creation of new modal text-worlds (Gavins 2005, 2007: 109–25). The possible answers to the question express, relative to their text-world of origin, two hypothetical possibilities: a world in which it is 'a crisis in economic capital' which is the source of the current problem, and a world in which it is 'a crisis of fiscal confidence'. As Figure 11.5 suggests, following the question there is a further world-switch, signalled by the narrator's answer to his own question, 'neither exactly'. Here, both the previous hypothetical worlds of fiscal confidence and economic crisis are discounted. Once more, the deictic shift is relational. The narrator shifts conversational role, moving from the perspective of the person asking the question, to the person answering it. The reader finds themselves in a text-world in which the 'global hysteria makes evident' which begins the TRUST IS GLUE megametaphor.

11.6   The rhetorical effect of situated metaphor

In the example from Barber's article, it is clear that the two megametaphors of the extract exist in discrete text-world networks, separated from one another by a series of world-switches that shift the role of the narrator from the position of asking a (rhetorical) question, to the position of answering it. In this respect, the megametaphors play two different roles in the discourse. The first

SEA STORM megametaphor plays the role of depicting the economic crisis as an intractable problem. The second megametaphor plays the role of replacing the SEA STORM megametaphor with a more amenable conceptualization, and thereby providing an answer to the problem. As it does so, it also establishes Barber as an expert voice in the debate because the narrative persona of the second megametaphor is capable of seeing through the faulty SEA STORM megametaphor and the false dichotomy it produces (the choice between 'a crisis in economic capital or in fiscal confidence'). The implication here is that this false conception of the economy is likely to be held by other commentators. Barber's article is therefore dialogical; it is an intervention into an ongoing debate about the economy. His use of metaphor is, accordingly, a representation of the other views in the debate and, as such, is a narrative device. It is a way of representing an enactor's point of view (in the same way that Johnson employed metaphor to represent the views of the governor of the Bank of England in his article 'Eat, Spend and be Merry'). It should be said that the connection between point of view in discourse and metaphor has been drawn before (e.g. Carraciolo 2013; Martens and Biebuyck 2013). It has not been my intention simply to restate this insight, but to argue that such a contextualized, holistic analysis of metaphor in discourse is well served by Text World Theory because of its ability to systematically describe the text-driven conceptual structures in which metaphor is embedded.

11.7   Conclusion

In this chapter I have used Text World Theory to present a situated analysis of metaphor in two op-ed articles about the 2008 financial crisis. Rather than start from the perspective of using the linguistic data as evidence for broader, socially shared metaphors for the crisis (which would also be immensely valuable research), I have instead focused on the rhetorical effects produced by the interaction of metaphor with the conceptual structures cued by the text. My concern here has been to examine metaphor as it is used on a particular occasion of discourse in a particular conceptual context, rather than focus on the patterns of metaphor used across a large corpus of op-ed articles about the economic crisis. Text World Theory is a useful framework for doing such a situated analysis because it offers a means of describing this conceptual context and the more 'subtle conceptual effects' (Werth 1994: 89) generated by metaphor in a particular instance of use.

References

Barber, B. (2008), 'Decades of Eroded Trust and Democracy Did the Damage', *Guardian*, <http://www.guardian.co.uk/commentisfree/2008/oct/20/economics-globaleconomy-creditcrunch> [accessed 1 November 2014].

Burt (2000), 'The Network Structure of Social Capital', in B. Staw and R. Sutton (eds), *Research in Organisational Behaviour Vol. 22*, New York: Elsevier Science: 345–423.

Carraciolo, M. (2013), 'Phenomenological Metaphors in Readers' Engagement with Characters: The Case of Ian McEwan's *Saturday*', *Language and Literature*, 22.1: 60–76.

Charteris-Black, J. (2004), *Corpus Approaches to Critical Metaphor Analysis*, Basingstoke: Palgrave MacMillan.

Chen, Y. M. (2011), 'The Ideological Construction of Solidarity in Translated Newspaper Commentaries: Context Models and Inter-Subjective Positioning', *Discourse and Society*, 22.6: 693–722.

Fillmore, C. (1982), 'Frame Semantics', in Linguistics Society of Korea (eds), *Linguistics in the Morning Calm*, Seoul: Hanshin Publishing Company: 111–37.

Gavins, J. (2005), '(Re)thinking Modality: A Text-World Perspective', *Journal of Literary Semantics*, 34.2: 79–93.

Gavins, J. (2007), *Text World Theory: An Introduction*, Edinburgh: Edinburgh University Press.

Gibbs, R. W. Jr. (1994), *The Poetics of Mind: Figurative Thought, Language and Understanding*, Cambridge: Cambridge University Press.

Givón, T. (1993), *English Grammar: A Function-Based Approach*, Amsterdam: John Benjamins.

Grady, J. (2005), 'Primary Metaphors as Inputs to Conceptual Integration', *Journal of Pragmatics*, 37.10: 1594–614.

Hidalgo Downing, L. (2000), 'Negation in Discourse: A Text-World Approach to Joseph Heller's *Catch-22*', *Language and Literature*, 9.4: 215–40.

Hidalgo Downing, L. (2002), 'Creating Things That are Not: The Role of Negation in the Poetry of Wislawa Szymborska', *Journal of Literary Semantics*, 30.2: 113–32.

Hidalgo Downing, L. (2003), 'Negation as a Stylistic Feature in Joseph Heller's *Catch-22*: A Corpus Study', *Style*, 37.3: 318–41.

Johnson, B. (2008), 'Eat, Spend and Be Merry – This is Not the End of the World', *Telegraph*, <http://www.telegraph.co.uk/comment/columnists/borisjohnson/3563092/Financial-crisis-Eat-spend-and-be-merry-this-is-not-the-end-of-the-world.html> [accessed 1 November 2014].

Koller, V. (2005), 'Critical Discourse Analysis and Social Cognition: Evidence from Business Media Discourse', *Discourse and Society*, 16.2: 199–224.

Lakoff, G. (1987), *Women, Fire and Dangerous Things: What Categories Reveal about the Mind*, Chicago, IL: Chicago University Press.

Lakoff, G. (1993), 'The Contemporary Theory of Metaphor', in A. Ortony (ed.), *Metaphor and Thought*, Cambridge: Cambridge University Press.

Lakoff, G. and Johnson, M. (1980), *Metaphors We Live By*, Chicago, IL: Chicago University Press.

Langacker, R. (1987), *Foundations of Cognitive Grammar Vol. 1: Theoretical Prerequisites*, Stanford, CA: Stanford University Press.

Martens, G. and Biebuyck, B. (2013), 'Channeling Figurativity through Narrative: The Paranarrative in Fiction and Non-Fiction', *Language and Literature*, 22.3: 249–62.

Pragglejaz (2007), 'MIP: A Method for Identifying Metaphorically Used Words in Discourse', *Metaphor and Symbol*, 22.1: 1–39.

van Dijk, T. (1989), 'Race, Riots and the Press: An Analysis of Editorials in The British Press about the 1985 Disorders', *Gazette*, 43: 229–53.

van Dijk, T. (1992), 'Racism and Argumentation: "Race Riot" Rhetoric in Tabloid Editorials', in F. H. van Eemereu (ed.), *Argumentation Illuminated*, Dordrecht: Foris: 243–57.

Werth, P. (1994), 'Extended Metaphor: A Text World Account', *Language and Literature*, 3.2: 79–103.

Werth, P. (1999), *Text Worlds: Representing Conceptual Space in Discourse*, Harlow: Longman.

The Humorous Worlds of Film Comedy

Agnes Marszalek

12.1   Introduction

While the creation of humour in narrative discourse has been the subject of extensive linguistic research (e.g. Attardo 2002; Ermida 2008; Larkin Galiñanes 2010; Triezenberg 2008), the cognitive stylistic frameworks associated with narrative world-creation provide an as-yet untapped source of highly relevant methodology. This chapter explores how an analysis of the world-building-related aspects of humorous film discourse allows us not only to identify common techniques used in the production of comic film texts, but also to pose hypotheses about the emotional effects such techniques can have on their receivers.

The texts analysed here are extracts from the screenplay of *In Bruges* by Martin McDonagh (2008) and from transcripts of *Bridesmaids* (Mumolo and Wiig 2011) and *In the Loop* (Armstrong et al. 2009). My analysis focuses on the written, linguistic layer of these films, and in particular the stylistic devices used in the creation of their narrative worlds. In the sections that follow, I explore the experiential qualities of these texts for their receivers by considering the affective responses of mood, empathy and suspense which are expected to be evoked by the films. I link each of these responses to specific world-building techniques to indicate how our emotional reactions to humorous film worlds can be cued by the stylistic devices used to create those worlds.

12.1.1   The experience of humorous worlds

This chapter is based on the premise that humour in comic narratives tends to be context-dependent – it is most effective when regarded as part of the whole narrative world to which it belongs. That is because it is the context, the world, which we will draw on to achieve a humorous interpretation of particular elements and which helps to 'unlock' the humour in them. A narrative world which has been meticulously constructed to enhance amusement, and which consequently elicits an overall impression of humour in the receiver, will be referred to as a 'humorous world' (Marszalek 2012, 2013).

The creation of humour in a comic narrative will be treated in what follows as closely bound with the construction of the narrative world – the space to which the narrative refers. This decision to equate the texts we read with the conceptual spaces that they enable us to build in our minds is grounded in various cognitive discourse theories, such as Contextual Frame Theory, which links narratives to the worlds which they allow readers to create (Emmott 1994, 1997) and Text World Theory, which applies the text-as-world metaphor to a wide range of texts (Gavins 2007; Werth 1999). In the discussion that follows, the creation and appreciation of humour in comic narratives will be related to our ability – as set out in those theories of discourse comprehension – to build and update mental representations of narrative worlds based on textual input. This ability to monitor the narrative world continuously and dynamically as discourse unfolds is significant because, as I will argue, readers' monitoring of narrative context is a key factor in their response to the humour in a humorous world.

The humour which appears in humorous worlds can be categorized into two different types: 'local' and 'extended' humour (Marszalek 2012, 2013). Local humour is contained within and restricted to the short form in which it appears and therefore has the potential to be funny in itself, regardless of the context in which it is found. Canned jokes and one-liners, which inform a number of linguistic theories of verbal humour (e.g. Coulson 2001; Giora 2003; Raskin 1985), can be classified as local humour, but there are also other types of quips, witticisms or sarcastic remarks common in conversational humour, which fall into this category. Understanding of local humour relies on our broad knowledge of the real world, rather than our knowledge of the particular narrative world of the text in which it occurs. In Text World Theory terms, this distinction can be compared to that between the 'discourse-world' and the 'text-world' (e.g. Gavins 2007: 9–10; Werth 1999: 17). Because of this, local humour is intrinsically amusing regardless of the immediate context in which it appears.

Humorous narratives, however, often contain humour which is not funny out of context, as it is part of a larger framework that can only be appreciated when the text is regarded as a whole. Such humour is referred to as extended humour, and the following excerpt – an extract from the transcript of the 2011 film *Bridesmaids* (dir. P. Feig) – should illustrate the concept.

Excerpt 12.1

WOMAN

I had a dream last night that we went down. Yup. It was terrible. You were in it.

(*Bridesmaids*)

In order to appreciate the humour in Excerpt 12.1, we need to be sufficiently familiar with the world of the film. At the very least, we should have knowledge about the immediate context in which the line is uttered – it is a comment made by a female passenger sitting next to the protagonist on the plane. Furthermore, our amusement is likely to be enhanced if we know that the protagonist, Annie, is terrified of flying and was not able to get a seat on the plane near her friends, and also that, when feeling nervous, she is prone to acting irrationally and eccentrically, which often alienates her from other people. Much of the humour of the line stems from the fact that, for once, Annie is not alone in her restlessness, as (rather unluckily) the woman sitting next to her seems even more hysterical. For most receivers, then, the Excerpt 12.1 will likely only be humorous when they recognize its place in the wider context of the narrative and notice that it belongs to one of the patterns of extended humour which run through it. Therefore, unlike a canned joke or a one-liner, the line in Excerpt 12.1 above cannot be considered an instance of local humour, as its comprehension relies not only on our knowledge of the real-world, but also (and crucially) on our knowledge of the context of the narrative.

Patterns of contextually bound extended humour are integral components of humorous worlds. The other vital ingredients, as I discuss in detail in the following sections, are (1) a humorous mode of comprehension cued in the receiver, (2) humorous world-building-blocks enhanced with incongruous features and (3) the use of repetition and recurrence for comic purposes. Since the particular stylistic techniques associated with each of these components have been discussed elsewhere (Marszalek 2012, 2013, in relation to comic novels), the focus here is on the emotional reactions which potentially accompany their cognitive processing; consideration is given to the experience of humorous worlds. The emotional aspects of experiencing those worlds explored here will be (1) the affective state of amusement-inducing mood that accompanies humorous mode cues, (2) the reaction of empathy which can complement our responses to certain humorous building-blocks and (3) the suspense experienced by receivers who anticipate the reoccurrence of certain elements.

12.1.2 Methodology: Stylistics of film

This chapter is based on a stylistic analysis of film narratives. The primary method used here is that of Short (1998), who emphasizes the value of the written dramatic text (play or screenplay) as material for stylistic analysis, with the assumption that the performance element so essential to the full experience of drama can be inferred from the linguistic layer. Short suggests that there are several 'informational systems' available to us to infer performance elements from written scripts and screenplays, for example background knowledge about the world, politeness conventions and grammatical or lexical patterns (1998: 13).

Although Short's approach allows for hypotheses to be made about the processing of films based on written dramatic texts, there are a number of limitations in relying exclusively on screenplays when analysing films. Apart from restricting the study of the multimodal aspects of films such as lighting or sound (as outlined by McIntyre 2008), the main problem lies in obtaining a version of the screenplay that closely matches the final film production. Richardson (2010) points out that in focusing on the written dramatic text, Short assumes that the screenplay is a faithful, stable form of the performance, while in fact 'the converse is true of popular drama: productions are fixed, whilst scripts are unstable' (Richardson 2010: 381). While many screenplays have not been published and are therefore not in circulation (as is the case with *Bridesmaids* and *In the Loop* used here), those that are accessible exist in various drafts, and even the seemingly conclusive published screenplays (like *In Bruges*) often differ from the films themselves. The final shooting scripts used in the making of films include the production crew's adjustments to the original screenplays – that, together with actors' improvisation, deleted scenes and significant editing choices are just a few of the many influences on the shape of the film in the post-production stage. In this chapter, the instability of the written film text is addressed by focusing on the transcripts of characters' utterances (with contextual information) as they appear in the film as the primary sources for analysis. The one extract from a screenplay used here (the opening section of McDonagh's *In Bruges* in

Excerpt 12.2) has been found not only to correspond directly to the final film production, but also to illustrate Short's argument about inference-making in processing written dramatic texts especially well.

12.2   Expecting amusement: The moods of humour

The feature that most clearly distinguishes humorous worlds from other narrative worlds is that humorous worlds have been designed to evoke an overall experience of humour by putting the receiver in a frame of mind that encourages a humorous response. The 'humorous mode' of comprehension can be thought of as a playful mind-set which facilitates a non-serious, whimsical interpretation of the narrative world. It is related to the more general motivational state associated with various kinds of playful activities – the 'paratelic state' (Apter 1982: 47, 1991: 15–18) or 'play mode' (Morreall 2009: 50) – where we are disengaged from practical concerns, and our motivations are oriented not towards reaching a goal, but towards engaging in the activity itself. While the paratelic and play mode are not specific to humour, the humorous mode is a frame of mind closely linked to the processing of humorous stimuli, which encourages a pursuit of humorous interpretations.

Once the humorous mode has been cued (or 'keyed', in the case of spoken discourse, as outlined by Dynel 2011: 221–2), the receiver is provided with a cognitive expectation of humour and therefore predisposed to experiencing the affective state of amusement ('amusement' is the term I give to the emotion evoked by humorous stimuli; see Martin 2007: 8 for others, like 'mirth' or 'merriment'). This process is similar to that described in Smith's (2003) 'mood-cue approach to filmic emotion', according to which, in order for emotion to occur in the course of watching a film, the viewer needs to have been cued into a lower-level emotional orientation called 'mood' (2003: 42). Smith's 'mood' can be seen as an affective form of the cognitive state of expectation called mode discussed above. Just as a humorous interpretation is reliant on the humorous mode of comprehension, a humorous emotional response of amusement will be dependent on the humorous mood experienced by the receiver of the text. If we assume that affect is guided by cognition and not vice versa (as argued in the cognitive 'appraisal theories' of emotion, e.g. Frijda 1986), then the humorous mood which facilitates amusement can be seen as an emotional reaction to the cognitive state which I call the humorous mode. As such, both can be associated with the same types of cues.

In order to explore how cueing this humorous mode/mood can be incorporated into the building of humorous worlds, it is worth investigating the opening fragments of comic narratives; if the world is supposed to elicit an overall humorous effect, this intent should be communicated to the receiver early on. The following excerpt from Martin McDonagh's screenplay of *In Bruges* is an example of how the introduction to a narrative world can cue us to enter that world with an expectation of humour. It is a series of external location shots accompanied by a voice-over:

Excerpt 12.2

EXT. BRUGES STREETS – NIGHT

Various shots of the empty, cobblestoned, other-worldly streets of Bruges, Belgium. It's winter, and a freezing fog covers everything; the Gothic churches, the narrow canals, their odd little bridges. We could be in any period of the last five hundred years. We happen to be in the present day. RAY speaks over all this.

RAY

(voice-over)

After I killed them I dropped the gun in the Thames, washed the residue off my hands in the bathroom of a Burger King, and walked home to await instructions. Shortly thereafter the instructions came through – 'Get the fuck out of London, yous dumb fucks. Get to Bruges.' I didn't even know where Bruges fucking was.

Fade to black.

RAY

(voice-over)

It's in Belgium.

(In Bruges: 3)

This example leads us to construct two different spatial worlds: the enchanting world of Bruges and the gritty world of London. These two distant worlds clash incongruously, thus illustrating two key features of comic discourse discussed in humour studies – incongruity in the humorous stimulus; and the ability of the receiver to distance oneself from the subject-matter. Incongruity – sometimes described as a clash of contrasting scripts (Attardo and Raskin 1991; Raskin 1985) – is seen as the vital ingredient of humour within the cognitive group of humour theories (see Clark 1970 and Suls 1972 for philosophical and psychological approaches, respectively). Concerning distance, within socially

focused theories of humour it is assumed that the object of a joke is only laugh-
able when we are not emotionally attached to it, which means that we can view
it from a detached position of superiority (Ferguson and Ford 2008; Zillmann
1983). A different take on humorous distance is the previously mentioned 'cognitive and practical disengagement from what is going on around us' (Morreall
2009: 32) associated with being in the humorous mode of comprehension,
which is said to facilitate a humorous mood.

In order to analyse the experience of incongruity and distance in the opening of *In Bruges*, it is worth exploring the stylistic cues which help us form
conceptualizations of the two worlds – that of Bruges and that of London.
Applying Smith's mood-cue method to McDonagh's stage directions to examine the filmic cues (e.g. lighting, set design, editing in Smith 2003: 42) which
can provide emotional information about the mood of the Bruges world, we can
describe the mood as enchanted, mysterious and slightly eerie. The entrancing
feel of this world relies primarily on the pre-modifiers used to characterize its
world-builders: streets are 'empty, cobblestoned, other-worldly' and bridges are
'odd' and 'little'. The stage directions indicate the spatio-temporal context of a
foggy winter's night ('It's winter, and a freezing fog covers everything'). This is
a world we might have come to associate with fairy tales, an association which
the screenwriter emphasizes by referring to the timelessness of the setting ('We
could be in any period of the last five hundred years.'). The stage directions suggest that these dreamlike elements of Bruges are presented to us through a series
of still images ('various shots'), not unlike illustrations in a children's book.

The London setting, by contrast, is described using a concentration of
active verbs ('killed,' 'dropped', 'washed'), which together with the relative
lack of extended adjective-rich depictions of scenery gives the world a sense
of urgency. What stands out – and can potentially be a source of humour – in
Ray's utterance is the disproportionately high use of swearwords. Apart from
the excessive swearing, it is unlikely that much else of the mood of the world of
London can be thought of as humorous. Rather, it is oppressive and unpleasant,
very distant from the magical, haunting feel of Bruges.

While neither of the worlds can be said to cue a humorous mood in the
receiver, the way they incongruously clash is characteristic of humorous discourse – a joke-carrying text, according to classic linguistic research, is one
that is compatible with two opposing semantic scripts (Raskin 1985: 99). The
incongruity between contrasting worlds, in the case of *In Bruges*, may draw
our attention to the fictionality of each, thus serving as a distancing cue which
suggests that neither of them should be taken too seriously. Once cued into

this somewhat disengaged mode of comprehension, we are open to experiencing moods congruent with amusement, alongside other, darker affective states which the introduction to the film's narrative world also prepares us for.

12.3   Enjoying the cringe: Empathy and humorous interaction

The humorous, amusement-enhancing mood associated with humorous worlds is vital for 'unlocking' the humour of narrative elements which could otherwise be treated simply as odd or unusual. In Text World Theory terms, these elements may be 'world-building elements' (meaning deictic and referential elements) or 'function-advancing propositions' (meaning elements which communicate what the text is actually about, Werth 1999: 180). In practice the distinction between world-builders and function-advancers is not absolute (Lahey 2006); both help us form the representations of the settings, objects, characters and situations which make up narrative worlds in our minds. Furthermore, world-building and function-advancing elements are partly informed by existing relevant 'schemata' (e.g. Emmott, Alexander and Marszalek 2014; Rumelhart 1980) – the mental stores of real-world knowledge which, when activated by textual elements, allow us to make sense of what we are reading.

Our schematic knowledge of the world can affect our responses to the world-builders and function-advancers which have been stylistically manipulated for comic effect. With their often unexpected, unusual choice and presentation of these elements, humorous worlds can be seen to 'disrupt' our stores of knowledge about the world, meaning that they distort 'the ordinary application of schemata' (Cook 1994: 152) in order to evoke amusement. 'Schema disruption' (Cook 1994: 191), then, can be seen as closely linked to the creation of humorous worlds. Abundant sources of schema disruption in humorous worlds are the manipulations of 'social schemata' that underlie the representations of people who inhabit those worlds, as character humour is often based on distortions or exaggerations of social stereotypes (Culpeper 2001: 156–7).

An illustration of such humorous social schema disruption could be the plane scene in *Bridesmaids* (Excerpt 12.1) in which a character torments the protagonist with the vision of their plane crashing. Irrational, unreasonable and contriving far-fetched scenarios, that character can be thought of as an exaggeration of the 'attitude schema' – an evaluative belief about a particular social group (van Dijk, e.g. 1988) – associated with people suffering from flight phobia. This humorous exaggeration of the link between a social group and a personal trait – a mechanism which Culpeper (2001: 156) refers to as a 'prototypicality distortion' – can be seen as an example of (social) schema disruption.

While some of the humour of the *Bridesmaids* line lies in the exaggeration-based distortion of our attitude towards a certain group, there is much more to character humour creation than simple schema disruption. The line is also humorous in its original context because of the 'investment' in the characters that the narrative world has evoked in us, such as the feelings of empathy and sympathy that we may have developed for the protagonists (Tan 1995: 192; see also Stockwell 2009: 94 for a more complex 'reading is investment' metaphor). 'Implication', 'the extent to which the viewer is encouraged to sympathize or empathize with character' (King 2002: 31) is, according to King, a feature which distinguishes comedy films with elaborate plots and developed characters (like those which are the subject of this chapter) from those based primarily on jokes and short gags. The importance of this kind of implication in comedy stems from the crucial role of the social dimension of humour discussed in psychology, where 'instances of laughter can usually be seen as "pseudo-social" in nature, because one is still responding to the characters in the television program or the author of the book, or reliving in memory an event that involved other people' (Martin 2007: 5).

Below, I show how another humorous extract from *Bridesmaids* can be seen as 'pseudo-social' in nature, in that its full appreciation relies on our implication with the protagonist and our ability to read other people's emotions. In the scene from an elegant engagement party attended mostly by married people, the single protagonist Annie finds herself talking to an enthusiastic newly-wed, Becca, who mistakenly assumes that the man standing behind Annie is Annie's husband. Annie corrects her:

Excerpt 12.3

ANNIE
Oh. No. No, no, no, no, I don't know him, I'm sorry.

MAN
Do you want to go for a walk later?

ANNIE
Oh … I can't. I can't, sorry.

BECCA
I'm so sorry.

(*Bridesmaids*)

There is a dimension to the humour here which stems from the viewers' ability to 'read the minds' of the characters in order to infer how they may be feeling. 'Mindreading', that is using our Theory-of-Mind Mechanism in order to attribute thoughts and emotions to other people (Baron-Cohen 1995: 51), has been linked to written narrative comprehension by Zunshine (2006), who proposes that one of the pleasures (if not the main pleasure) of entering fictional worlds is that it can test the functioning of our mindreading abilities. 'Intensely social species that we are', she argues, 'we thus read fiction because it engages, in a variety of particularly focused ways, our Theory of Mind' (2006: 162).

The full comic potential of the above *Bridesmaids* scene is only apparent when we use mindreading – or 'mind-modelling' (Stockwell's 2009 cognitive stylistic take on this term) – to attempt to infer, or model, the mental states of the characters. Since the interaction revolves around mitigating the effects of a misunderstanding, the basic principles of Brown and Levinson's (1987) politeness theory can be especially useful to account for the reasoning behind characters' utterances, particularly those associated with the use of the word 'sorry'. While the man seems oblivious to the awkwardness of the situation, the two flustered women are relying on apology as a politeness strategy in order to preserve the positive self-image ('positive face', based on Goffman's 1967 notion of 'face') of each of the participant after Becca's blunder. Annie, whose face was initially threatened, apologizes first to mollify Becca's potential embarrassment at having blundered, and subsequently to soften the rejection of the man's offer of a walk. Becca's apology suggests that she realizes the face-threatening nature of both her own faux pas and of Annie's turndown of the stranger. The repetition of the word 'sorry' (which continues in the rest of the dialogue) highlights the excessive politeness of this humorously disrupted communication breakdown.

While some of the experience of witnessing the situation relies on our mind-modelling skills, its emotional effect is accessible when we both *know* what the characters are going through and when we *feel for* them, or perhaps even *with* them. My choice of a scene from the romantic comedy *Bridesmaids* is not coincidental, as it is a text whose protagonist is constructed in a way that makes her thoughts and feelings easily accessible to a certain target audience. *Bridesmaids* can be considered an example of what Montoro (2007, 2012) calls 'cappuccino fiction' – 'feel good' narratives which centre around female protagonists who tend to be rather similar to each other. Montoro suggests that 'behind these narratives' success lies an attempt at a quasi-faithful representation of certain female values and beliefs drawn from our social world so that their readership can recognize, sympathize and maybe even empathize with those values' (2007: 71), where 'sympathy' can be understood as feeling for someone and 'empathy' as feeling with someone (Keen 2006: 209; Mar et al. 2011: 824).

It is the sharing of some of the values on which the cappuccino fiction protagonists are built that causes us to feel for and with those characters. The extent to which we sympathize or empathize with Annie's embarrassment will, then, depend partly on whether we can be manipulated to take on her qualities, plans and goals, and consequently 'identify' with her as a character (Oatley 1994, 2011). Classic research in the psychology of humour (e.g. Zillmann and Cantor 1976) suggests that laughing at someone's misfortune requires a detached perspective of superiority and ideally a negative disposition towards the object of the joke. When someone is experiencing embarrassment, we laugh at their expense, not 'with them' to show our support. Is it possible then, that we both feel Annie's awkwardness and are amused by the situation she is in? Some comedy relies on the ability to make us cringe and laugh at the same time (see Woodward 2010 and Wright 2011: 662 for 'cringe comedy' and 'cringe humour', respectively), and that might also be the case for the humorous world of *Bridesmaids*.

12.4   Looking for trouble: Enduring comic suspense

One technique for assembling the disrupted elements which make up humorous worlds is the use of recurrence as a world-building strategy. Repetition, re-emergence or recurrence as tools for narrative humour creation are emphasized not only within linguistic approaches to humorous novels and short stories (Attardo 2002; Ermida 2008), but they are also known to be found in other forms of comedy, such as stand-up comedy. Comedian Stewart Lee outlines the mechanism of a 'callback', which is when 'the mere reincorporation of an idea from earlier in the set can seem funny in and of itself, if its re-emergence happens at a surprising or satisfying enough point' (Lee 2010: 301). A callback is a stand-up equivalent of the literary device of 'repetition and variation' (Triezenberg 2004), which enables the writer to use the same element or its variant throughout the whole narrative to achieve humorous effects.

Humorous recurrence not only creates an emotional background which facilitates amusement, but it can also add to our experience of humorous worlds in ways not typically linked to humour. The following set of examples from *In the Loop* (2009, dir. A. Iannucci) can demonstrate how recurrence can operate on a large, narrative-wide scale; how this can be used in characterization; and how it can contribute to the creation of suspense. One of the elements which is spread across the narrative through recurrence is the appalling public speaking of the character Simon Foster (the UK Minister for International Development), which is expressed in various forms with such consistency that there comes a point when the viewer starts equally dreading and looking forward to Simon's amusing blunders. It starts with a comment about the situation in the Middle East which Simon makes while being interviewed on the radio:

Excerpt 12.4

SIMON

Well, personally, I think that war is unforeseeable.

(*In the Loop*)

This is the type of flippant comment that the Minister for International Development should avoid at all costs, as it suggests that he has no knowledge or control over the situation. Below is how the party's spin doctor, Malcolm Tucker, angrily greets Simon upon hearing the unfortunate comment:

Excerpt 12.5

MALCOLM

In the words of the late, great Nat King Fucking Cole, 'Unforeseeable, that's what you are...'

(*In the Loop*)

Malcolm is playing on the first line from Nat King Cole's song 'Unforgettable' in a way that foregrounds the word 'unforeseeable'. The humorous potential of this comment would be lost on a receiver unfamiliar with Simon's original use of 'unforeseeable', but is easily understood to someone aware of the previous context in which the word was uttered. 'Unforeseeable' subsequently reoccurs a number of times until reaching its humorous climax in the following scene, where Simon is surrounded by a press pack of reporters and photographers, and there is pressure on him to revoke the earlier comment about the war:

Excerpt 12.6

REPORTER

So, is war unforeseeable, Minister?

SIMON

Look, all sorts of things that are actually very likely are also unforeseeable. For the plane in the fog, um, the mountain is unforeseeable, but then it is suddenly very real and inevitable.

(*In the Loop*)

Simon had the opportunity to reclaim his image as a competent politician, but ended up accidentally declaring war. His lack of professionalism and verbal ineptitude become fundamental qualities of his character, as they confirm the preconceptions about his public-speaking abilities and competence generally which we might have been formulating up to this point. From this scene onwards, witnessing any situation in which Simon engages in public speaking is even more likely to result in us either cringing in anticipation of an embarrassing blunder or enjoying the anticipation of the humorous potential of the blunder, or both at the same time.

This type of comic anticipation where the repetition of misunderstandings or misfortunes presented in a humorous mode creates an expectation of amusing trouble to come, can be associated with narrative suspense (e.g. Brewer and Lichtenstein 1982; Vorderer, Wulff and Friedrichsen 1996). The feeling of suspense – including comic suspense which appears in humorous worlds – can be linked to Allbritton and Gerrig's (1991) notion of 'participatory responses' ('p-responses') in experiencing narrative worlds. A discourse structure organized by uncertainty about the outcome of a situation invites a certain kind of p-response in the reader/viewer. Suspense is one of such p-responses, as it engages the participant in problem-solving. According to Gerrig, suspense occurs when a reader '(1) lacks knowledge about (2) some sufficiently important target outcome. Feelings of suspense will be heightened to the extent that (3) the target outcome maps out a challenging problem space and (4) the author is able to sustain participatory responses over a period of delay' (1993: 79). In the case of Simon's blunders in *In the Loop*, we (1) lack knowledge about (2) what exactly he will say publically, which is important because (3) what he says will affect not only the way people react, but can potentially also influence high-level politics, and (4) the film production team sustain our problem-solving during the periods between Simon being asked to comment on something and the final words of his reply.

12.5   Conclusion

Comic narratives including films have their own set of techniques used in humour creation, many of which are related to the construction of the narrative world. A humorous world is a context which, by eliciting an overall impression of humour, helps to 'unlock' the comic potential of elements which would not otherwise be perceived as amusing. Such a world relies on cueing the receiver into a non-serious mode of comprehension that facilitates the experience of amusement. Its building-blocks can be manipulated to trigger schema disruption for comic purposes, and it uses recurrence as a structural device for extended humour, allowing comedy to permeate the whole text. Those features not only make the world amusing as a whole, but also elicit a number of effects seemingly unrelated to humour. Ostensibly negative affective states such as a bleak, austere mood, a vicarious discomfort of embarrassment through empathy with a character, or a tense anticipation of something going wrong can all be seen to enhance amusement in film comedy and, more generally, enrich the experience of inhabiting the humorous worlds of film texts.

References

Allbritton, D. W. and Gerrig, R. J. (1991), 'Participatory Responses in Text Understanding', *Journal of Memory and Language*, 30: 603–26.

Apter, M. J. (1982), *The Experience of Motivation: The Theory of Psychological Motivation*, London and New York: Academic Press.

Apter, M. J. (1991), 'A Structural Phenomenology of Play', in J. H. Kerr and M. J. Apter (eds), *Adult Play: A Reversal Theory Approach*, Amsterdam: Swets & Zeitlinger: 13–42.

Armstrong, J., Blackwell, S., Iannucci, A. and Roche, T. (2009), *In the Loop* (dir. A. Iannucci), UK: Optimum Releasing.

Attardo, S. (2002), 'Cognitive Stylistics of Humorous Texts', in E. Semino and J. Culpeper (eds), *Cognitive Stylistics: Language and Cognition in Text Analysis*, Amsterdam: John Benjamins: 231–50.

Attardo, S. and Raskin, V. (1991), 'Script Theory Revis(it)ed: Joke Similarity and Joke Representation Model', *Humor*, 4.3–4: 293–347.

Baron-Cohen, S. (1995), *Mindblindness: An Essay on Autism and Theory of Mind*, Cambridge, MA: MIT Press.

Brewer, W. F. and Lichtenstein, E. H. (1982), 'Stories Are to Entertain: A Structural-Affect Theory of Stories', *Journal of Pragmatics*, 6: 473–86.

Brown, P. and Levinson, S. C. (1987), *Politeness: Some Universals in Language Use*, Cambridge: Cambridge University Press.

Clark, M. (1970), 'Humour and Incongruity', *Philosophy*, 45: 20–32.

Cook, G. (1994), *Discourse and Literature: The Interplay of Form and Mind*, Oxford: Oxford University Press.

Coulson, S. (2001), *Semantic Leaps*, Cambridge: Cambridge University Press.

Culpeper, J. (2001), *Language & Characterisation: People in Plays and Other Texts*, Harlow: Pearson.

Dynel, M. (2011), 'Joker in the Pack: Towards Determining the Status of Humorous Framing in Conversations', in M. Dynel (ed.), *The Pragmatics of Humour across Discourse Domains*, Amsterdam: John Benjamins: 217–41.

Emmott, C. (1994), 'Frames of Reference: Contextual Monitoring and Narrative Discourse', in M. R. Coulthard (ed.), *Advances in Written Text Analysis*, London: Routledge: 157–66.

Emmott, C. (1997), *Narrative Comprehension*, Oxford: Clarendon Press.

Emmott, C., Alexander, M. and Marszalek, A. (2014), 'Schema Theory in Stylistics', in M. Burke (ed.), *The Routledge Handbook of Stylistics*, London: Routledge: 268–83.

Ermida, I. (2008), *The Language of Comic Narratives: Humor Construction in Short Stories*, Berlin: Mouton de Gruyter.

Ferguson, M. A. and Ford, T. E. (2008), 'Disparagement Humor: A Theoretical and Empirical Review of Psychoanalytic, Superiority, and Social Identity Theories', *Humor*, 21.3: 283–312.

Frijda, N. (1986), *The Emotions*, Cambridge: Cambridge University Press.

Gavins, J. (2007), *Text World Theory: An Introduction*, Edinburgh: Edinburgh University Press.

Gerrig, R. J. (1993), *Experiencing Narrative Worlds: On the Psychological Activities of Reading*, New Haven, CT: Yale University Press.

Giora, R. (2003), *On Our Mind: Salience, Context, and Figurative Language*, Oxford: Oxford University Press.

Goffman, E. (1972 [1967]), *Interaction Ritual: Essays on Face-to-Face Behavior*, Harmondsworth: Penguin.

Keen, S. (2006), 'A Theory of Narrative Empathy', *Narrative*, 14.3: 207–36.

King, G. (2002), *Film Comedy*, London: Wallflower.

Lahey, E. (2006), 'Re-Thinking World-Building: Locating the Text-Worlds of Canadian Lyric Poetry', *Journal of Literary Semantics*, 35: 145–64.

Larkin Galiñanes, C. (2010), 'How to Tackle Humour in Literary Narratives', in C. Valero-Garcés (ed.), *Dimensions of Humor. Explorations in Linguistics, Literature, Cultural Studies and Translation*, Valencia: Servicio de Publicaciones de la Universidad: 199–223.

Lee, S. (2010), *How I Escaped My Certain Fate: The Life and Deaths of a Stand-Up Comedian*, London: Faber and Faber.

Mar, R. A., Oatley, K., Djikic, M. and Mullin, J. (2011), 'Emotion and Narrative Fiction: Interactive Influences Before, During, and After Reading', *Cognition & Emotion*, 25.5: 818–33.

Marszalek, A. (2012), *Humorous Worlds: A Cognitive Stylistic Approach to the Creation of Humour in Comic Narratives*, Unpublished MPhil Thesis, University of Glasgow.

Marszalek, A. (2013), ' "It's Not Funny out of Context!": A Cognitive Stylistic Approach to Humorous Narratives', in M. Dynel (ed.), *Developments in Linguistic Humour Theory*, Amsterdam: John Benjamins: 393–421.

Martin, R. (2007), *The Psychology of Humor: An Integrative Approach*, London: Elsevier.

McDonagh, M. (2008), *In Bruges*, London: Faber and Faber.

McIntyre, D. (2008), 'Integrating Multimodal Analysis and the Stylistics of Drama: A Multimodal Perspective on Ian McKellen's *Richard III*', *Language and Literature*, 17.4: 309–34.

Montoro, R. (2007), 'Stylistics of Cappuccino Fiction: A Socio-cognitive Perspective', in M. Lambrou and P. Stockwell (eds), *Contemporary Stylistics*, London: Continuum: 68–80.

Montoro, R. (2012), *Chick Lit: The Stylistics of Cappuccino Fiction*, London: Bloomsbury.

Morreall, J. (2009), *Comic Relief: A Comprehensive Philosophy of Humor*, Chichester: Wiley-Blackwell.

Mumolo, A. and Wiig, K. (2011), *Bridesmaids* (dir. P. Feig), USA: Universal Pictures.

Oatley, K. (1994), 'A Taxonomy of the Emotions of Literary Response and a Theory of Identification in Fictional Narrative', *Poetics*, 23: 53–74.

Oatley, K. (2011), *Such Stuff as Dreams: The Psychology of Fiction*, Chichester: Wiley-Blackwell.

Raskin, V. (1985), *Semantic Mechanisms of Humor*, Dordrecht: D. Reidel Publishing.

Richardson, K. (2010), 'Multimodality and the Study of Popular Drama', *Language and Literature*, 19.4: 378–95.

Rumelhart, D. E. (1980), 'Schemata: The Building Blocks of Cognition', in R. J. Spiro, B. C. Bruce and W. F. Brewer (eds), *Theoretical Issues in Reading Comprehension: Perspectives from Cognitive Psychology, Linguistics, Artificial Intelligence and Education*, Hillsdale, NJ: Lawrence Erlbaum Associates: 33–58.

Short, M. (1998), 'From Dramatic Text to Dramatic Performance', in J. Culpeper, P. Verdonk and M. Short (eds), *Exploring the Language of Drama: From Text to Context*, London: Routledge: 6–18.

Smith, G. M. (2003), *Film Structure and the Emotion System*, Cambridge: Cambridge University Press.

Stockwell, P. (2009), *Texture: A Cognitive Aesthetics of Reading*, Edinburgh: Edinburgh University Press.

Suls, J. M. (1972), 'A Two-stage Model for the Appreciation of Jokes and Cartoons: An Information-processing Analysis', in J. H. Goldstein and P. E. McGhee (eds), *The Psychology of Humour: Theoretical Perspectives and Empirical Issues*, New York, London: Academic Press: 81–99.

Tan, E. (1995), *Emotion and the Structure of Narrative Film: Film as an Emotion Machine*, Hillsdale, NJ: Lawrence Erlbaum.

Triezenberg, K. E. (2004), 'Humor Enhancers in the Study of Humorous Literature', *Humor*, 17.4: 411–18.

Triezenberg, K. E. (2008), 'Humor in Literature', in V. Raskin (ed.), *The Primer of Humor Research*, Berlin: Mouton de Gruyter: 523–42.

van Dijk, T. A. (1988), 'Social Cognition, Social Power and Social Discourse', *Text*, 8.1–2: 129–57.

Vorderer, P., Wulff, H. J., Friedrichsen, M. (eds), (1996), *Suspense: Conceptualizations, Theoretical Analyses, and Empirical Explorations*, London: Routledge.

Werth, P. (1999), *Text Worlds: Representing Conceptual Space in Discourse*, Harlow: Longman.

Woodward, S. (2010) 'Curbing Our Enthusiasm: The Cringe Comedy of Sacha Baron Cohen, Ricky Gervais, and Larry David', *Tea and Talk* lecture series, Bishop's University.

Wright, B. (2011), ' "Why Would You do That, Larry?": Identity Formation and Humor in *Curb Your Enthusiasm*', *The Journal of Popular Culture*, 44.3: 661–77.

Zillmann, D. (1983), 'Disparagement Humor', in P. E. McGhee and J. H. Goldstein (eds), *Handbook of Humor Research, Vol. 1: Basic Issues*, New York: Springer: 85–107.

Zillmann, D. and Cantor, J. R. (1996 [1976]), 'A Disposition Theory of Humour and Mirth', in A. J. Chapman and H. C. Foot (eds), *Humor and Laughter: Theory, Research and Applications*, New Brunswick, NJ: Transaction Publishers: 93–116.

Zunshine, L. (2006), *Why We Read Fiction: Theory of Mind and the Novel*, Columbus, OH: Ohio State University Press.

13

Spanglish Dialogue in *You and Me*: An Absurd World and Senile Mind Style

Jane Lugea

13.1 Introduction

In this chapter, I use Text World Theory (Gavins 2007; Werth 1999) in conjunction with other stylistic models to analyse a play called *You and Me* (Simeon 2011; Shanahan 2013). The play revolves around two elderly sisters and is set in the confines of their home. The production company behind *You and Me* (Little Soldier Productions 2013: 3) and several theatre critics (Dillon 2013; Teo 2012; Yorston 2013) describe the play as 'absurd(ist)' and my aim in the discussion which follows is to show the cognitive-stylistic means through which this absurdity is achieved. I begin by outlining the few previous stylistic studies of absurd drama which have attempted to characterize an absurd dramatic aesthetic. I then suggest that Gavins's (2013) comprehensive account of the stylistic characteristics of absurd prose fiction might be additionally useful for the analysis of absurd drama (Section 13.2). Section 13.3 uses Text World Theory to analyse several excerpts from the play, demonstrating the many ways *You and Me* conforms with the label 'absurd'.

As I outline in Section 13.4, several of the dialogue features identified – including the use of code-switching and dysfunctional communication – also contribute to a realistic depiction of the characters' senile 'mind style' (Fowler 1977; Semino 2002). According to clinical psychologists, senile dementia includes 'chronic progressive deteriorization in intellect, personality and communicative functioning' (Bayles and Kaszniak 1987: 1) and many of the features of the characters' dialogue outlined in Section 13.3 are consistent with these symptoms. On the basis of this evidence, it may be suggested that *You and Me* presents a realistic depiction of the senile mind style, as well as features consistent with absurd drama. I argue, however, that these two phenomena need not be mutually exclusive, as linguistic absurdity is certainly not the exclusive property of absurd drama and may also be found in natural speech (Simpson 2002). In Section 13.4, I use Text World Theory again to account for how absurdism and realism are dispersed across the worlds of the play.

13.1.1   About the play

Originally a monolingual Catalan play (Simeon 2011), *You and Me* is an adaptation and translation into English for a UK audience (Shanahan 2013). Although the setting is never confirmed, the characters express the desire to be flown back to Spain for their funerals, which suggests that the play is set in the United Kingdom. In the Shanahan (2013) production, the actress who plays Angeleta is Catalan while the actress who plays Etelbina is from Asturias and the actresses often code-switch from English into their native languages, with Catalan and Castilian Spanish interspersed throughout the English dialogue. It seems strange that one sister is Catalan and the other is from Asturias, but this logical anomaly is one of many which contributes towards an absurd reading of the play. In the ambiguity of its spatio-temporal context, *You and Me* conforms with canonical 'Theatre of the Absurd' texts, where settings are often ill-defined and timeless (Esslin 1980/1961; Sherzer 1978).

You and Me employs interesting strategies through which the fictional world of the play is built and that invite a text-world analysis. The play centres around the two ageing protagonists in their home and never leaves the confines of that space through any explicit spatial world-switch. As sisters, Etelbina and Angeleta argue frequently and these exchanges are the source of much of the play's humour. However, Etelbina is also very caring toward Angeleta, who shows more acute behavioural and linguistic signs of dementia (summarized in Section 13.4). The two women discuss their daily existence, reminisce about the past and speculate about their future. These conversations result in flashbacks and hypothetical flash-forwards to imagined or remembered events. These departures from the matrix text-world provide rich data for analysis from a text-world perspective.

Although no published version of *You and Me* exists, Little Soldier Productions were kind enough to grant me access to their script, upon which my analysis is based. Although I make reference to some multimodal elements in support of the theatrical world-building, for reasons of limited space my focus here is on the written word. Although Werth (1995b, 1999) designed Text World Theory for the analysis of all kinds of discourse, there have been limited applications of the model to dramatic discourse (see Cruikshank and

Lahey 2010; and Lugea 2013 for exceptions) and this chapter goes some way to redressing that imbalance.

In the discourse situation of a written play script, the discourse-world consists of the discourse participants, which in this case include the playwright, the translator and the reader. Each of these participants brings their individual schematic and cultural knowledge, their bank of experience and their background to bear on the construction of the text-world. Although some world-building information is provided in the stage directions, the characters' use of reference also helps us to furnish this text-world. It is further developed through function-advancing propositions, which are essentially the clauses in the stage directions or the dialogue that advance the action. Changes in the spatio-temporal coordinates of the text-world initiate world-switches, and the matrix text-world can be departed from through the use of modality or hypothetical expressions in the same way as in other discourse types. As this chapter demonstrates, a structured approach to informational accessibility and to spatio-temporal reference allows the text-world analyst to identify how meaning is made across ontological and referential levels.

13.2   Absurd text-worlds

Simpson (2002) and Gavins (2013) observe that previous scholarship on absurd fiction has suffered from a lack of precision with regard to the stylistic features that constitute the genre. Absurd drama in particular remains largely ignored by stylisticians, with the exception of a few isolated studies (Cruikshank and Lahey 2010; Sherzer 1978; Simpson 2002; Vassilopoulou 2008). Sherzer (1978) and Simpson (2002) focus on the dialogic features of absurd drama and their insights prove useful in identifying whether the dialogue of *You and Me* conforms with the absurd tradition (Section 13.3). Given that they take a worlds-based perspective on absurd dramas, Cruikshank and Lahey (2010) and Vassilopoulou (2008) are closer to the text-world approach that this chapter applies to *You and Me*. To analyse several canonical absurd plays, Vassilopoulou (2008) applies Ryan's model of fictional worlds (1991a, 1991b), a useful framework for understanding how literary worlds relate to the 'real world'. In their text-world analysis of Tom Stoppard's *Rosencrantz and Guildenstern are Dead* (1967), Cruikshank and Lahey (2010) demonstrate how Text World Theory, previously applied mainly to narrative texts, can indeed be useful in the analysis of drama. Although the play they analyse is in the absurd tradition, they are less focused on its conformity with this genre and more interested in developing the text-world model for application to dramatic discourse. Thus, this chapter constitutes the first exposition of the features of drama that contribute to an absurd reading, from a text-world perspective.

Gavins has provided a detailed account of the stylistic features of absurd prose (2000, 2001, 2013), analysing a wide variety of canonical and less-prototypical absurd texts. She demonstrates that numerous features pertinent to absurd narratives can also be found in poetry (Gavins 2013), suggesting that they transcend absurd narrative to other kinds of fictional texts. As well as classic concepts from stylistics, Gavins uses Text World Theory to account for the stylistic features she encounters. Given the breadth and depth of her study into absurd prose fiction, as well as her use of a text-world approach, Gavins's account of absurd prose fiction is evaluated here for its possible application to absurd drama.

Gavins identifies an 'unreliable narrator' as 'a key trait in absurdist narratives' (2013: 137) and describes several narrative techniques by which such unreliability is achieved. Using terminology borrowed from Simpson's (1993) modal grammar, she identifies 'negatively shaded modality' as a common strategy in constructing narratorial unreliability. This describes a narrator whose frequent use of epistemic modality (e.g. 'I think', 'maybe', 'I see') foregrounds a sense of doubt and uncertainty in the narrative. Gavins notes that a narrator's use of logical fallacies or incongruities can also point to unreliability in the construction of a text-world, reflecting Simpson's (2002) and Sherzer's (1978) observations with regard to Theatre of the Absurd's character dialogue. While world-building is achieved through different means in narrative prose and in plays, the usual lack of a narrator in drama does not mean that there are no means of expressing viewpoint (McIntyre 2006). Instead, we rely on stage directions and character dialogue, where unreliability and incongruities may also be found.

Gavins goes on to observe that absurd narratives often manipulate spatio-temporal deixis for surreal effect (2013: 132), referring to the ways in which references to space and time can be at odds with our discourse-world understanding of how these dimensions work, contributing towards a difficulty in 'knowing' or in cognitively processing absurd texts. Throughout, Gavins stresses that the stylistic features she identifies are not definitive but can be traced as 'linguistic family resemblances' (2013: 160) within the genre. Among some of the texts she analyses, Gavins finds that multimodal elements such as font, layout and images can be employed in innovative ways (2013: 133), disrupting the reading process and foregrounding of the physicality and fictionality of the text. Fictionality may also be foregrounded through other means, such as the use of a narrator who inhibits immersion in the text-world through their unreliability, reminding the reader of the creative process behind the text. The breakdown of the boundary between the real world and the text, what Gavins (2013: 133) (drawing on McHale 1987: 34) calls a 'semi-permeable membrane', can disrupt the distinction between fact and fiction in absurd discourse, as the analysis in Section 13.3 of this chapter demonstrates. The features summarized here may appear to be a taxonomy of postmodern fiction in general, but Gavins points out that they are accompanied with an existential message or philosophy that contributes towards an absurd reading (2013: 133).

13.3   The text-worlds of *You and Me*

The discourse-world of this play involves the spatio-temporal coordinates of the discourse context, the discourse participants and all their schematic knowledge activated in processing the discourse. The play opens with the following stage directions (Excerpt 13.1), which initiate the building of the matrix text-world, illustrated in Figure 13.1:

Excerpt 13.1

Two old women, sisters, sit silently next to each other, staring out. They have been here for hours. Neither says a word and both appear to be in their own, separate, worlds. They sit for a while. Out of nowhere ANGELETA lets out an enormous fart. Both are frozen. A very tense moment. ANGELETA then begins to laugh hysterically. ETELBINA is not impressed.

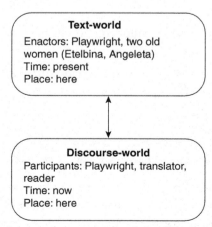

Figure 13.1 Excerpt 13.1: The discourse-world and initial text-world

The opening stage direction refers to 'two old women, sisters' and later gives their names, Angeleta and Etelbina; these characters are 'enactors' in text-world terms. As Cruikshank and Lahey (2010) maintain, the stage directions originate from the playwright, who is both a discourse participant and an enactor in the text-world. This occurs as, although a 'playwright/narrator' is not overtly mentioned in the stage directions, there are textual clues that such a perceiving enactor exists at the text-world level, through the use of evidential verbs such as 'appear to be'. While the reader might make some guesses, there is no information given about the location, 'here', where the women sit. However, the stage directions are given in the present tense (e.g. 'They sit'), denoting a shared time between the narrated event and its narration.

The excerpt also includes function-advancing propositions (not shown in Figure 13.1), such as 'Angeleta lets out an enormous fart', an action which is incongruous with discourse-world expectations of behaviour either on-stage or from elderly ladies and is thus a source of humour. Simpson identifies 'incongruity' as a key feature of absurd drama, arising as 'the consequence of speakers not observing the familiar or expected routines that are cued by a particular context' (2002: 40). However on its own, this incongruity does not necessarily result in absurdity. Rather it is the accumulation of features revealed in the analysis below that contributes to the emergence of an absurd style.

Following the opening stage directions, the character dialogue begins, as follows:

Excerpt 13.2

ETELBINA Disgusting.

More laughter.

ETELBINA Disgusting. Disgusting, you are an old fart!... Disgusting ... Disgusting!

With some effort, and with her sister still laughing, ETELBINA gets herself off the sofa and goes to the tower of boxes, beginning to label them.

ANGELETA Hey, I'm sorry.

Werth recognizes that directly represented discourse is embedded in basic-level discourse, stating that for characters in a text-world:

The world they inhabit is equivalent to the participants' discourse world: it is, as it were, simply around them. Now suppose a character in a story himself tells a story: then the world of that story is for the characters a text world; but for the participants, it is one step further removed. (Werth 1995a: 60–1)

Werth goes on to describe character dialogue as generating a sub-world, but as Gavins (2005, 2007) points out, this label houses too many kinds of world to be effective. As such, I propose that character dialogue – and indeed any kind of directly represented discourse – be regarded as generating an 'enactor text-world' at a remove from the originating text-world (see also Lugea 2013). This descriptive term better reflects Werth's contention that all levels within Text World Theory are subject to the same rules (1999: 353). Thus, as discourse participants create text-worlds, text-world enactors create enactor text-worlds, for which they are responsible and which operate according to the ontological rules of that level of the discourse. Figure 13.2 illustrates the enactor text-world created in the initial few lines of dialogue quoted above:

As shown in Figure 13.2, Etelbina describes her sister as 'disgusting' and 'an old fart'. This world-building information feeds back into our conceptualization of the overall discourse, the matrix text-world. As readers, we process Etelbina's accusation as indicative of her own character (perhaps irritable or prudish?), of the character of her sister (is she truly disgusting?) and of the relationship that holds between them (disgust, intolerance?). Furthermore, the unnecessary

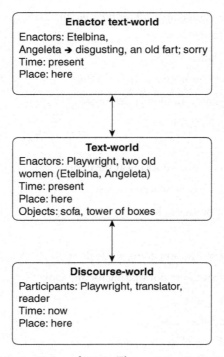

Figure 13.2 Excerpts 13.1 and 13.2: The enactor text-world informs the initial text-world

repetition of the word 'disgusting' infringes Grice's (1975) maxim of quantity. In her analysis of canonical Theatre of the Absurd plays, Sherzer (1978) demonstrates that Gricean maxims are often broken by characters therein. There is a brief switch back to the matrix text-world with the use of stage directions, beginning with 'with some effort', which reveals the laboured physicality of the elderly characters. The playwright develops the matrix text-world with function-advancing propositions which tell us the movements of the characters (Etelbina gets off the sofa, goes, labels etc.). Angeleta's verbal apology, 'I'm sorry', brings us back into the enactor text-world, where her use of the relational copula verb provides further world-building information about the enactors.

13.3.1   Verbal play in the enactor text-world

While the opening of *You and Me* serves to show the initial text-world structure, we can find clear examples of absurd dramatic dialogue in the excerpt below, which occurs after an unanswered knock at the door:

Excerpt 13.3

ANGELETA *Straightening up a bit on the sofa and looking discreetly towards the door.* Are they gone?

ETELBINA Yes... who?

ANGELETA Whoever was knocking at the door.

ETELBINA I don't know. But I am guessing so.

ANGELETA And who was it?

ETELBINA Who?

ANGELETA Whoever was knocking at the door.

ETELBINA No one... someone who got lost.

ANGELETA And how do you know that they were lost?

ETELBINA Who?

ANGELETA Whoever was knocking at the door.

ETELBINA Because we were not waiting for anybody.

ANGELETA Maybe I was.

ETELBINA Then he'll be back.

ANGELETA Who?

ETELBINA Whoever was knocking at the door.

ANGELETA But was it not you?

ETELBINA. Who?

ANGELETA. *In Catalan.* Qui trucava la porta, collons! [Whoever was knocking at the door, dammit!]

Sherzer observes the tendency of characters in absurd drama to participate
in 'verbal ping-pong', whereby they seem to momentarily lose interest in the
propositional content of their utterances and instead 'are carried away by the
rhythm of speech' (1978: 276) in a back-and-forth exchange. This absurd aesthetic is clearly represented here in the repetition and rhythm across turns.
Extending from the discourse level to the phonic level, Sherzer likewise finds
that there is often a repetition of similar sounds, to the extent that 'phonic
properties of language are foregrounded' (1978: 278), evident in the repetition
of 'who/whoever'. Playing with discourse and phonic structure happens at the
expense of plot-driving information and Sherzer identifies the 'dramatization
of banality achieved by overly performative elements that are of low informational content' (1978: 282). Angeleta's use of code-switching into Catalan to
end the pointless exchange contributes to an emphasis on phonic properties
over propositional content, given that the audience are likely to be unfamiliar
with Catalan.

In this excerpt, the characters also break Gricean maxims of manner and
quantity, by being unclear and repetitive. We can use our discourse-world
schematic knowledge to surmise that given their cognitive decline, the elderly
characters may not break these maxims purposefully, infringing them without meaning to do so. However, the presence of additional, absurdist features
of style in the play may lead to a separate implicature being drawn – that the
playwright is violating the maxims in order to make the implicature that life
is meaningless. Thus, what might be an unconscious infringement of Gricean
maxims at the enactor text-world level, is a deliberate flout by the playwright
at the text-world level. It could also be argued that Angeleta's suggestion that
she was waiting for someone (in 'Maybe I was') is a similarly purposeful violation of the maxim of quality, for there is no evidence to support her claim
elsewhere in the play. This, combined with her use of epistemic marker 'maybe',
lends negative modal shading to the dialogue and calls into question the enactors' reliability and our emergent understanding of the text-world, one of many
examples in the play. As such, Gavins's (2013) identification of 'unreliable narrators' as key in absurd prose may also be relevant to drama, where unreliable
characters can contribute to a difficulty in 'knowing' the text-world.

13.3.2   Modal-worlds

Although the two characters in *You and Me* never physically depart from the matrix text-world in terms of space or time, they do imagine, desire and wish for alternate states-of-affairs. This is usually performed through dialogue, which generates various kinds of modal-worlds, extraneous to the matrix text-world. Paralinguistic and non-verbal elements of performance also combine with linguistic features to transport us to these modal-worlds. The following excerpt is taken from early in the play and demonstrates a theme that recurs throughout, death. The scene also exemplifies a recurrent logic in the play that 'one can choose whether to live or die':

Excerpt 13.4

ETELBINA *Climbing up to stand on her chair.* I've made up my mind. I don't want to be a problem to anyone and I am aware that it is a huge sacrifice that no one else is prepared to do . . .

ANGELETA Cuidado [Careful]

ETELBINA . . . but I've decided that I will never die.

ANGELETA What?

ETELBINA That I'll live forever. Oye [Listen] Don't get me wrong, it's not that I enjoy being here, but I'm kind of used to it and I move around easily, and now, to think about all the hassle of dying.

Mozart's requiem begins to play, as this sequence is physically played out with ANGELETA playing various characters from the coffin bearer to mourners, while ETELBINA enacts her own death.

The last bit of breath leaving my lungs . . . so much effort. And then the ambulance arriving and them spending an hour trying to resuscitate me when all I want to do is sleep. And then finally when they have given up they zip me into a body bag and dump me in a freezing mortuary just for some doctor to drag me back out. He pokes and prods me, cutting me open pulling out my intestines, squishing my lungs before he eventually decides that I died of old age. Then they measure me for my coffin, dress me in my Sunday best and put awful make up on my face and drag my lips into a hideous smile. And then the plane journey! Aargh! I'm put in the cargo storage and sent to Barcelona because my stupid sister wants me to be buried there, even though I tell her I want to go to Asturias! And then the funeral! No! I have to endure my service. The church is full of people I don't even know all wearing horrible black. Then men of all different heights march me in, making me feel sick in my coffin, all to depressing, morbid music. Then set me down and open the lid for everyone to see and I am freezing. And then the priest begins to pray and tells everyone how wonderful I am ... which I already know!

ANGELETA *whispers the prayers of the priest in Catalan.*

ETELBINA And all the never-ending tears and the people bothering me open-ing the lid to kiss me and fill my cheeks with saliva and makeup Quita, quita! [Get off, get off!] and then throwing flowers on my face. Nah! Such a pain! So many unnecessary complications. I accept my condition of martyrdom and I remain here and that's that.

ANGELETA Oh! I didn't know that you could choose. I haven't thought what I want to do.

Before examining the hypothetical events around Etelbina's undesired death, I want to consider the proposition underscoring this scene, namely that death is a choice. In her fictional-worlds analysis of several canonical absurd plays, Vassilopoulou (2008) reveals that absurd dramas often have a logical incompat-ibility with the real world, noting that absurdist plays present the reader with 'a world that is similar to theirs but all their expectations for a realistic plot are then disrupted due to the impossibilities that take place' (2008: 174). Furthermore, Vassilopoulou also finds that 'authentication' (Doležel 1989) is blocked in absurd plays, as the characters – like narrators in absurd prose – make it dif-ficult for readers to form an understanding of the fictional world through their unreliability. Like Sherzer (1978) and Simpson (2002), Vassilopoulou finds that, 'absurdity does not result only from the logical contradictions that render the world partially impossible but mainly from the characters' reaction to these impossibilities' (2008: 163). Thus, when Angeleta replies 'Oh! I didn't know that you could choose', her unquestioning acceptance of and contribution to Etelbina's use of flawed logic contributes to the drama's overall absurdity.

Applying a text-world approach to this excerpt, Etelbina's use of 'will' in the first line 'I will never die' activates a future world in which her dying does not happen. It is unclear whether the subsequent propositional content (Etelbina's not dying) produces a temporal world-switch to the future, or a modal-world. This is because the modal auxiliary 'will' can be used in English to mark the future tense, as well as three kinds of modality: boulomaic modality (express-ing desire), epistemic modality (expressing belief) or deontic modality (express-ing obligation) (Coates 1983; Simpson 1993). Indeed, we could read Etelbina's intention not to die as either a future prediction, a desire, a firm belief or per-haps even a personal obligation. The ambiguity in the meaning of this auxiliary demonstrates how a replicable text-world analysis can prove difficult (see Lugea forthcoming). Nevertheless, as a discourse-world participant who knows that death is inevitable, I read Etelbina's use of 'will' as expressing desire, which is stored in a boulomaic modal-world (see Figure 13.3 for this and subsequent modal-worlds). This same boulomaic modal-world is revisited throughout the course of the play as the characters discuss and advance the desire to not die. Like most of the other modal-worlds in the play, it is generated from character dialogue and so stems from the 'enactor text-world' as depicted in Figure 13.3.

Advancing the enactor text-world, Etelbina's monologue develops with her stating the reasons why she does not want to die and she begins 'to think about all the hassle of dying'. The use of the epistemic lexical verb 'to think' triggers the generation of an epistemic modal-world where the imagined events around dying occur (Figure 13.3). The stage directions cue the start of Mozart's requiem at this point, using music to further indicate a switch from the matrix text-world to an imagined world. The epistemic modal-world is not just realized verbally and musically, but also physically enacted by both characters. Etelbina enacts her dead self, pulling her face into a hideous smile, shivering in her coffin and code-switching into Spanish to tell mourners to 'get off!'. Angeleta takes on various roles from the airplane, to the coffin bearers and to

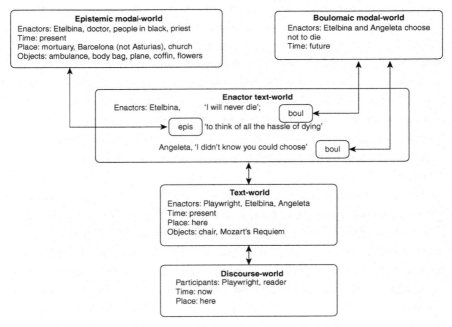

Figure 13.3 Excerpt 13.4: Modal-worlds

the priest, code-switching into Catalan to perform the priest's funeral blessing. Just as Gavins has found absurd narrative fiction to use a mixture of modes and genres, it seems that absurd drama can also employ the aural and physical modes available in performance for a similar effect. I would also argue that these re-enactments constitute a manipulation of spatio-temporal deixis, in the sense that the epistemic modal-world we are presented with in this scene constitutes a complete shift from the spatio-temporal coordinates of the matrix text-world of the play (from a timeless scene in the sisters' home to an imagined living death), crossing many spatio-temporal boundaries (including a three-second plane journey to Barcelona), as well as ontological ones.

Many of the features described so far contribute towards foregrounding the fictionality of the play, drawing attention to the semi-permeable membrane between the text-world and the discourse-world. Throughout the epistemic modal-world in the excerpt above, Etelbina uses the present tense to make the imagined scene as immediate to the time frame of the text-world and thus the discourse-world of the performance as possible. This trick of tense is mirrored in the characters' performances, as they enact the imagined events live. What were fragile, slow-moving elderly ladies in the matrix text-world become agile, animated actors in the epistemic modal-world that their enactor text-world creates, leaping on chairs and channelling various other characters, objects and events. The young actresses' discourse-world agility is brought into the performance, dropping the old-lady act from the matrix text-world and reminding us of the fictionality of the play. This permeation of discourse-world features into the enactor text-world is not just physical but also linguistic, as the actresses' native Spanish and Catalan permeate the English text-world of *You and Me*. The significance of these code-switches is explored in the next section, which examines whether the features observed in the play contribute towards the absurdity of the text, or whether they can be read as contributing towards a realistic representation of a senile mind style.

13.4   Realism and Absurdism in *You and Me*

The version of *You and Me* discussed here is aimed at an Anglophone audience, so the code-switching exemplified in the excerpts above does not contribute to the ideational meaning (Halliday 1973) and so does not serve an informative function. The fact that isolated, non-clausal elements are in Spanish and Catalan means that the code-switching does not inhibit Anglophone understanding. However, the question as to why include it at all still remains. If we recall Sherzer's assertion that, in Theatre of the Absurd, 'phonic properties of language are foregrounded' and 'language makes itself conspicuous in its materiality' (1978: 282), the code-switching in the play could simply be interpreted as adding to its meaninglessness and hence its absurdism.

Nevertheless, the code-switching strategies used reflect real code-switching practices. Research has shown that discourse markers, fillers and interjections tend to be code-switched (Gumperz 1982; Poplack 1980), as in Etelbina's use of *oye* ('listen') in Excerpt 13.3. Furthermore, natural code-switches are often repetitions to emphasize or clarify the message (Gumperz 1982), as in Etelbina's use of *quita, quita*, meaning 'get off, get off' in Excerpt 13.3. The play abounds with realistic examples of code-switching and all conform to the 'equivalence constraint' (Poplack 1980), whereby syntactic rules of both languages are upheld when bilinguals switch between languages. Not only is the code-switching a realistic portrayal of bilingual performance, but also of bilingual practices in the elderly, as senile dementia sufferers 'often revert to their first language in second language contexts and tend to use the same code-switching strategies as healthy speakers' (Hyltenstam 1995: 334). Given the realism in the use of code-switching, it could be argued that *You and Me* does not necessarily use alternate codes to foreground the phonic properties of language in line with an absurd aesthetic, but rather realistically portrays ageing bilingual characters.

It may also be argued that *You and Me* quite accurately represents a senile mind style. Semino defines mind style as follows:

> ... world views that are primarily personal and cognitive in origin, and which are peculiar to a particular individual, or common to people who have the same cognitive characteristics (for example, as a result of a similar mental illness or of a shared stage of cognitive development [...]). (Semino 2002: 97)

Previous research has focused on literary creations of 'deviant' mind styles (Halliday 1971; Leech and Short 1981; Semino 2002), especially in characters on the autism spectrum (Semino 2011, 2014a, 2014b). Although the mind style of characters in narrative fiction has been explored widely, mind style in drama has received relatively little attention. One notable exception is McIntyre (2005, , 2006), who explored the mind style of the elderly character Miss Shepherd in Alan Bennett's play *The Lady in the Van*. He shows that the character's flawed use of inductive logic, where she jumps to conclusions 'on the basis of little evidence and wrong assumptions' (2005: 28), cumulatively contributes to her mind style. In Section 13.3, we saw a similar use of inductive logic in Etelbina's claim, 'I have decided that I will never die!', where the logic is, 'I don't want to die, therefore I will not'. As with Miss Shepherd, it is the repetition of such patterns that leads to the emergence of a particular mind style.

However, no study has specifically examined a senile mind style, which may derive from features that tally with our schematic and clinical knowledge about cognitive ageing. I have chosen to use the term 'senile' mind style, as senility refers to general cognitive deterioration due to age. Dementia is an umbrella term for a broad-spectrum syndrome which entails a progressive deficit in cognitive functions, affecting the communicative, cognitive and memory faculties. Alzheimer's disease is the most common form of dementia, although not restricted to the elderly, and displays more specific symptoms, including confusion and impaired thought and speech (Román 2006). While both sisters display symptoms of senile dementia, Angeleta certainly seems to display more symptoms related to Alzheimer's, culminating in an incoherent, violent and confused breakdown towards the end of the play. De Bot and Makoni (2005) emphasize the effect of non-linguistic factors, such as memory and perception, on language processing in the elderly. According to inhibition deficit theory (e.g. Hasher and Zacks 1988; Hasher, Lustig and Zacks 2007), the inhibitory processes that regulate information entering and leaving working memory are weakened with age. De Bot and Makoni relate this phenomenon to several key communicative dysfunctions:

> A reduction of the inhibition capacity may lead to both verbosity in production and a slowing down of language production and decline in language comprehension because of the inability to suppress irrelevant candidates in selection processes. (De Bot and Makoni 2005: 43)

Inhibition deficiency may lead to violations of the Gricean maxims of relevance, quantity and manner, as displayed in the repetitive and irrelevant contributions advanced by both characters in the play. As Semino notes, medical accuracy is not necessary for a successful fictional depiction of character, yet 'stories involving characters with illnesses or disorders tend to be valued, among other things, for their degree of realism' (2014b: 143).

The evidence from clinical accounts of senile dementia suggests that some of the features found in the character dialogue of *You and Me* could actually be interpreted as symptoms of cognitive ageing. This would mean that these features do not foreground fictionality, but instead realistically represent a senile mind style. However, I should stress again that a realistic depiction of a senile mind style and an absurd dramatic aesthetic need not be mutually exclusive. As observed

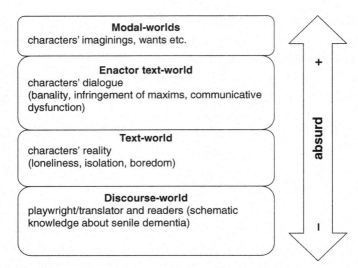

Figure 13.4 A cline of absurdity across the worlds of *You and Me*

by Simpson (2002), linguistic absurdity may not be the sole property of absurd drama, but may also pertain to other unsuccessful communicative events where communicative norms are broken. Nevertheless, *You and Me* poses a problem as to how these two seemingly incompatible fictional strategies can work together.

13.4.1 A text-world resolution

The answer to this question can be found by examining the structure of the play using Text World Theory. In Figure 13.4, a familiar Text World Theory diagram is presented, this time without the micro-level details from the text, and instead representing the overall macro-structure of the worlds of *You and Me*.

I suggest that events depicted at the text-world level, which include the characters' lonely reality, their isolation and their boredom, set the scene for the discourse participants' empathetic engagement with the elderly characters. Once the characters begin to converse, some of the features at the enactor text-world level tally with our discourse-world perceptions of cognitive ageing. These features include the code-switching and the communicative dysfunction created by logical incongruities, repetitions and infringements of Gricean maxims. At this level, the dialogue can be understood as contributing either towards realistic depictions of cognitive ageing and/or conforming to classic stylistic features of absurd drama. What happens at either side of the enactor text-world enriches this double reading, as our discourse-world schematic knowledge of ageing and the text-world representation of the elderly characters' lonely exist-ence can support the realist reading. Esslin observes that:

> The Theatre of the Absurd can actually coincide with the highest degree of realism. For if the real conversation of human beings is in fact absurd and non-sensical, then it is the well-made play with its polished logical dialogue that is unrealistic, while the absurdist play may well be a tape-recorded reproduction of reality. Or, in a world that has become absurd, the Theatre of the Absurd is the most realistic comment on, the most accurate reproduction of, reality. (Esslin 1965: 17)

You and Me's strategy of realistically portraying the absurdity of these elderly characters' lonely and isolated existence at the text-world and enactor text-world levels coincides with a high degree of realism. This strategy does not preclude an absurd reading, but actually contributes to a reading of *You and Me* as a genuine piece of Theatre of the Absurd. Going beyond the text-world and enactor text-world levels, the use of multiple modal-worlds to portray fan-tastical events supports an absurd reading, as it coincides with Gavins's (2013) findings with absurd prose. At the modal-world level, the characters depart from the confines of their banal reality and operate at the level of imagination, memory and hypothetically, bringing the play to its absurd heights. As Esslin observes, 'the reality with which the Theatre of the Absurd is concerned is a psychological reality expressed in images that are the outward projection of states of mind, features, dreams nightmares and conflicts ...' (1980 [1961]: 415). While many critics have commented on the sense of alienation and meaning-lessness that absurd fiction can convey, I believe that this play's integration of truly absurd stylistic features with a realistic portrayal of the elderly characters' existence and dialogue contributes towards a very human and heartfelt work.

13.5   Concluding remarks

By analysing several excerpts from *You and Me* with reference to previous research on absurd fiction, I have found that the play indeed conforms with the absurdist tradition. I demonstrated how Gavins's account of absurd prose fiction can pro-vide some insight into the analysis of absurd drama, but I recognize that much more work is needed in order to characterize the stylistic features of absurd drama in its own right. A text-world approach, supported by other stylistic frameworks, has proven useful for considering both the micro-level word-building in this play as well as the macro-level structures in operation. Ultimately, Text World Theory has enabled me to tease out the layers at which realistic and absurd features operate, in order to account for the co-existence of an absurd aesthetic and a realistic representation of a bilingual senile mind style. Further research into fictional constructions of the senile mind style is necessary to expand on the brief and unique examples provided by the characters in *You and Me*.

Given the bias of text-world research towards fictional narrative, Text World Theory can only benefit from further application to drama and integration with stylistic models for the analysis of dramatic dialogue. Furthermore, the text-world framework was developed in and for the analysis of English discourse and although Werth (1999: 85) made claims to the applicability of the model to any text type, there has been no attempt to test the framework's broader suitability to a wider range of languages other than English (see Lugea forthcoming). Given that languages other than English have different means to express deixis, modality and other key world-building information, Text World Theory would need to be adapted for non-Anglophone discourse analysis. With regards to *You and Me* specifically, future research might explore the unified use of the three languages in one text further and the potential implications of the play's multilingualism for the readerly experience.

References

Bayles, K. A. and Kaszniak, A. W. (1987), *Communication and Cognition in Normal Aging and Dementia*, Boston, MA: College Hill Press.

Coates, J. (1983), *The Semantics of Modal Auxiliaries*, London: Croom Helm.

Cruikshank, T. and Lahey, E. (2010), 'Building the Stages of Drama: Towards a Text-World Theory Account of Dramatic Play-Texts', *Journal of Literary Semantics*, 39: 67–91.

de Bot, K. and Makoni, S. (2005), *Language and Aging in Multilingual Societies: Dynamic Perspectives*, Clevedon: Multilingual Matters.

Dillon, B. (2013), 'Review of *You and Me* at Bike Shed Theatre', *Exeunt Magazine*, <http://exeuntmagazine.com/reviews/you-and-me/> [accessed 8 September 2015].

Doležel, L. (1989), 'Possible Words and Literary Fictions', in S. Allén (ed.), *Possible Worlds in Humanities, Arts and Sciences: Proceedings of Nobel Symposium 65*, New York: de Gruyter: 223–42.

Esslin, M. (1965), *Absurd Drama*, Harmondsworth: Penguin.

Esslin, M. (1980 [1961]), *The Theatre of the Absurd*, Harmondsworth: Penguin.

Fowler, R. (1977), *Linguistics and the Novel*, London: Methuen.

Gavins, J. (2000), 'Absurd Tricks with Bicycles Frames in the Text World of *The Third Policeman*', *Nottingham Linguistic Circular*, 15: 17–33.

Gavins, J. (2001), 'The Absurd Worlds of Billy Pilgrim', in I. Biermann and A. Combrink (eds), *Poetics, Linguistics and History: Discourses of War and Conflict*, Potchefstroom: Potchefstroom University Press: 402–16.

Gavins, J. (2005), '(Re)Thinking Modality: A Text-World Perspective', *Journal of Literary Semantics*, 34: 79–93.

Gavins, J. (2007), *Text World Theory: An Introduction*, Edinburgh: Edinburgh University Press.

Gavins, J. (2013), *Reading the Absurd*, Edinburgh: Edinburgh University Press.

Grice, P. (1975), 'Logic and Conversation', in P. Cole and J. Morgan (eds), *Syntax and Semantics 3: Speech Acts*, New York: Academic Press: 41–58.

Gumperz, J. (1982), *Discourse Strategies*, Cambridge: Cambridge University Press.

Halliday, M. A. K. (1971), 'Linguistic Function and Literary Style: An Enquiry into the Language of William Golding's *The Inheritors*', in S. Chapman (ed.), *Literary Style: A Symposium*, Oxford: Oxford University Press: 330–68.

Halliday, M. A. K. (1973), *Explorations in the Functions of Language*, London: Edward Arnold.

Hasher, L. and Zacks, R. T. (1988), 'Working Memory, Comprehension, and Aging: A Review and a New View', in G. H. Bower (ed.), *The Psychology of Learning and Motivation, Vol. 2*, San Diego, CA: Academic Press: 193–255.

Hasher, L., Lustig, C. and Zacks, R. (2007), 'Inhibitory Mechanisms and the Control of Attention', in A. Conway, C. Jarrold, M. Kane, A. Miyake and A. Towse (eds), *Variation in Working Memory*, Oxford: Oxford University Press: 227–49.

Hyltenstam, K. (1995), 'The Code-Switching Behaviour of Adults with Language Disorders – With Special Reference to Aphasia and Dementia', in L. Milroy and P. Muysken (eds), *One Speaker, Two Languages*, Cambridge: Cambridge University Press: 302–43.

Leech, G. N. and Short, M. (1981), *Style in Fiction: A Linguistic Introduction to English Fictional Prose*, Harlow: Longman.

Little Soldier Productions (2013), *You and Me: Marketing Pack.*

Lugea, J. (forthcoming), *World-Building in Spanish and English Spoken Narratives*, London: Bloomsbury Academic.

Lugea, J. (2013), 'Embedded Dialogue and Dreams: The Worlds and Accessibility Relations of Inception', *Language and Literature*, 22.2: 133–53.

McHale, B. (1987), *Postmodernist Fiction*, London: Methuen.

McIntyre, D. (2005), 'Logic, Reality and Mind Style in Alan Bennett's *The Lady in the Van*', *Journal of Literary Semantics*, 34.1: 21–40.

McIntyre, D. (2006), *Point of View in Plays*, Amsterdam: John Benjamins Publishing.

Poplack, S. (1980), 'Sometimes I'll Start a Sentence in Spanish y Termino En Español', *Linguistics*, 18: 581–618.

Román, G. C. (2006), 'Defining Dementia: Clinical Criteria for the Diagnosis of Vascular Dementia', *Acta Neurologica Scandinavica*, 106: 6–9.

Ryan, M. L. (1991a), 'Possible Worlds and Accessibility Relations: A Semantic Typology of Fiction', *Poetics Today*, 12.3: 553–76.

Ryan, M. L. (1991b), *Possible Worlds, Artificial Intelligence and Narrative Theory*, Bloomington, IN: Indiana University Press.

Semino, E. (2002), 'A Cognitive Stylistic Approach to Mind Style in Narrative Fiction', in E. Semino and J. Culpeper (eds), *Cognitive Stylistics: Language and Cognition in Text Analysis*, Amsterdam: John Benjamins: 95–121.

Semino, E. (2011), 'Deixis and Fictional Minds', *Style*, 45.3: 418–40.

Semino, E. (2014a), 'Language, Mind and Autism in Mark Haddon's *The Curious Incident of the Dog in the Night-Time*', in M. Fludernik and D. Jacob (eds), *Linguistics and Literary Studies*, Berlin: Mouton de Gruyter: 279–303.

Semino, E. (2014b), 'Pragmatic Failure, Mind Style and Characterisation in Fiction about Autism', *Language and Literature*, 23.2: 141–58.

Shanahan, B. (2013), *You and Me*. Theatre production. Little Soldier Productions.

Sherzer, D. (1978), 'Dialogic Incongruities in the Theater of the Absurd', *Semiotica*, 22.3–4: 269–86.

Simeon, R. (2011), *Tu i Jo*. Theatre production. Filòmans.

Simpson, P. (1993), *Language, Ideology and Point of View*, London: Routledge.

Simpson, P. (2002), 'Odd Talk: Discovering Discourses of Incongruity', in J. Culpeper, M. Short and P. Verdonk (eds), *Exploring the Language of Drama: From Text to Context*, London: Routledge: 34–53.

Stoppard, T. (1967), *Rosencrantz and Guildenstern are Dead*, London: Faber and Faber.

Teo, S. (2012), 'Review: *You and Me*', A Younger Theatre, <http://www.ayoungertheatre.com/review-you-and-me-little-soldier-productions-rich-mix/> [accessed 2 October 2015].

Vassilopoulou, K. (2008), 'Possible Worlds in the Theatre of the Absurd', in G. Watson (ed.), *The State of Stylistics*, Amsterdam: Rodopi: 157–76.

Werth, P. (1995a), 'How to Build a World (in a Lot Less that Six Days, and using Only What's in Your Head)', in K. Green (ed.), *New Essays on Deixis: Discourse, Narrative, Literature*, Amsterdam: Rodopi: 49–80.

Werth, P. (1995b), ' "World Enough, and Time": Deictic Space and the Interpretation of Prose', in P. Verdonk and J.-J. Weber (eds), *Twentieth Century Fiction: From Text to Context*, London: Routledge: 181–205.

Werth, P. (1999), *Text Worlds: Representing Conceptual Space in Discourse*, Harlow: Longman.

Yorston, A. (2013), 'Review of *You and Me*', British Theatre Guide, <http://britishtheatreguide.info/reviews/you-and-me-yvonne-arnaud-m-9580> [accessed 2 October 2015].

14

Autofocus and Remote Text-World Building in the Earliest English Narrative Poetry

Antonina Harbus

14.1   Introduction

This chapter considers the process of world-building done in the minds of present-day readers of culturally and temporally remote literary texts. It explores how empathetic engagement and narrative coherence are constructed across the barriers of fiction and timespan in a medieval poem written in Old English, the oldest form of the language. To trace this process, the discussion below applies Text World Theory to translated excerpts from *Beowulf*, the best-known poem from Anglo-Saxon England (probably composed in the eighth-century CE [Fulk, Bjork and Niles 2008: clxxix]). This text is particularly appropriate for the literary application of a text-world framework, as it is not only one of the longest and finest Old English poems still in existence, but also features appealing fantasy elements – including a battle between the hero and a dragon-guardian of a treasure hoard – that contribute vividly to world-building. This engaging subject matter is communicated via a narrative technique that is reflective and retrospective, a combination that produces a strong invitation to the reader's conceptual and emotional investment in the text-world. These discursive properties of meaning-making are examined below, with a particular focus on the emotional component of world-building. This framework and text sample are deployed to propose here that the inter-reliance of cognitive and emotional processing can be examined at work in textual interpretation beyond the contemporary context, using the analytical tools offered by Text World Theory.

The apparent ease with which present-day readers are able to build worlds from such a remote text, and have an emotional reaction to it, operates as the result of a phenomenon that is defined here as 'autofocus': the use of discursively cued familiar conceptualization and habitual emotional response in configuring meaning within unfamiliar textual and/or cultural territory. This spontaneous cognitive and emotional orientation and enactment operates in similar ways in both actual-life and fictional encounters, even when transmitted from a foreign culture. Autofocus is shown below to operate via textual cueing and emotive language processing, to result in recourse to habituated default affective positions as part of pragmatic sense-making, world-building and textual interpretation, even with products of a remote culture. As the following discussion will show, an early medieval English text, perhaps contrary to expectations, can feature comparatively complex text-worlds, especially given its likely oral composition and reception, as well as its historical/fantastic subject matter. A further aim of this discussion, then, is to highlight the value of considering, via discursive analysis, the long-term continuities of literary technique and reception, as they can be disclosed and examined via a text-world approach.

14.2   World-building in literary narrative

Text World Theory – originally developed by Werth (1999), and augmented by Gavins (2007) and others – provides a way of understanding and analysing the mind's complex yet organized responses to any textual encounter, especially to those processes that occur below conscious awareness. This discourse processing theory assumes that to understand language we have to conceptualize its propositions; to create coherence from extended pieces of discourse (such as a long narrative text), we have to keep track of those propositions systematically, make inferences from them as a whole and synthesize them with customized selections from stored knowledge (cued by the text). We make sense of discourse through the creation of mental representations of the ideas provoked by that discourse: conceptual systems that provide a way of managing and integrating collections of propositions. These provisional worlds must be imagined and then continuously updated in order to make sense of the text, and to accommodate its emerging premises and assumptions. The process of creating coherence from these scenarios is cumulative and adaptive: the reader incrementally takes information from the text, with which general knowledge, stored schemas, inferencing – and acts of the imagination – are selectively combined.

This activity of world-building is a customized and flexible collaboration between textual cueing and the reader's cognitive processing. The text defines those areas of the knowledge-base immediately relevant to its meaning, to be supplied by the recipient, a process that is possible even beyond the text's contemporary context. Of course, the more remote the text becomes, the larger the gaps to be filled by translation, glossing, historical and critical knowledge become. In the first instance, though, the specific collection of words on the page, along with associations evoked, prompt the reader to prioritize specific pieces of knowledge, relationship schemas and personal memories from the whole store of these ideas held in the mind, and to disregard other information; to make assumptions about information, beliefs and emotional states shared with the textual producer; and to create certain expectations for further details in order to continue the established pattern.

Text World Theory is particularly useful for literary-linguistic analyses, as it provides a means of accounting for the complex creation and synthesis of imaginative representations during reading. What has not yet been considered in detail in relation to this conceptual framework, though, is the interplay between emotion and the cognitive processing of pre-modern texts (but see Harbus 2012), especially in terms of automatic emotional priming and reactions cued textually, a contribution to which is made here. Even explicitly fictional texts provide the opportunity for readers to imagine alternative realities and emotional states that nevertheless bear some relationship to those pertaining in the actual world, and to create and update those models over the course of the text, despite instances when the text treats counterfactual situations, as in *Beowulf*, whose narrative features three major battles between the eponymous hero and supernatural adversaries. In negotiating the propositions of this text, the reader is called upon to conceptualize a world in which monsters exist, certain unfamiliar cultural norms prevail and yet recognizable human behaviour and emotional states operate.

Because *Beowulf* was composed over 1,200 years ago, we can expect a degree of discrepancy in the author's and present-day reader's common ground, or 'the totality of information which the speaker(s) and hearer(s) have agreed to accept as relevant for their discourse' (Werth 1999: 119). It is proposed here that this commonality encompasses not only conceptual propositions, which might be very foreign, but also their emotional dimensions, which are not. This silent and approximate co-operation between the writer and reader leaves not only a great deal of flexibility in terms of relevance, but also huge scope for various selection and deployment of ideas and, in turn, reaction and interpretation.

The common ground evolves as the discourse progresses, changing as information is provided and new concepts and images are introduced. This process of incrementation means that each new piece of information is managed to cohere with and to modify the common ground, as the text-world and its emotional aspects are updated. Because most of this information is implied and called upon rather than explicitly stated, it is useful to imagine the text as a 'network of inference' (Werth 1999: 122), and for reading to be seen as the activation of that deductive process of sense-making, which requires sharing a set of propositions and emotional keys relevant to a specific text. Indeed, the text drives the specific construction of context, which is negotiated by the reader and writer through the process of incrementation. The way textual clues act to trigger that process of text-driven coherence is a guiding principle of Text World Theory, which sees the accumulation of information as being determined by its immediate relevance to the textual context. It is argued here that there is an emotional, as well as a conceptual dimension to that relevance test.

Like other literary texts, the text-world in *Beowulf* is rich, in that it is lifelike, with characters (including monsters) that are created by the reader to resemble actual people, including in terms of emotional range and experience. They represent human experience in complex and detailed ways, since they call upon cognitive and affective models, and are filled out with information from the reader's own memories, knowledge, emotional experience and conceptual schemas. They therefore have a large degree of 'internal structure' (Werth 1999: 204) that requires active creation and negotiation. This internal structure allows the text-world to be further broken up into world-switches, which are different aspects or perspectives marked by a shift in time or space, triggered by a flashback, or a movement of the text into the mind of a particular character, and also to mark wishes and obligations ('boulomaic' and 'deontic' modal-worlds in Gavins's terminology [2007: 94 and 98]). These switches involve cognitive repositioning, so are therefore noticeable and marked as potentially significant, because when a world-switch occurs, a reader must reorient themselves both spatially and temporally in response to the new deictic markers. These 'sub-worlds' (Werth 1999) are embedded in the main text-world, and can be grouped into those that are able to be accessed and therefore verified by characters within the text-world (character-accessible sub-worlds), and those verifiable directly by readers (participant-accessible sub-worlds). This distinction is important because it separates what can be verified as coming from the narrator and what has been filtered through a character.

An important feature of Text World Theory in relation to fictional narrative is its recognition of a text's capacity to reorient a reader's perspective via a switch to a new time and place. When the textual 'here-and-now' moves to a new position, the reader has to project their viewing position (deictic centre) into the new sub-world, in order to keep track of what is going on. This repositioning is part of a new conceptualization (text-world or sub-world) that must be created in the mind. Gavins explains this process as the projection of a reader's 'notion of a zero reference point onto someone or something else in the text-world' as a form of 'imagined transportation' (2007: 40–1). Such transportation occurs regularly in *Beowulf* through retrospective repositioning by both the narrator and characters, via memory, and is characterized by emotional priming cues that direct readerly engagement and world-building.

14.2.1   Text World Theory, pre-modern literature and emotion

Because little use of Text World Theory has been made in relation to pre-modern literature and emotion, introducing medieval examples will broaden the opportunities for investigation. For instance, the probability that the present-day reader will share less common ground with the producer of the discourse-world than the medieval textual recipient would have done – and also acknowledge and try to accommodate that deficit of cultural knowledge – deserves scrutiny, especially in terms of implications for meaning. Even more interesting is how this theory can account for the potential for emotional similarity: how we can conceptualize and even share represented emotional states, and perhaps even be moved by texts written so long ago.

Stockwell addresses some of these issues in relation to a range of modern and early-modern literary texts. He extends Text World Theory in his analysis of the role of emotion in the aesthetics of reading, or 'texture': 'the experienced quality of textuality' (2009: 1). This more literary development of the theory is particularly useful because it seeks to account for the mechanisms of literary reading: how certain ideas and knowledge from a reader's whole store of information are selectively recalled and deployed in response to textual cues in a particular act of reading; and how texts foreground and group certain ideas, inviting certain associations and cumulative responses in the mind of the reader. Specifically, Stockwell has developed an approach that accounts for the literary creation of ambiguity, tone and the affective reading experience. He looks at how the reading mind is primed below the level of consciousness to create certain connections in the text at hand and to derive a particular sort of reading experience from that text (11).

While Stockwell has opened up the affective dimension of world-building, there is still work to be done on how literary texts can exploit an evolved, embodied human universal: the connection between cognitive and emotional processing. As Semino shows, 'no existing approach caters fully for the potential complexity and variety of the relationships between fictional minds and text-worlds in fiction and literature' (2009: 68). Texts can invite intense, involved readings from a culturally remote, modern audience because they evoke and thereby produce emotional experiences and genuine sensations, notwithstanding their acknowledged fictionality. Stockwell is broadly in agreement with Gerrig's argument that fictionality does not affect actual cognitive processing: 'the experience of narratives is largely unaffected by their announced correspondence with reality' (Gerrig 1993: 102). Readers' emotional investment is implicated in world-building and sense-making, even in a medieval fantasy text such as *Beowulf.*

14.2.2   Autofocus

This affective potential of a fictional text from long ago can be explored via the idea of autofocus, or emotional f-stops, to continue the photographic metaphor: default positions developed during lived experience as habituated and pragmatic emotional reactions to types of situations. Of course, there is a complexity and nuance to such reactions that is not being discounted here, as a result of context-specific and individuated experience and reaction, but the idea of pragmatically taking recourse to a learned emotional approximation as part of world-building via autofocus is the one being proposed here. It is likely that in the process of making sense of literary narrative, emotional, as well as cognitive orientation occurs, along with recourse to emotional models, as well as story patterns or schemas. Just as readers make use of background knowledge made pertinent via textual cues, similarly, they deploy emotional background information, and experienced affective states, during the process of comprehension. In other words, emotional priming happens through world-building, in which there is an interdependence of thinking and feeling.

Neuroscientist Antonio Damasio has shown convincingly that the emotional life is thoroughly embedded in and interacts with cognitive functioning and embodied experience, and is consistent across cultures (1994, 2003). For example, the experience of a flush of heat during the sensation of feeling angry is an embodied emotional reaction that interplays with mental functioning when apprehending behaviour or context. It is an immediate, repeatable response that occurs in particular types of situations. Philosophers and literary scholars have embraced this idea, to consider the emotional impact of reading literary fiction (Coplan 2004; Feagin 2010; Robinson 2005), and having an empathetic response to it (Keen 2007). Part of the process of making sense, or world-building, then, engages the emotions, as well as the cognitive capacity of the reader. Just as there are conceptual schemas and scripts that are relied on during sense-making, in the world and in textual interpretation, similarly, there are somewhat formularized and recurring emotional reactions that are traceable. Part of the way in which readers imagine the text-world, its characters and their experiences, is the emotional landscape: dynamic conceptualization must entail dynamic affect too. It would seem useful, then, to combine these ideas with those already established in Text World Theory, in order to consider more comprehensively the complexity of world-building in the mind, especially the way in which textual cues can trigger emotional, as well as cognitive reactions.

14.3   Building a text-world of the battle between Beowulf and the dragon

These lines of inquiry can be developed further through a consideration of the interpretative processes triggered by a temporally remote, evidently fictional narrative, *Beowulf*. Specifically, the discussion below will consider how textual discourse primes the recipient to conceptualize multiple textual frames and to configure meaning and affective responses from stated and implied information, and from contributed perceptual and experiential knowledge.

Beowulf depicts three battles: with the semi-human monster Grendel, with that creature's avenging mother and finally with a dragon. The reader is invited to perceive that incrementally the stakes are raised with each fight, permitting the hero to demonstrate his grit, resolve and superiority. Below are four fragments of this long narrative poem (3182 ll) depicting the impetus for and outcome of the final battle between the hero and a dragon, provided in both the original Old English, and a literal, syntactically similar translation. When its hoard is plundered, the dragon takes motivated action:

Excerpt 14.1
Þa se wyrm onwoc,   wroht wæs geniwad;
stonc ða æfter stane,   stearcheort onfand
feondes fotlast;   he to forð gestop
dyrnan cræfte   dracan heafde neah.

```
    ...          Hordweard sohte
georne æfter grunde,   wolde guman findan,
þone þe him on sweofote   sare geteode;
hat ond hrohmod   hlæw oft ymbehwearf
ealne utanweardne;   ne ðær ænig mon
on þam westenne - hwæðre wiges gefeh,
beadwe weorces; ...
Ða se gæst ongan   gledum spiwan,
beorht hofu bærnan -   bryneleoma stod
eldum on andan; no ðær aht cwices
lað lyftfloga   læfan wolde. (Fulk, Bjork and Niles, eds, ll. 2287-2315)
```

Then the serpent awoke, [and] strife was renewed. Smelling along the rock, the hardhearted one perceived his enemy's footprint; in skilful stealth, he had stepped right beside the dragon's head ... The guardian of the hoard sought eagerly along the ground, intending to find the man, the one who had wrought him an injury in his sleep. Hot and sad at heart, he flew often all around the mound, but there was no-one in that wasteland. However, he thought with joy of battle, of waging war .... Then the invader began to spew forth flames, to burn the shining halls – the blazing light stood out as a woe to people. That loathsome winged creature did not intend to leave any being alive. (My translation)

This passage notably explains the dragon's reasons for its wrathful rampage, and its emotional response to the theft of a precious item of its treasure – a cup – the motivation and desire for excessive revenge. The stolen cup thereby becomes an item elevated from the text-world ground to be a central figure in the emotions and events of the narrative. We are given the dragon's point of view, in order to appreciate its drive for destruction, and its status as a highly charged adversary for the hero, but also to create an emotional schema of angry revenge-seeking as part of world-building. The very first line of the excerpt links the concept of 'roused serpent' with 'the inevitable renewal of strife', cueing the reader to imagine a state of affairs where not only do dragons exist and routinely sit upon treasure-hoards, but also short-temperedly and furiously guard those hoards to the death. The dragon configures the man who came into the cave as an 'enemy', and all living things as its target; the reader is invited to align with that enemy group, and to construct via autofocus an opposing cognitive/emotional position to the dragon. This affective situation is reinforced by the descriptor 'invader' to characterize the rampaging dragon, a term that similarly primes the construal of an adversarial role for this beast in the mind of the reader.

Besides such discursive cueing, the reader is permitted via world-switches into the sub-world of the dragon's detection and planned revenge: 'sought eagerly along the ground, intending to find the man' and 'did not intend to leave any being alive'. The human level of intentionality depicted through these world-switches characterizes the dragon as a motivated rather than an instinctive adversary. The mental models the reader is encouraged to create to make sense of this excerpt, then, call upon dragon schemas, blended with those of property acquisition and protection, and recognizable human emotional models of insulted pride, anger and blood-thirst. The world-building elements are unfamiliar and generically fantastic, yet the affective referential frame is familiar and not specific to fiction.

In the narrative, Beowulf, as king, decides himself to respond, in order to protect his kingdom:

Excerpt 14.2
Þa was Biowulfe   broga gecyðed
snude to soðe,   þæt his sylfes ham,
bolda selest,   brynewylmum mealt,
giftstol Geata.   Þæt ðam godan wæs
hreow on hreðre,   hygesorga mæst;
wende se wisa   þæt he wealdende
ofer ealde riht,   ecean dryhtne
bitre gebulge;   breost innan weoll
þeostrum ge þoncum,   swa him geþywe ne wæs. (ll. 2324–32)

Then the terror was made known to Beowulf, swiftly and in truth, that his own home, the best of houses, the gift-throne of the Geats, was being destroyed in the surging blaze. That was a heart-sorrow to the good man, the greatest grief in the mind. The wise one thought that he had bitterly offended the ruler, the everlasting lord, by breaking some ancient law. His breast within welled with dark thoughts, which was not customary for him.

The event of news delivery triggers a world-switch to the hero's inner world of thought and emotion, and links grief with the destruction of the royal house, a symbolic coupling that recurs throughout this text. The reader has already been emotionally primed to associate Beowulf with stock heroic emotions, so here, the process of autofocus is contextually enhanced. Unlike the dragon, Beowulf experiences remorse for an imagined affront to his deity, and unusually negative thoughts. The state of affairs the reader is cued to imagine is one in which dragons behave wrathfully and heroes behave reflectively. So, even before these two adversaries come to grips and battle to the death, we are told in these two excerpts of their contrasting motivations for action and their emotional states – continuing the pattern that has been established by the earlier encounters with Grendel and his mother. Throughout the text, the habitual world-switches into memory or reflection (or the legendary past), especially by the hero, organize information into contemplative rather than event-filled patterns, suggesting a logical relationship between heroism and the cognitive/emotional life.

This discursively created connection is played out emphatically at the climax of the narrative. After the battle, in which the dragon is slain and the hero mortally wounded, and Beowulf is deserted by all but one of his followers, the dying hero recalls key events from his youth, including the tragic accident that paved the way for his path to the Geatish throne, in the household of his uncle, Hrethel, who loved Beowulf like a son:

Excerpt 14.3
Fela ic on gioguðe   guðræsa genæs,
orleghwila;   ic þæt eall gemon.
Ic wæs syfanwintre   þa mec since baldor,
freawine folca   æt minum fæder genam;
heold mec ond hæfde   Hreðel cyning,
geaf me sinc ond symbel,   sibbe gemunde;
næs ic him to life   laðra owihte,
beorn in burgum,   þonne his bearna hwylc,
Herebeald ond Hæðcyn   oððe   Hygelac min.
Was þam yldestan   ungedefelice
mæges dædum   morþorbed stred,
syððan hyne Hæðcyn   of hornbogan,
his freawine   flane geswencte,
miste mercelses ond   his mæg ofscet,
broðor oðerne   blodigan gare.
Þæt wæs feohles gefeoht,   fyrenum gesyngad,
hreðre hygemeðe;   sceolde hwæðre swa þeah
æþeling unwrecen   ealdres linnan.
Swa bið geomorlic   gomelum ceorle
to gebidanne,   þæt his byre ride
giong on galgan.   Þonne he gyd wrece,
sarigne sang,   þonne his sunu hangað
hrefne to hroðre,   ond he him helpe ne mæg
eald ond infrod   ænige gefremman,

symble bið gemyndgad   morna gehwylce
eoforan ellorsið; oðres ne gemyð
to gebiddan   burgum in innan
yrfeweardas,   þonne se an hafað
þurh deaðes nyd   dæda gefondad.
Gesyhð sorhcearig   on his suna bure
winsele westne,   windge reste,
reotge berofene;   ridend swefað,
hæleð in hoðman;   nis þær hearpan sweg,
gomen in geardum,   swylce ðær iu wæron.
Gewitteð þone on sealman,   sorhleoð gæleð
an æfter anum;   þuhte him eall to rum,
wongas ond wicstede. (ll. 2426–2602a)

In youth, I survived many onslaughts of war; I remember it all. I was seven
years old when the lord of the treasure, the friend of the people, accepted me
from my father. King Hrethel kept and protected me, granted me treasure
and feasting, remembering our relationship. I was not, while he lived, a whit
the less loved by him in the strongholds than his own sons, Herebeald and
Heathcyn, or my Hygelac. For the eldest, unfittingly by the deeds of a kinsman,
there was prepared a bed of violent death, when Heathcyn with an arrow from
his horn bow struck his lord, missed his mark and shot his kinsman, brother
slew brother with a bloody shaft. That was a fight without compensation, a terrible crime, wretched to contemplate in the heart, but nevertheless the prince
had to lose his life unavenged. Yet, it is a sad thing if an old man has to endure
that his still young son should swing on the gallows. Then he will utter a dirge,
a sad song, while his son hangs, as sport for the raven, and he, old and very
aged, cannot help him at all. He is always reminded, each morning, of his son's
passing. Little does he care to wait in his stronghold for another heir, when
this one has, through evil deeds, tasted death. In wretched sorrow he sees his
son's dwelling, the deserted wine-hall, the wind-swept resting-place, bereft of
laughter. The riders sleep, the men into the darkness. There is no sound of the
harp, no joy in the courts, as there once were. Then he goes back to his bed,
alone sings a song for the loved-one. To him the fields and dwelling place seem
too vast.

This narrative excerpt is one of the so-called digressions in the poem, where
incidents from the past or future are recounted, and which have received a lot of
critical attention in terms of their role in the text (e.g. Bjork 1997; Bonjour 1950).
Using a text-world approach, we could perceive here a convergence or slippage

between world-building elements and function-advancing propositions: the memory recounted both provides context for the state of events (including ongoing current action and behavioural motivation), and itself constitutes a definable story event sequence. The gnomic generalization in the last part of the excerpt, especially the line 'There is no sound of the harp, no joy in the courts, as there once were', creates a conceptual and emotional bridge between past and present. We could thereby view this piece of discourse as a lengthy world-switch into memory, with autofocus cueing for universally recognizable feelings around love and loss at a narratively significant moment. This capacity to evoke emotional resonance via context-neutral autofocus prompts relates to strong and cross-cultural familial emotions. The loaded image of the father contemplating his son's material absence invites an empathetic response in the reader, in light of the universal reaction of a parent to the loss of a child. Yet, the accidental killing of one brother by another is presented as not only having caused paternal grief and the added frustration of the inability to exact vengeance (the latter a culturally specific element of the common ground that the modern reader might have to imagine), but also of producing long-lasting implications for the leadership and stability of the kingdom.

Incrementally, the reader is cued in this world-switch to build a text-world in which social detriment is linked to personal tragedy, and where old age is coupled with helplessness ('old and very aged, cannot help him at all'). The switch is facilitated via the affective autofocus, where an imagined scenario is ushered into the text-world via a familiar emotion. In a further world-switch within the sub-world ('in wretched sorrow he sees his son's dwelling'), the reader is drawn more deeply into the observations, reflections and sensory perceptions of one fictional speaker, the old man himself ('no sound of the harp, no joy in the courts'), and his thoughts imagined by the next-level fictional speaker, Beowulf ('to him the fields and dwelling place seem too vast'), both transmitted through the narrator's voice. This system of story-telling and slipping into characters' consciousnesses is repeated throughout the poem, and primes the reader to draw inferences and to synthesize information along particular lines. In making sense of this excerpt, for instance, the reader comes to rely on the pattern of attractors clustered around loneliness and sorrow, both of which reflect and inform the situation in which the dying hero finds himself, and thereby establish the tone of the wider textual moment and prime the interpretation of what follows.

The context of the account, within a speech made by the dying and childless Beowulf, creates a depth to the tragedy of the situation, and a fatalistic intimation of the end of the safety for the Geats that is crucial to world-building. Through negotiating the sequence of information provision, the reader has to create mental representations of all the sub-worlds in this reported memory in order to make sense of the text, and thereby to recalibrate the conceptual and affective relationships among propositions, setting up a chain of inference-making that leads to a certain type of textual coherence, resonance and emotional positioning. In this system, Beowulf has become emblematic not only of heroism, but of kingship, security and success, as well as emotional depth, textual attention takers or 'attractors' (Stockwell 2009: 20) that elevate this character to a superlative status at the poem's conclusion.

The hero is also distinguished from his fellows behaviourally in the text-world. During the dragon's final onslaught, Beowulf is abandoned by all but one of his companions:

Excerpt 14.4
Nealles him on heape   handgesteallan,
æþelinga bearn   ymbe gestodon
hildecystum,   ac hy on holt bugon,
ealdre burgan.   Hiora in anum weoll
sefa wið sorgum;   sibb' æfre ne mæg
wiht onwendan   þam ðe wel þenceð.
Wiglaf wæs haten... (ll. 2596–62a)

Not at all did his close companions, sons of princes, stand by him in a group, virtuous in battle, but they ran away into the woods to save their lives. In one of them, the mind was moved with grief. Nothing may put aside kinship for the one who thinks well. He was called Wiglaf.

As with the other excerpts, here, the narrator provides commentary on the mental functioning and emotional motivation of the characters. With the generalized utterance, 'Nothing may put aside kinship for the one who thinks well', such commentary is simultaneously world-building and function-advancing, in that it contributes to context and event-advancement. The contrast created between shameful and loyal behaviour is made starkly, and the common ground understanding that character determines action underpins that contrast, and organizes the textual response along lines that privilege cognitive/emotional motivation for behaviour. This excerpt, like the previous one, depicts love as implicated in loyalty and social impact. Additionally, the textual attractors, in Stockwell's terms, 'aloneness' and 'helplessness' are expressed in this excerpt, where the hero is left to die almost alone, an element that deepens the tragic aspect of the scenario under construction. The autofocus prompts in this excerpt are more culturally specific than in the earlier ones, as this is an imagined society where retainer loyalty (reinforced by ritualized gift-giving) is deeply embedded and highly valued. The behaviour described, of fleeing one's bound lord at a moment of crisis for self-preservation, is culturally condemned, and goes against the model built up in the text-world throughout the poem, so is recruited accordingly by the reader in the organized response to the text.

14.4   The emotional world of Beowulf

As these excerpts show, the text-world of *Beowulf* is emotionally and conceptually rich, and the invited emotional reaction is complex. Incrementally, the text encourages the reader, in conceptualizing discursive propositions, to build a picture of Beowulf as all-mighty and thoroughly good, a paragon felled by a highly motivated and angry dragon and let down by his supporters. Information is presented as a part of the common ground of Beowulf's context, rather than as a matter of opinion: the use of firm indicative and deictic-free gnomic statements rather than modalized ones creates a set of confident assertions of truth rather than of opinion (e.g. 'Nothing may put aside kinship for the one who thinks well'). It treats the past as preparation for the present challenge, and the future its already known outcome, a context in which the existence of monsters, and in turn heroes to defeat them, is part of the established state of affairs. This expressed and implied common ground is in keeping with the way it is invoked right from the outset of the poem, with the addressee potentially included in the plural pronoun used by the 'authenticating voice' of the narrator (Greenfield 1976): 'We have heard of the glory of the Spear Danes' (line 1). Even if this reference and those within Beowulf's speech are allusive for the modern reader without some knowledge of Anglo-Saxon history, culture and literary style, they immediately create a referential frame that forces the reader towards interpretative and emotional multitasking in order to keep up and create coherence.

The text establishes Beowulf as a moral victor in the hero-versus-monster schema it calls up, and a righteous defender of his kingdom, in a construal effect that accumulates focus on his success in the forthcoming battle. The built-up textual attractor, Beowulf-as-hero, is conceptualized by the reader at the centre of the world being built; his imminent death brings on not only the end of the narrative, but also the end of the civilization of which he is the leader and defender. This poem thereby persuasively invites a 'prototypical reading'

(Stockwell 2009: 162) that cooperatively accepts the speaker's expressed views. The reader is not encouraged, for instance, to align with the dragon, but rather to recognize it as a mighty adversary, and thereby to appreciate the hero's efforts against it all the more. This co-operation results not only from the reader's collection and synthesis of accumulated information, but as a result of being invited to project their minds into the hero's past and present, poised to imagine certain outcomes in his future, and to appreciate his emotional position. The result is a form of psychological projection whereby the reader is invited to model Beowulf's mind in terms of his motivation to succeed in the task and his affective commitedness to it.

At the end of his speech, the reader is able to create a text-world combining Beowulf and the concept of fate (Excerpt 14.3) – a pairing that is reiterated elsewhere in the poem – as a direct result of being led via narrative control from the past exploits of Beowulf to his new intentions. The shifting text-worlds in the particular chain of events narrated facilitate this connection through what Langacker has conceptualized via a billiard-ball metaphor as the supply, transfer and absorption of grammaticalized energy in texts (2008: 103). In this case, attributes are attracted to the central character and gather dynamic momentum via specific clausal structure and clustering in the text. This experiential investment is reinforced as the reader is encouraged to synthesize the attributes Beowulf collects from the world-switches (Stockwell 2009: 149), thereby creating momentum for a conceptual trajectory of Beowulf + heroic success + tragic loss. If we consider these lines in terms of the 'force dynamics' outlined by Langacker and used by Stockwell, we can trace the arc of the metaphoric billiard ball of the attractors 'heroism', 'loss' and 'loneliness', to Beowulf, in the build up to the poem's conclusion, which features the hero's funeral, and the (emphatically rhymed) closing lines:

Excerpt 14.5
Swa begnornodon   Geata leode
hlafordes hryre,   heorðgeneatas;
cwædon þæt he wære   woruldcyninga
manna mildust   ond monðwærust,
leodum liðost   ond lofgeornost. (ll. 3178–82)

So, the people of the Geats, the companions of the hearth, lamented the fall of their lord. They said that he was, among the world's kings, the most generous and gracious of men, to his people the most kindly and the most eager for renown.

This character summary reinforces the incrementally produced portrait of the hero and his imputed motivations, where behaviour and reputation are configured as centrally important in the internal structure of the produced text-world. The reader has been primed, particularly through the many world-switches into his emotions and thoughts (and those of his adversaries), to believe that the loss of such a superlative human being is tragic, and has wide-reaching consequences. Indeed, the mental representations we modern readers create from the textual clues of *Beowulf* arise from multiple world-shifts into memory and imagination within the text, enacted with minimal or apparently non-existent textual markers of those shifts. The reader is required to shift attention in time and space without very clear or prominent deictic or referential indicators, especially in the cases of items from memory or generalized gnomic utterances that apply equally to remembered and ongoing events, as discussed above. We are required to manage and negotiate several provisional scenarios at once, via the narrative digressions, and to perceive their relevance, as well as that of several generalized, gnomic utterances that fill out the assumed common ground and operate within the pattern of meaning-making in the text. Within this process, the reader has to make a considerable conceptual and emotional investment in decoding the text via the creation simultaneously of several possibly suitable and at times incomplete text-worlds: tentative or vague configurations of textual propositions that have clearer affective than conceptual shape. The result is the creation of an 'emotional feedback loop' (Stockwell 2009: 95 and 98) – one that relies fundamentally on autofocus. This complex information delivery technique indicates not only the intensely affective fabric of the possible worlds the Anglo-Saxon audience would have created in order to make sense of this text, but also demonstrates how narrative ambiguity has been used as a vehicle for emotional power here specifically, and points more broadly to the affective potential of poetry. The mental representation the text triggers is thereby, for modern readers, like its own contemporary medieval audiences, an affective rather than a narrative one.

The richness of this long heroic poem – its emotional intensity – is the result of the reader's contribution of emotional disposition, experience and involvement, or 'literary resonance' (Stockwell 2009: 63), enacted through the process of autofocus as described here. Readers are up to this task of responding to the demands placed on them precisely because the text drives inference-making and the process of making coherence from its propositions, mental representations and emotional events and states it gives rise to. Recognizable emotional models are evoked and triggered by charged situations and discursive cueing that instigate autofocus, where familiar cognitive and emotional states are called up by memory to draw together the textual clues and to build a meaningful text-world. Even in the case of a text such as *Beowulf*, with evident fantasy elements, and produced long ago, familiar human conceptualization and emotional states are depicted, evoked and recruited in literary sense-making, a process that Text World Theory can help us to understand.

References

Bjork, R. E. (1997), 'Digressions and Episodes', in R. E. Bjork and J. D. Niles (eds), *A Beowulf Handbook*, Lincoln, NE: University of Nebraska Press: 193–212.

Bonjour, A. (1950), *The Digressions in Beowulf*, Medium Ævum Monographs 5, Oxford: Blackwell.

Coplan, A. (2004), 'Empathetic Engagement with Narrative Fictions', *Journal of Aesthetics and Art Criticism*, 62.2: 141–52.

Damasio, A. (1994), *Descartes' Error: Emotion, Reason and the Human Brain*, New York: Putnam.

Damasio, A. (2003), *Looking for Spinoza: Joy, Sorrow, and the Feeling Brain*, Orlando, FL: Harcourt.

Feagin, S. L. (2010), 'Affects in Appreciation', in P. Goldie (ed.), *The Oxford Handbook of Philosophy of Emotion*, Oxford: Oxford University Press: 617–50.

Fulk, R. D., Bjork, R. E. and Niles, J. D. (eds) (2008), *Klaeber's Beowulf*, 4th ed., Toronto: University of Toronto Press.

Gavins, J. (2007), *Text World Theory: An Introduction*, Edinburgh: Edinburgh University Press.

Gerrig, R. J. (1993), *Experiencing Narrative Worlds: On the Psychological Activities of Reading*, New Haven and London: Yale University Press.

Greenfield, S. B. (1976), 'The Authenticating Voice in *Beowulf*', *Anglo-Saxon England*, 5: 51–62.

Harbus, A. (2012), *Cognitive Approaches to Old English Poetry*, Cambridge: D.S. Brewer.

Keen, S. (2007), *Empathy and the Novel*, Oxford: Oxford University Press.

Langacker, R. W. (2008), *Cognitive Grammar: A Basic Introduction*, Oxford: Oxford University Press.

Robinson, J. (2005), *Deeper than Reason: Emotion and its Role in Literature, Music and Art*, Oxford: Oxford University Press.

Semino, E. (2009), 'Text Worlds', in G. Brone and J. Vandaele (eds), *Cognitive Poetics: Goals, Gains and Gaps*, Berlin: Mouton de Gruyter: 33–71.

Stockwell, P. (2009), *Texture: A Cognitive Aesthetics of Reading*, Edinburgh: Edinburgh University Press.

Werth, P. (1999), *Text Worlds: Representing Textual Space in Discourse*, Harlow: Longman.

'Into the Futures of their Makers': A Cognitive Poetic Analysis of Reversals, Accelerations and Shifts in Time in the Poems of Eavan Boland

Nigel McLoughlin

15.1 Introduction

In the chapter that follows I intend to examine the theoretical crossing points between the new mobilities paradigm (Sheller and Urry 2006), Text World Theory (Gavins 2007; Werth 1999) and Stockwell's (2009, 2011) model of literary resonance, in order to generate a framework through which the reversals, accelerations and shifts in time in the work of contemporary Irish poet, Eavan Boland may be effectively analysed. Several of Boland's poems contain challenges to temporal and/or spatial normality in order to make wider points about the nature of reality as we remember and re-experience it. For this reason her work offers a challenging test to the framework proposed.

I will begin by outlining the new mobilities paradigm, and follow this with brief outlines of Text World Theory and Stockwell's model of literary resonance in order to show why they may be effectively combined as a theoretical framework which can be used to address imaginative movement and mobile sense-making. This is followed by the analysis of several examples, and some conclusions drawn from those analyses.

15.2 The new mobilities paradigm

According to Sheller and Urry (2006: 217) mobilities research is primarily concerned with the patterning, timing and causation of face-to-face co-presence and the observation of the ways in which people may move. The paradigm emerged from the social sciences and has developed out of work in a wide variety of disciplines including anthropology, geography and sociology (208). Sheller and Urry assert that this new paradigm calls into question conventional sedentarist approaches that normalize place and stability, and their attendant meanings, while positioning change and placelessness as abnormal (208). They identified several research directions that focus on mobile ethnographies, imagination and memory, and cyber research. Sheller and Urry also highlight new directions which are emerging in the paradigm such as examinations of the mechanisms by which one can be virtually present while physically absent and other transformations of 'time-space scapes' (209); connective networks and systems which contribute to our 'liquid modernity' through 'zones of connectivity' and 'attachments' (210–11); and re-territorializations which allow us to reimagine our relationship to place. They suggest that this approach can also lead to a questioning of our 'linear assumptions about temporality' (214) and how we experience the narrative of events through the 'affective vehicle' of our corporeal bodies in order to construct 'emotional geographies' as we move through and make sense of the world (216).

Several different but analogous facets of mobilities research were identified by Büscher and Urry (2009: 101). These differentiate between corporeal movement, physical movement, imaginative travel, virtual travel and communicative travel. Both sets of researchers also discuss 'places of inbetweenness' (Sheller and Urry 2006: 218) or interspaces (Büscher and Urry 2009: 110; Sheller and Urry 2006: 219) which may be defined as places of 'connected co-presence in which various kinds of meeting-ness are held' (Sheller and Urry 2006: 219).

Such a definition of 'interspace' may apply to the medium which facilitates imagined meeting or imagined travel by acting as the 'interspace' between the imaginations of the sender and the receiver (the written text in literature, for example) and also to imagined 'places on the move' (Büscher and Urry 2009: 110) evoked by the text in the mind of the reader. Imagined travel can open up the possibility of studying counterfactual or impossible co-presences and movements such as reversals of time which often occur in metaphoric journeys and visitations in literature, and afford us the opportunity to analyse how literature uses such movements to tell us something about the real world and about ourselves. In this way, the work of literature can function as an interspace, which facilitates the meeting or journey that would not otherwise be possible, and facilitates the 'connected co-presence' of the reader and the characters, and the reader's journey into the text as that text is realized, both in the sense of being understood, and in the sense of being made 'real' in the mind of the reader.

Urry (2004: 32) talks of inhabited machines, giving the examples of mobile phones and individual televisions, as machines which 're-order Euclidian time-space relations' (35) through various acts of bending, stretching and compressing. Through interactions with these inhabited machines others can be made 'uncannily present' by being near and distant, present and absent simultaneously. Richards in the preface to his *Principles of Literary Criticism* argued that 'a book is a machine to think with' (1925: 1). I would argue that extends to poems too. If that is true, and I believe that it is, then they too are inhabited machines, less obviously technological, but no less capable of making the distant proximate, and the absent present, sometimes very uncannily so. In the imagination presence and absence, proximity and distance are not opposed, and in literature, which is a product of the imagination, some interesting answers may be found to Callon and Law's (2004: 3) question about what happens when they are not.

The new mobilities paradigm is in part intended to undermine 'existing linear assumptions' related to temporality and time, for instance, the assumption that actors perform only one action at a time and that events occur in linear order. A poem is a cohabited vehicle containing a poet and a reader in a discourse-world, which permits virtual or mental travel to other places or times in the act of imaginative creation and recreation. As readers moving through a poem, our normal experience of time can be challenged by sudden temporal shifts, reversals or co-presences of older and younger enactors, and other devices which act to problematize our perception of time in the real world. Such challenges can foreground the relationship between the temporal ordering of the elements that the poem presents, and the way the poet has chosen to represent them. In Section 15.5 of this chapter, I analyse example poems by Eavan Boland in order to understand what insights such manipulations and underminings of existing linear temporal and narrative structures offer their readers. In order to achieve this, I have used a cognitive poetic framework that combines Text World Theory and Stockwell's model of literary resonance, both of which are described in the following sections.

15.3 Text World Theory

Text World Theory was developed by Werth (1999) and has been further modified in recent years by Gavins (2007). While Gavins's version of the theory reconfigures several aspects of Werth's original structure, particularly in relation to the way 'departures' are seen as operating, the basic theory remains structurally very similar. Both versions include a discourse-world where participants interact in a language act, and include the cultural and contextual information that informs the language act. Both versions include the text-world, which is the reader's mental representation of the world as it is built up using information contained in the text. This information includes the various world-building elements referred to, as well as function-advancing propositions which may be descriptive of the environment, tell us more about character, offer points of view, or move the narrative plot forward.

The main structural differences in Werth's and Gavins's versions of the theory are apparent in how they deal with the reader's imaginative movements from the main text-world into other text-worlds. Werth positions these movements at the level below the main text-world, and refers to them as 'departures' into 'sub-worlds'. These departures are classified according to three main types: deictic, attitudinal and epistemic departures (Werth 1999: 216). Deictic departures are initiated by movements in time or space; attitudinal departures offer representations of character's thoughts, intentions and beliefs; epistemic departures are engendered by propositions that are hypothetical, counterfactual, conditional or otherwise modal.

Gavins's version of the theory resists this notion of hierarchy by using the terms 'world-switch' and 'modal-worlds'. World-switches are equivalent to Werth's deictic departures. Modal-worlds reconceptualize attitudinal and epistemic departures in terms of three types of modality: deontic (relating to duty or compulsion); boulomaic (relating to wishes and desires); and epistemic (concerned with perceptions of truth as well as hypothetical or conditional worlds). The epistemic category also includes indirect speech and thought, and free indirect speech, since any type of filtering through the viewpoint of a character is unverifiable. Gavins's model and terminology indicates that the world being switched to, or the world expressed by a particular modality can exist at the same level as the main text-world, and does not have to be subordinate to it.

The two versions also differ in the way they approach negation. In Werth's model, negation may be described as an epistemic 'sub-world' since it involves a change of world definition through deletion (Werth 1999: 252). In Gavins's model, which draws on work by Hidalgo Downing (2000, 2002), various types of 'negative world' may be created, for example, a negative epistemic modal-world may be created, where a character believes that another character does not wish them harm, when in fact they do.

Because Gavins's version of the theory removes the hierarchical aspects with regard to the main text-world and other worlds that arise in the text, this also has important implications for how metaphor can operate within Text World Theory. As we process metaphor, both the representation of the originating text-world and the other worlds created by the metaphor remain active in attention; this means that we may produce a blended world at the same level as the originating world, and readers process these text-worlds at the same time. This can allow the reader to 'toggle' between them, just as one perceptually toggles between bi-stable reversible figures of duck and rabbit in that visual illusion.

15.4   Resonance

In his model of literary resonance, Peter Stockwell (2009, 2011) has adapted Carstensen's (2007) ideas on how attentional foci may be established and moved, and applied them to inform literary readings. In Carstensen's terms, figures may be thought of as positive blobs, possessing edges that are processed simultaneously as part of the shape. In the same way, negative blobs consist only of edges, and focus attention on the gap or absence. This gestalt processing can be extended to structured or unstructured collections of blobs, so structures such as children in a class photo, or a herd of animals are perceived as connected or contiguous. Likewise, attentional foci can change through processes that signify apparent motion (shifts), changes in apparent size (zooms) or through sudden appearance or colour change (changes of state).

Attractors, described by Stockwell as conceptual effects, such as newness, agency or aesthetic difference from the norm, can also be said to be figures. These will operate on a salience scale, depending on whether they relate, from most to least salient, to people (particularly speaking people), ill-defined groups, objects, landscape or abstractions. Figures that are attended to may be maintained in attention, they may be occluded in our attention by another more salient figure, or they may decay as our attention gradually disengages because they have ceased to do anything salient or interesting. A 'lacuna' or 'felt absence' may be experienced where an attractor is occluded in attention by another attractor, but still possess some resonance. Stockwell describes this 'felt absence' as 'something unspecified or removed, rather than never having been mentioned at all' (Stockwell 2011: 43).

Text World Theory and Stockwell's model of literary resonance act as complementary ways of analysing the cognitive effects of imagined movements in
time and space which are created in the mind of a reader by the experience of
reading a literary text. Text World Theory offers a way of analysing the structural relations of the various worlds within a text, and identifying the linguistic cues and structures that cause them to come into being. What Stockwell's
model adds is a way of seeing these structures and movements between them
in dynamic relation through the monitoring of attentional focus, and how that
changes, and why it changes, as the reader progresses through the text. This
enriches the analysis of texts by adding a 'real time' aspect to the analysis that
captures the very fluid movements between text-worlds, and mechanisms by
which these worlds may change in terms of their attentional relation, moving
forward and back in the reader's attentional focus, and in some cases, being re-
activated several times after periods of occlusion and decay.

This theoretical framework can be integrated with the concerns of the new
mobilities paradigm, because 'mobilities theorists pay close attention to the
infrastructures, technical objects, prostheses and embodied practices' that
inform the spatial and material conditions related to mobility (Sheller 2011: 4).
These include items as basic as shoes or road networks, or as advanced as satel-
lite navigation systems, computer coding systems and air traffic control systems that play a part in population movements, and consideration of structural
aspects of the world which may facilitate or impede movement. However, there
is also a growing concern with the temporal aspects of mobility, and this can
extend to 'mobile sense-making' (Jensen 2010 cited in Sheller 2011: 4). Text-
world theorists pay close attention to the infrastructure of the worlds they analyse, both in terms of the imaginative movements within and between them that
the reader engages in, but also in their imaginative relation to each other within
the wider structure, and infrastructure of the text. The technical objects, prostheses and embodied practices mentioned above can also be drawn into parallel relation with the world-building elements and processes that the text-world
theorist analyses in terms of not only their function in building and sustaining
the text-world, but also in certain cases, the linguistic cues and mechanisms
from which readers infer the need to construct alternate text-worlds.

Stockwell's literary resonance model affords the opportunity to analyse
these relationships and movements in terms of their dynamics, the changes in
attentional privilege afforded to each at a particular time, and the mechanisms
by which these changes operate. This allows a way of discussing the inter- and
intra-world movements that are made in attention around the imaginative

spaces constructed by the text-worlds. In this way, Text World Theory offers a way of approaching the spatial and material aspects of imaginative movement and mobile sense-making, while the resonance model offers a way of integrating the temporal aspects with the spatial and material, to produce a deeper and more three-dimensional analytical model for understanding the sense-making mechanisms of the reader as they imaginatively travel through the text.

The following section shows this framework in action by applying it to a number of examples drawn from the poetry of the Irish poet Eavan Boland, whose work is widely admired for its vision in making the personal political, representing the female experience, and also for the use of tropes which are related to metamorphosis, transition and sometimes elision or absence. My interest in using her work for this chapter stems from her striking use of the counterfactual image, particularly in relation to manipulations of time-space relations.

15.5   Analysis

In her Petrarchan sonnet 'Is it Still the Same' from the collection *Code* (2001: 47), Boland uses a series of questions, beginning with the run-on title, to create in the mind of the reader affirmative and negative versions of the resulting text-world, while at the same time populating both versions with the same world-building elements. The title itself contains the pronoun 'it', which is anaphorically ambiguous at this point, and since it cannot be resolved backwards, because it is right at the beginning of the poem, the reader must attempt to resolve it forwards.

Is It Still the Same

young woman who climbs the stairs,
who closes a child's door,
who goes to her table
in a room at the back of a house?
The same unlighted corridor?
The same night air
over the wheelbarrows and rain-tanks?
The same inky sky and pin-bright stars?

Boland (2001: 47)

Owing to the reader's prior experience with similar utterances, the title, as a unit of sense, is taken to be a question, which may relate to the previous memory of a place or action. This initial interpretation is fleeting however, as the 'it' of the title is soon resolved as 'the young woman' of line one. The set of questions, which begin with the run-on title and which extend over the first eight lines of the poem, open two geminal (or twin) epistemic worlds created by the potential for affirmative and negative responses to the questions. These are epistemic modal-worlds because they relate to the potential beliefs of the speaker (and reader) of the poem in relation to whether the world-building elements described are 'the same' or not. In one epistemic world, we imagine it *is* still the same young woman who climbs the stairs, closes a child's door and goes to her table in a room at the back of the house to write, and in another epistemic world we imagine that it *is not* the same woman. The 'it' of the title is attached in turn to each of the world-building elements 'the same unlighted corridor' (line 5); 'the same night air' (line 6); 'the same inky sky and pin-bright stars' (line 8). The reader, since they cannot know which of these geminal epistemic text-worlds is true, is invited to hold both possibilities equally active in mind. The reader at this point can be thought of as imaginatively inhabiting both worlds. This, of course, goes against the reader's normal corporeal experience, but may also suggest to them the opening up of imaginative possibilities that the physical world does not allow. This in turn makes the poem the 'inhabited vehicle' through which the reader undergoes this imaginative transition. The poem contains, but also constrains the worlds that the reader is invited into.

The poem's use of a series of different elements in quick succession as possible candidates to attach to the 'it' of the title allows the affirmative and negative possibilities to be repeatedly reinforced in each case. Both possibilities (and the corresponding affirmative and negative epistemic worlds associated with them) are maintained in the reader's attention as attractors, foregrounding the anaphoric ambiguity generated by the pronoun and reinforcing the equal possibilities of truth as each world-building element is, in turn, assigned as referent for the 'it' of the title. At the same time, in focusing the reader's attention first on the actions of the young woman, and then introducing these new questions related to her environment, the reader's attention is disengaged from her, and moved to the various attractors which emerge through the actions in the questions. She is subject to decay as a figure, while the actions and particulars of the environment are drawn forward in attention by being zoomed in on, in the process becoming figures separated from their ground. One might see this as allowing the reader's imaginative re-enactment of the corporeal experience of physically encountering an unfamiliar place, looking around them, focusing on different elements, in order to build up a coherent image of the new surroundings.

The reader constructs the identity of the speaker of the poem as Boland herself, because in the absence of any information to the contrary we tend to assume a deictic centre for the speaker as I, here, now, for the narrative voice which Werth (1994: 82) takes by convention to operate in the discourse-world. In the affirmative epistemic world, the reader constructs the idea that the older Boland watches her younger self, in her memory, performing these actions. In the negative epistemic world, the reader must believe that the older Boland imagines watching another young woman, who must therefore be a generation below Boland, undertake the same actions that Boland herself had done.

In both these worlds there is a tension between what is possible or likely in the real world, and what is possible in the imaginative world. It is not possible in the real world to be physically co-present in the act of observation of an earlier version of the self, but one can imaginatively do so quite easily. One can do this as an act of remembering the circumstances and feelings at the time, but one can also re-experience events from the perspective of the current self, where one knows outcomes and consequences, and where one has developed perspective and perhaps detachment from the original situation. It is also not usually possible to observe strangers at such close quarters in intimate surroundings without having some form of interaction with them, and without the very fact of one's presence changing the circumstances of what is being observed. However, again the poem draws attention to the fact that we can quite easily do so in the imaginative space, and that this can be a very privileged viewpoint.

From line 9 after the *volta* Boland enters a different phase of the poem. The negation 'you can see nothing of her' teases the reader using the ambiguous pronoun 'you' to either directly address the reader or as a generic 'you' which in Hiberno-English is commonly used instead of the Standard English 'one'.

> You can see nothing of her, but her head
> bent over the page, her hand moving,
> moving again, and her hair.
> I wrote like that once.
> But this is different:
> This time, when she looks up, I will be there.

(Boland 2001: 47)

The reader, of course, can see nothing of the woman, unless the poet chooses to show them. And what she chooses to show them is significant. The poet focuses on the bowed head and the moving hand of the writer. But the head bowed in the act of writing obscures the identity of the young woman and maintains the indeterminacy instigated by the questions as an attractor in the poem. In line 11 the poet observes 'I wrote like that once.' This deictic world-switch into the past originates from both the affirmative and negative versions of the text-world. This may be taken either to reinforce the perceived identity between the younger and older versions of Boland, or as a more general observation that she too had faced the same challenges. The comparison maintains the twinned aspect of the text-worlds, prevents the decay of either, and reinforces the indeterminacy. The final two lines are similarly ambiguous: 'But this is different: / This time, when she looks up, I will be there.' In the deictic shift that occurs from the 'affirmative' version of the epistemic modal-world, it will indeed be different, if the younger Boland looks up to find the older Boland there. Since the younger Boland had never looked up from writing to find herself observed by an older iteration, and since her younger iteration has up to this point been unaware of the older iteration's presence, and given the context of the utterance as part of a poem – where we are conditioned to expect metaphoric use of language – the reader is invited to infer a metaphoric reading, one in which established female writers were not present to be looked up to by the younger Boland.

In the equivalent deictic shift from the 'negative' version of the epistemic modal-world, a young writer will find an older writer present when she 'looks up'. Again, since in the real world writers tend not to find older, more established poets observing them when they look up from writing, we are again invited to infer that in the metaphoric sense there will be an older female writer present to look up to for this young writer (perhaps as representative of her generation), where there wasn't for the younger Boland. Both readings are true. Female poets of the generation before Boland were not visible in the canon of Irish literature; indeed several influential anthologies of Irish poetry have no female representation at all, and Anne Fogarty (1999: 257) has drawn attention to what she calls

> the unwritten history of Irish women's poetry from the 1930s onwards and to the way in which even in absentia it succeeds in casting a shadow over and shaping later pronouncements about the thwarted nature of a female literary tradition in the country.

So the two versions of the epistemic worlds operate to reinforce the idea of the felt absence of senior female poets when the younger Boland was beginning to write, but also assert that Boland is herself now such a presence for the young female poets currently emerging. The question in the title 'Is it Still the Same' now takes on a new resonance and finds a new answer through Boland's virtual journey. Some of the challenges faced by women writers are still the same, particularly in terms of managing demanding roles, but it is different, and it is different because she has been, and is, present. Through the construction of these two text-worlds, Boland questions the nature of what it means to be 'present' for the next generation of writers. She is virtually present in the poem because she is the unseen observer. At the same time, she embodies the absence she felt as a young writer, of visible senior female poets she could 'look up to'. The young woman is portrayed as being surrounded by darkness: 'unlighted corridor', 'night air', 'inky sky', and she is obscured. This may be taken to resonate metaphorically as signifying the young poet's isolation and struggle in the darkness without a major female 'guiding light' while Boland was a young, unpublished and 'obscure' poet.

In this way, the poem draws attention to Boland's struggle, in the darkness of a formative part of her career, to create for herself a poetry that addressed the cultural circumstances in which she found herself, both as woman and poet. It highlights the fact that this struggle was carried on without the benefit of a valued and apparent lineage of Irish female poets to draw upon or use as a model to help her reconcile the various demands upon her as she struggled to initiate her career. The poem also draws attention to the duality of Boland's presence now, as just such an inspirational figure for poets coming after her. She is physically present as a model of what can be achieved in terms of career and status, but she is also metaphorically present as a 'body of work' which will remain for other poets after her physical presence. This body of work serves to demonstrate to women in similar circumstances that it is possible to succeed, despite the conflicting demands that may be made upon them. Boland's figure embodies the absence, both in terms of a physical poet that could be turned to as a model, and in terms of the sustained, successful and valued body of work from Irish women poets absent from the canon during her own formative years as a poet. The ambiguous nature of Boland's figure in the poem draws attention to both. She is 'there' for them, but the younger poet in both cases cannot 'see' her.

The poem serves as an inhabited machine, with Boland uncannily both present and absent. As the writer of the poem she is present as voice, but she is physically separated from the reader in space and time, as well as from the woman she observes, who occupies a different text-world. Boland is a character in her own poem, the embodiment of an absence and an observing presence. This is an important aspect of the poem; the watching figure we take to be Boland is an empowered figure, privileged as observer, able to move imaginatively between worlds, and able to dictate what the reader sees and experiences in her role of narrative mediator. She exemplifies the powerful and privileged position of the poet, a position too often denied to women writing in Ireland during Boland's formative years, but one that, as Boland shows, is achievable now, and for which she can serve as guide.

This figuring of the self in the poem resonates strongly with Boland's lines from 'Anna Liffey' (Boland 1995: 201) that '[i]t has taken me / All my strength to do this. Becoming a figure in a poem'. The relationship between these different text-worlds is presented diagrammatically in Figure 15.1.

As a second example, we can examine another imagined journey Boland makes in the same collection. In 'A Marriage for the Millennium', the narrator of the poem leaves the house and undertakes a journey that involves 'driving the whole distance of [her] marriage'. What we witness next is a series of reversals and unravellings:

Ceramic turned to glass, circuits to transistors.

Old rowans were saplings.
Roads were no longer wide.
Children disappeared from their beds.
Wives, without warning, suddenly became children.
Computer games became codes again.
The codes were folded
back into the futures of their makers.
Their makers woke from sleep, weeping for milk.

(Boland 2001: 22)

This is a very striking way of imaginatively travelling back to the start of the marriage, both in the sense of the amount of time that these reversals signify (because the writers of computer games are babies and radios have transistors again) and also because the reversals create a deictic world-switch by using different versions of world-building elements that make up the current text-world to map directly back to different versions of themselves in the earlier text-world (so wives become children, old rowans become saplings, roads become narrower). It's the same people, same trees, same roads, just earlier versions as they were in an earlier text-world. This strategy makes the reader feel both the pace of the reversal, which is almost instantaneous, but also, because the world-building elements are basically the same, just earlier enactors of the same entities, the past is rendered familiar and accessible. This is also striking because of the fact that it engenders a co-presence, because each early enactor

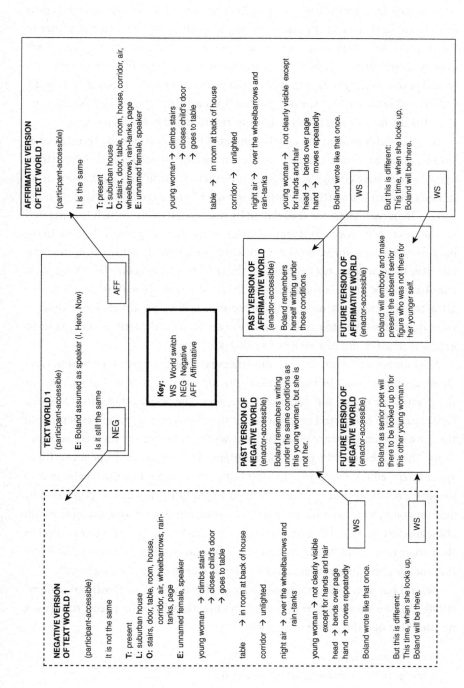

AFFIRMATIVE VERSION OF TEXT WORLD 1

(participant-accessible)

It is the same

T: present
L: suburban house
O: stairs, door, table, room, house, corridor, air, wheelbarrows, rain-tanks, page
E: unnamed female, speaker

young woman → climbs stairs
→ closes child's door
→ goes to table

table → in room at back of house

corridor → unlighted

night air → over the wheelbarrows and rain-tanks

young woman → not clearly visible except for hands and hair
head → bends over page
hand → moves repeatedly

Boland wrote like that once.

WS

But this is different:
This time, when she looks up,
Boland will be there.

WS

TEXT WORLD 1

(participant-accessible)

E: Boland assumed as speaker (I, Here, Now)

Is it still the same

NEG   AFF

Key:
WS World switch
NEG Negative
AFF Affirmative

PAST VERSION OF AFFIRMATIVE WORLD

(enactor-accessible)

Boland remembers herself writing under those conditions.

FUTURE VERSION OF AFFIRMATIVE WORLD

(enactor-accessible)

Boland will embody and make present the absent senior figure who was not there for her younger self.

PAST VERSION OF NEGATIVE WORLD

(enactor-accessible)

Boland remembers writing under the same conditions as this young woman, but she is not her.

FUTURE VERSION OF NEGATIVE WORLD

(enactor-accessible)

Boland as senior poet will there to be looked up to for this other young woman.

WS

WS

NEGATIVE VERSION OF TEXT WORLD 1

(participant-accessible)

It is not the same

T: present
L: suburban house
O: stairs, door, table, room, house, corridor, air, wheelbarrows, rain-tanks, page
E: unnamed female, speaker

young woman → climbs stairs
→ closes child's door
→ goes to table

table → in room at back of house

corridor → unlighted

night air → over the wheelbarrows and rain-tanks

young woman → not clearly visible except for hands and hair
head → bends over page
hand → moves repeatedly

Boland wrote like that once.

But this is different:
This time, when she looks up,
Boland will be there.

Figure 15.1 Text-world diagram for 'Is it Still the Same'

is presented in direct reference to its later version. This imaginative bringing of the two versions into apposition allows us both to see the unusual nature of the reversal, and also to experience the power of the imaginative journey which evokes them. This suggests that we need not think about the narrative of our lives linearly, as the prevailing sedentarist paradigm would indicate that we do, but that we are capable of thinking about this narrative much more flexibly, and that this flexibility creates some striking emotional effects and insights.

In Stockwell's model, the effects generated by the text may be thought of as shifts, zooms and state changes which can capture attention and form attractors. As each state change is focused on in turn, we shift to it, and zoom in on it. Each in turn is an attractor, which we are asked to attend to while it transforms. Then each attractor is occluded by the new attractor, which is generated by the next shift, zoom and state change as the list progresses. Interestingly, because these transformations are presented in language, which operates serially over time, it obscures the fact that the transformations may be taking place simultaneously. There is some sense of this in the rapidity with which each new attractor is presented almost as though our gaze is being directed very quickly from one to the other to catch them in the act of transformation. The imagined action is reminiscent of a series of saccades.

As readers we find ourselves in the 'interspace' between two text-worlds, travelling simultaneously in two vehicles. We are in the car with the narrator of the poem, and also in the poem with the poet. The poem acts as an interspace facilitating the connected co-presence of the two versions of each enactor, and the connected co-presence of the two text-worlds generated by their transformations. The machine of the poem has reordered and compressed Euclidean timespace (Urry 2004), rendering the past both proximate and distant, absent and present: proximate and present by being evoked in the poem and populated by enactors of entities from the present text-world, but distant and absent through showing the extent of the change each enactor undergoes in order to manifest in the earlier text-world. Some enactors disappear altogether. Such an act of negation makes their disappearance into a felt absence in the earlier text-world.

Boland has also used this same strategy elsewhere. In 'A Dream of Colony' (1998: 27), she uses reversal to create a text-world where the effects of war are negated through the power of language:

> Each phrase of ours,
> holding still for a moment in the stormy air,
> raised an unburned house
>
> . . . .

Unturned that corner
the assassin eased around and aimed from.
Undid. Unsaid:

This undoing signalled in the last line above creates two versions of the text-world, using a twinning effect through the deictic shift to a time before the house was burned, and before the assassin crept around the corner and fired. This is similar to the twinning effect achieved by the deictic switch created by the reversal discussed in 'A Marriage for the Millennium', in that the world-building elements in each of the worlds are the same. However, in this case the effect of the deictic world-switch is not simply to restore the world-building elements to their former states, but also to allow them to imaginatively exist as both negative and positive versions, both unburned and burned house, real and potential assassin, who, in the earlier version has not yet carried out the act of violence, and may still change tack. It also strikingly evokes a felt absence in the poem. The assassin's victim is simultaneously murdered and restored to life. This evokes – through the morphological negations – the potential for healing through the poem, the potential to undo the violence and suggest a restorative function. This resonates with Boland's assertion of the power of language that 'We say *like* or *as* and the world is' (Boland 2007: 36 italics in original) expressed in the poem 'Of Shadow. Of Simile'.

'A Dream of Colony' exemplifies this power of language to create and change worlds, and to make conflicting worlds co-present, by keeping both versions of the text-world, before and after, negative and positive, available and prominent in attention, in such a way as to allow the reader to toggle between them bringing the reality of the acts and their consequences into sharp focus. It also problematizes the negative and positive versions of the world, because the linguistically positive world, where the house is burned and the assassin has acted, is more inherently negative than the linguistically negative version of the world, where the house is unburned and the assassin's act is undone. This linguistically negative world is inherently positive through its imaginative act of restoration, exposing the tension between the linguistic polarity and the actual polarity described by the circumstances.

15.6   Conclusion

In many of her poems Boland poses a version of Callon and Law's question regarding what happens when presence and absence, proximity and distance are not mutually exclusive. As we have seen in the examples analysed, Boland's use of twin text-worlds can be both startling and potent, making the reader both see and feel the effects of imagined journeys and juxtapositions of past and present and different enactors of the same character within a single space. As Boland put it an interview (Villar and Boland 2006: 64):

> Where poetry excels is as a method of experience, not expression. It has a unique capacity to render an experience in a fresh, unsettling way. I don't write a poem to express an experience, but to experience it again.

This quotation demonstrates that Boland sees poetry as a way of collapsing temporal and spatial boundaries in order to place both the poet and the reader 'in the moment', to re-embody remembered experience in order to experience it anew, and to change how the experiencer thinks about the experience.

Poetry is a cultural practice that allows the mobilization of a changed context to re-experience and to change experiences. It makes 'the familiar strange, and the strange familiar' (attributed to Coleridge by Eliot 1950: 259). Applying a cognitive poetic framework constructed from Text World Theory and Stockwell's model of literary resonance allows us to track the reader's progress and processes through the text and rigorously analyse the linguistic cues and mental spaces activated at different times. The analysis presented in this chapter demonstrates how such a framework may elucidate the ways in which poetry can address the new mobilities paradigm's concerns and questions regarding the infrastructures of imaginative travel, and how these may be 'mobilized, or performed, through ongoing sociotechnical and cultural practices' (Sheller 2011: 2). The framework provides a way to describe, analyse and understand how poetry collapses boundaries between then and now, and between here and there, making them co-present. It draws out the mechanisms by which a poem operates as an interspace where meeting-ness is facilitated, and as an inhabited machine which, through its workings, has the potential to problematize the very nature of presences and absences, distance and proximity.

References

Boland, E. (1995), *Collected Poems*, Manchester: Carcanet.
Boland, E. (1998), *The Lost Land*, Manchester: Carcanet.
Boland, E. (2001), *Code*, Manchester: Carcanet.
Boland, E. (2007), *Domestic Violence*, Manchester: Carcanet.

Büscher, M., and Urry, J. (2009), 'Mobile Methods and the Empirical', *European Journal of Social Theory*, 12: 99–116.

Callon, M. and Law, J. (2004), 'Guest Editorial', *Journal of Environment and Planning D: Society and Space*, 22: 3–11.

Carstensen, K. U. (2007), 'Spatio-Temporal Ontologies and Attention', *Spatial Cognition and Computation*, 7.1: 13–32.

Eliot, T. S. (1950). *Selected Essays* (new edition), New York: Harcourt, Brace and Company.

Fogarty, A. (1999), ' "The Influence of Absences": Eavan Boland and the Silenced History of Irish Women's Poetry', *Colby Quarterly*, 35.4: 256–74.

Gavins, J. (2007), *Text World Theory: An Introduction*, Edinburgh: Edinburgh University Press.

Hidalgo Downing, L. (2000), 'Negation in Discourse: A Text-World Approach to Joseph Heller's *Catch-22*', *Language and Literature*, 9.4: 215–40.

Hidalgo Downing, L. (2002), 'Creating Things That Are Not: The Role of Negation in the Poetry of Wislawa Szymborska', *Journal of Literary Semantics*, 30.2: 113–32.

Richards, I. A. (1925), *Principles of Literary Criticism*, New York: Harcourt Brace Jovanovich.

Sheller, M. (2011), 'Mobility', *Sociopedia.isa*, <http://www.sagepub.net/isa/resources/pdf/Mobility.pdf> [accessed 15 July 2014].

Sheller, M. and Urry, J. (2006), 'The New Mobilities Paradigm', *Journal of Environment and Planning A*, 38: 207–26.

Stockwell, P. (2009), 'The Cognitive Poetics of Literary Resonance', *Language and Cognition*, 1.1: 25–44.

Stockwell, P. (2011), 'Ethics and Imagination in Literary Reading', in R. Jones (ed.), *Discourse and Creativity*, London: Pearson: 35–51.

Urry, J. (2004), 'Connections', *Journal of Environment and Planning D: Society and Space*, 22: 27–37.

Villar, P. and Boland, E. (2006), ' "The Text of It": A Conversation with Eavan Boland', *New Hibernia Review*, 10.2: 52–67.

Werth, P. (1994), 'Extended Metaphor: A Text World Account', *Language and Literature*, 3.2: 79–103.

Werth, P. (1999), *Text Worlds: Representing Conceptual Space in Discourse*, Harlow: Longman.

Stylistic Interanimation and Apophatic Poetics in Jacob Polley's 'Hide and Seek'

Joanna Gavins

16.1   Introduction

The core appeal of Text World Theory as a framework for poetic analysis is its provision of a unified apparatus under which the context surrounding the production and reception of a poem, the poetic text itself, and its conceptual effects can all be examined systematically and rigorously. The usefulness of a text-world approach to poetry has been widely demonstrated over recent years (see Gavins 2010, 2012, 2013, 2014, 2015; Gavins and Stockwell 2012; Giovanelli 2010, 2013; Harbus 2012, this volume; Lahey 2005, 2006, 2010; McLoughlin 2013, 2014, this volume; Nahajec 2009; Stockwell 2002, 2005, 2009, 2011a, 2011b, 2014, this volume, 2016). I have also argued elsewhere (see Gavins 2012, 2015; Gavins and Stockwell 2012) that the three-tiered structure of Text World Theory can help to ensure that key aspects of the poetic reading experience are not overlooked in stylistics, as contemporary scholars rush to incorporate new viewpoints and methodologies into their analyses from associated fields such as corpus linguistics, cognitive science, sociolinguistics and anthropology. In this chapter I develop this argument further by examining the poem 'Hide and Seek' by British poet, Jacob Polley, from a text-world perspective. I show that a full understanding of the poem's eerie and unnerving effects cannot be achieved without a proper consideration of the interanimation of particular stylistic features across the text as a whole. I argue that Text World Theory can enable such a coherent analysis, focusing in great part on the interaction between repeated instances of negation and negativity more broadly in the poem and surrounding stylistic elements of the poetic co-text.

16.2   Co-text, whole text and poetic cohesion

As a means of facilitating a discussion around the necessity for a fully integrated approach to the analysis of poetic style, I have chosen to examine Jacob
Polley's poem, 'Hide and Seek', from his (2012) collection, *The Havocs*. The
poem is reproduced in full below with the kind permission of the author:

Hide and Seek
I wasn't in the chicken coop,
watching. I didn't put my head
through the frayed and dusty loop
slung from the rafter in the pig shed.
I wasn't in the warm brown egg.
I wasn't in the barrel of rain
or in Grandma Dolly's beige plastic leg.
I wasn't in the rookery. I wasn't in the lanes
that powdered the cow-parsleyed hedgerows
those year-long late-summer afternoons.
I wasn't planted. I didn't grow
or constellate. I wasn't field-mushrooms,
milk or mould. I wasn't in the rabbit hole
or under the cowpat. I didn't hang
from the fence with six brother moles.
I didn't do what scarecrows can.
I didn't bark or howl or hoot.
That wasn't me in the frogspawn.
I wasn't brought in off my father's boot.
I wouldn't move like that through a field of corn.
I wasn't under my parents' bed,
listening. I wasn't in the earth
with the bones and broken crockery.
I wasn't in the cold brown Firth
with the flounders. I wasn't Lockerbie,
Annan or Langholm. I wasn't the South
or the North. I didn't wet the bed.
I wasn't in the snapdragon's mouth
or under the heap of severed heads
or under the heap of turnip heads.
I didn't rust. I wasn't waterproof

or catching. I didn't spread.
I wasn't sunburn or the truth.
I wasn't in the slurry pit.
I wasn't the accordion of baled hay
that drew breath when the string was cut.
I wasn't what I didn't say.
I wasn't the echo of the trout
ringing silently through the slow-
flowing bronze. I didn't shout
and stamp. I wasn't under the snow
that kept me from school. I wasn't slammed.
I didn't leak or scratch or smell.
I didn't go to pieces in a stranger's hands.
That wasn't my voice coming from down the well.

I also chose this poem as a subject for analysis because of the profoundly unsettling effect it had on me on my first encounter with it. Although no scholarly literary criticism has yet been published on this text to my knowledge, many of the press reviews of the poem and of the rest of *The Havocs* collection which appeared on its release seem to concur with my initial response to the text. Some note the dark undertones to Polley's work (McAuliffe 2013), others his interest in 'the darker reaches of the psyche and contemporary life' (Johnson 2012), or 'the persistent aura of unease' (Wilkinson 2013) which runs throughout *The Havocs*; how that aura of unease is created and sustained through language is the central focus of the present discussion. It is my contention that no single linguistic feature of the text can possibly be responsible for the overarching and resonant sense of disquiet 'Hide and Seek' provokes. Rather, many different but interconnecting stylistic elements have an accumulative and interanimating effect on each other in this as in most other poetic discourses.

First to appear among the co-dependent stylistic features of Polley's text is the first-person poetic voice, which is created in the opening line ('I wasn't in the chicken coop') and remains the consistent reflector of the world of the poem throughout the rest of the text. This enactor occupies the subject position in all but two of the thirty-seven sentences which make up 'Hide and Seek' (where the same enactor is nominated through other means, as I discuss later), ensuring that it remains a persistently central figure in the poetic text-world and one which becomes increasingly foregrounded through the repetition of the personal pronoun 'I'. The overall cohesion of the poem is further enhanced by the similarly repetitive, limited set of sentence structures within which the poetic voice is positioned: the first clauses of twelve of the poem's sentences take an 'I wasn't + *prepositional phrase*' form; eleven take an 'I didn't + *verb phrase*' structure (plus a further two passives in 'I wasn't planted' in line eleven and 'I wasn't slammed' in line forty-two); and seven take the form of 'I wasn't + *noun phrase*'. Together, these recurring syntactic constructions, along with the complete lack of stanza breaks and frequent enjambment, help give the poem a strongly cohesive configuration, as well as a somewhat hypnotic feel on reading aloud in particular. The simple rhyme scheme created elsewhere in the co-text adds greatly to this effect, with its regular ABAB pattern (e.g. 'coop/loop', 'head/shed', 'egg/leg' and so on). The majority of these rhymes are highly prototypical, being full rhymes in the main, with only a handful of pararhyme or slant rhyme exceptions (e.g. 'afternoon/mushroom', 'hedgerows/grow', 'crockery/Lockerbie', 'pit/cut', 'slammed/hands').

In these ways, 'Hide and Seek' is so cohesive as to be almost child-like in its composition. The repetition of the subject position 'I', in particular, lends a self-centred quality to the text, which aligns neatly with an immature perspective on the world. This, of course, dovetails with the title of the poem, a childhood game, and with an accompanying prevalent lexis evocative of the day-to-day childhood experience of family and play (e.g. 'Grandma Dolly', 'scarecrows', 'frogspawn', 'father's boot', 'parents', 'wet the bed', 'snapdragon's mouth', 'shout', 'stamp', 'school'). Intermingled here, too, is another, complementary lexical field which also runs consistently throughout the text and adds a distinctly rural flavour to the world of the poem (e.g. 'chicken coop', 'pig shed', 'cow-parsleyed hedgerows', 'field-mushrooms', 'rabbit hole', 'cowpat', 'turnip heads', 'baled hay' and so on). Specifically, readers are strongly led to infer a Scottish setting to the text, by the mention of 'Lockerbie', 'Annan' and 'Langholm', towns all situated within a few miles of one another near the border between Scotland and England, as well as by the lines which follow their mention: 'I wasn't the South / or the North'.

Poetic cohesion on this whole-text scale is necessarily built on parallel, repeated and co-dependent features, the results of which can only be appreciated in an examination of the poem in its entirety. This is not to suggest, however, that cohesion is the defining characteristic of this text; rather, the carefully constructed aggregate of stylistic elements identified so far can be seen as a kind of initial poetic building block, against which Polley sets other, similarly co-dependent features of poetic style in opposition or tension.

16.3   Stylistic interanimation and poetic dissonance

Perhaps the most obviously dissonant feature of Polley's poem is the presence of a third lexical field, which provides a stark contrast against the established themes of childhood and rural life: that of death and violence. Among the idyllic mental imagery conjured up by 'year-long late-summer afternoons', 'the echo of the trout / ringing silently through the slow- / flowing bronze', and 'the accordion of baled hay / that drew breath when the string was cut' are woven numerous far darker descriptions. These include an allusion to suicide by hanging ('I didn't put my head / through the frayed and dusty loop / slung from the rafter in the pig shed'); reference to the diminishing, but grisly, British rural tradition of mole-catchers pegging their victims around the borders of fields ('I didn't hang / from the fence with six brother moles'); briefer mentions of 'mould', 'bones' and a 'heap of severed heads'; as well as the more subtly disconcerting 'beige plastic leg' and the closing 'voice coming from down the well'. These elements interact with the co-text which surrounds them to cast wider shadows on other text-world components which, in different circumstances, might not appear quite so bleak or so menacing, such as 'the rookery', 'scarecrows', 'the frogspawn', 'the snapdragon's mouth' and 'a stranger's hands', among others.

The close textual co-location of various other key world-building elements in the poem has similarly echoic and interanimative effects, many of them realized through the use of the additive conjunctions 'or' and 'and'. In some cases, clauses containing lexical items from the same field of experience are conjoined in logical ways: 'I didn't *bark* or *howl* or *hoot*'; 'I wasn't in the *rabbit-hole* / or under the *cowpat*'; 'I wasn't the *South* / or the *North*' (my emphasis). In others, the metaphorical blending of one text-world element with another is encouraged through the presentation of visually similar objects as equal alternatives, for example in 'I wasn't in the earth / with the bones and broken crockery', and 'under the heap of severed heads / or under the heap of turnip heads'. Interestingly, in each of these examples, the more grisly item comes first, foregrounding the darker themes in the poem in each case. Elsewhere, however, the alternatives presented through the same sorts of conjoined clauses are incongruous with one another, producing a much more conceptually dissonant and surrealistic effect. For example, in 'I wasn't planted. I didn't grow / or constellate' a common, cohesive connection is initially set up between 'planted' and 'grow', bringing a metaphor of the child as a seed or plant to mind. However, this is then immediately deviated from with the inclusion of 'constellate' in the same sentence. This verb form is highly novel and not common usage in contemporary British English, with no occurrences of it recorded in the 100-million word British National Corpus, compared with 182 occurrences for the nominalized form 'constellation', all of which describe the movement or arrangement or multiple objects (most frequently stars), not the action of a single entity (Brigham Young University 2015). Similar incongruity occurs in 'I wasn't waterproof / or catching', 'I wasn't sunburn / or the truth', where no semantic connection is identifiable between the two clauses at all, and even to some extent in 'I wasn't field-mushrooms, / milk or mould', where the conceptual link between each item is tenuous, even though they could all be said to belong to the broad rural theme of the poem.

Even the highly regular rhyme scheme established in the first twenty lines of the poem is deviated from in one isolated instance on the twenty-first line, where 'I wasn't under my parents' bed' breaks the ABAB end-rhyme pattern which has been observed consistently until this point. This pattern then returns again, unbroken, for the remaining twenty-four lines. Again taking a whole-text perspective, I found the fact that this is a single break in the rhyme patterning of the poem particularly jarring in my own reading, since this not only interrupted a sustained parallelism, but led me to anticipate a further deviation at a later point which then never materialized.

All of the stylistic features I have identified so far are linguistic components in the construction of a series of discrete scenes in 'Hide and Seek'. Each of these scenes builds a text-world, which comes into focus through its description in the poem, occluding the scene which preceded it, to use Stockwell's (2009: 21-2) terms, and creating a world-switch from a Text World Theory point of view. The amalgamation of Stockwell's approach with a text-world view here is useful, as it gives a deeper sense of the textural effect such switches between worlds can have in literature. Stockwell points out that the conceptual spaces generated in literary reading contain a 'cluttered array' (Spelke 1990) of perceptual elements, vying for attention, and that shifts in attention between objects and scenes are not always instant or clean-cut:

> . . . elements which are either no longer the focus of attention, were never prominent features, or have been deliberately backgrounded can be said to be relatively *neglected*. Neglect can be a matter primarily of reader disengagement, and this can take the form of a reader consciously *lifting* the element out of the focused domain of awareness: there is a sense that the element is still 'there' but is on its way out of focus. Alternatively, the readerly disengagement can be

more a matter of attentional *drag*, with a sense that the element is now part of the background but there is still a whiff of it in the air. Lastly, the neglect can be seen to be more a matter of textual patterning, such that another focused element can *occlude* the previously focused figure. This occlusion can be instant for an element that is linguistically removed from the scene (for example, by negation or a verb of disappearance, death or removal), or it can be gradual, where the element fades away by not being mentioned for a duration of several clauses. (Stockwell 2009: 21–2, original emphasis)

Stockwell goes on to argue that the crossing of world-boundaries as our attention shifts in reading is a *felt* experience. He uses the metaphor of reading as a journey to liken shifting scenes in texts to the effort required to negotiate a bicycle over an uneven and fractured surface, as opposed to smooth, consistent ground (Stockwell 2009: 89–90). From this perspective, then, the transitions between text-worlds in Polley's poem are another repeated feature of the text, and cohesive from that point of view. However, their end, felt result is in multiple breaks in the poem's surface and a conceptually bumpy ride for the reader.

The repeated world-switching in Polley's text reflects, of course, the title of the poem and enacts a game of hide and seek through each shift in scene. As noted earlier, the 'I' poetic voice narrates each of these text-worlds; however the occurrence of the first-person pronoun in this way does not necessarily entail the viewing perspective of that textual enactor. Although the poem is narrated by the 'I' persona, each scene he describes is one defined by his own absence from it. The poem switches from one separate world to another – from a chicken coop, to a pig shed, to the inside of an egg, to a barrel of rain and so on – each of which possesses its own, distinct spatial and temporal parameters, but each of which is united by *not* being the location of the first-person poetic voice. This creates another dissonant disjunction in the poem, as the 'I' reflects the point of view of his seeker, rather than of himself. Our perspective as readers, then, is a curious one which seems to follow the pursuit of the 'I' persona – an enactor who is present in the textual universe as a whole, but who never reveals the specific text-world in which he can be found – across numerous spatio-temporal locations. The sense the reader gains as the poem progresses of having performed the hunt for the poetic voice for themselves is further aided by the use of the definite article throughout the text. All but two of the nominal items in 'Hide and Seek' take a definite form and the consistent simple-past tense also serves to concretize the numerous text-worlds, described as familiar scenes, containing fixed, completed actions and events.

However, perhaps the most important complicating factor in all of the worlds depicted in 'Hide and Seek' is their negated nature, which is linguistically realized in various ways. As outlined earlier, the poem repeats a limited set of syntactic structures, some of which describe the poetic voice *not* being in a particular location, some of which describe him *not* doing an action (or *not* having an action done to him in two cases), and some describe him *not* being a place or object or *not* possessing a quality. Negation, particularly in poetic texts, has received a significant amount of attention from text-world theorists over recent years (see e.g. Gavins 2013, 2014; Gavins and Stockwell 2012; Giovanelli 2013; Hidalgo Downing 2000a, 2000b, 2002; Nahajec 2009), all of whom agree upon the essentially foregrounding effect of this linguistic feature, which demands that a text-world element (whether world-building or function-advancing) be called to mind in order to then be negated (see also Lakoff 2004). Linguists are also in broad agreement over the fact that negation has an important pragmatic function to defeat discourse-world expectations and generate implicature as a result. As Nahajec explains:

> The notion that negation not only acts upon the proposition it occurs in, but also on a previous assertion, either within the text itself or in common knowledge, furthers the argument for a readerly interpretation of negative assertions, and indicates that negation is, in fact, pragmatically loaded; it is not simply the propositional content of a negated expressions that generates meaning, but its context in a discourse that triggers its intended meaning. (Nahajec 2009: 113)

Thus, when in Polley's poem we are told 'I wasn't in the warm brown egg', not only must we complete the challenging task of mentally representing a textual enactor inside a warm brown egg before we can comprehend the absence of this state of affairs, but we also understand the expression to be generating implied meaning: that someone was looking for him in that location (and perhaps also that this was a reasonable thing to do), and that he was somewhere else. The same applies for each of the negated prepositional phrases expressed in the poem: 'in the chicken coop', 'in the barrel of rain', 'in Grandma Dolly's beige plastic leg', 'in the rookery', 'in the lanes', 'in the rabbit hole', 'under the cowpat' and so on. Each of these statements of 'not being located' generates an implicature that an unspecified entity was looking for the 'I' enactor in that place, but that he inhabited some other text-world parameters. Again, however, these details remain undisclosed and the places where the enactor wasn't are foregrounded instead.

Other negated expressions in the poem have a slightly different conceptual effect. Those clauses which take a 'I wasn't + *noun phrase*' structure, such as in 'I wasn't field mushrooms, / milk or mould', 'I wasn't Lockerbie, / Annan or Langholm. I wasn't the South / or the North', 'I wasn't sunburn or the truth' and so on, all require the reader to conceptualize the poetic voice as a place or object, before an understanding of this textual entity as something other than those things can be reached. Once again, the implicature generated is that the poetic voice is a different, but unspecified object or place, and that it might be reasonable to expect this. In these examples, though, a more complex conceptual blending of 'I' enactor with a variety of other world-building elements, some of them more concrete ('field-mushrooms', 'milk', 'mould') than others ('the truth', 'the echo of the trout') is involved. For example, in the lines 'I wasn't Lockerbie, / Annan or Langholm', the reader's mental representations of each of these Dumfriesshire towns, located close to the Scottish border with England, form compressed inputs (in Fauconnier and Turner's 2003 terms) into blended text-worlds, in which the poetic voice takes on aspects of each location, before this blend can then be negated. The inputs themselves are compressed in the sense that it is impossible for us to conceptualize the whole of Lockerbie, Annan or Langholm, all of their inhabitants, buildings, geographical features and so on, so we reduce our mental representations of such unmanageable linguistic items to 'human scale' (see Fauconnier and Turner 2003: 8). The key historical significance of Lockerbie as a site of terrorist mass-murder in 1988 comes into play here and, I would argue, echoes out from the text even more strongly as a result of the underlying darkness to be found elsewhere throughout the poem. Although Lockerbie (and Annan and Langholm) are positioned as noun phrases syntactically in the poem, in the blended text-worlds these lines produce, they function adjectivally as far more ethereal, descriptive qualities. In my own reading of 'Hide and Seek', my sense of 'Lockerbie-ness' as a quality which the 'I' enactor did not possess, was greatly defined by my discourse-world knowledge of the historical events which took place in that town. The notoriety of this location contrasted sharply with my lack of real-world knowledge of Annan or Langholm, which formed far less detailed inputs into my conceptual blend.

The negated expressions contained in the 'I didn't + *verb*' constructions in 'Hide and Seek' work differently again. In these cases, the negation generates an implicature that someone else performed an action or was involved in an event which the 'I' enactor claims not to have participated in or done. For example, in the lines 'I didn't put my head / through the frayed and dusty loop / slung from the rafter in the pig shed', the strong suggestion is that someone else *did* put their head through the loop, or that the narrator *ought* to have. From this perspective, the repeated use of negation throughout the whole text can be seen to imply that the 'I' narrator should have done a number of other foregrounded actions, but did not: 'hang', 'grow', 'constellate', 'hang', 'bark', 'howl', 'hoot', 'wet the bed', 'rust', 'spread', 'shout', 'stamp', 'leak', 'scratch', 'smell', 'go to pieces'.

Although these constructions differ syntactically from the negated noun phrases, negated conceptual blends and negated prepositional phrases in the poem, all of these various expressions in 'Hide and Seek' represent examples of what Werth terms 'negative accommodation' (Werth 1999: 254). This type of negation, according to Werth, suggests certain readerly expectations, bringing them into the realm of the discourse, by the very act of negating them. What is interesting to note about Polley's poem is that this is accompanied in several cases, regardless of the syntactic structure of the negated expressions, by extended world-building and function-advancing in the text-worlds for the discrete scenes the poem presents. So, the 'I' enactor is not simply absent from the chicken coop in the opening line, but the inclusion of a sub-clause in this sentence, 'watching', adds further function-advancing information about what he did not do (but again ought to have done, or someone else did) while he was not there. When we are told 'I wasn't under my parents' bed / listening', these lines evoke another eavesdropping presence through indirect implication. A similar example can be found in the lines 'I wasn't in the lanes / that powdered the cow-parsleyed hedgerows / those year-long late-summer afternoons'. Here, another sub-clause again provides post-modifying detail, which in this case extends the negated situation of being in the lanes to one which not only includes highly specific world-building information about the nature of the lanes and hedgerows, but also positions this text-world as a familiar and repeated situation through the use of the demonstrative 'those' and plural 'afternoons'.

Elsewhere, Polley appears to be playing with the conceptual effects of negation in even more deliberate and curious ways, and particularly with the effects of pairing negated expressions with specific or familiar deictics. In two separate lines, he uses 'that' as a dummy subject – 'That wasn't me in the frogspawn' and 'That wasn't my voice coming from down the well' – where in both cases 'that' suggests a definite and jointly perceived object or phenomenon. This has the effect of concretizing the implicature that 'that' was not only the 'I' enactor, but *was* someone else. Note, too, the odd perspective in the text-world produced by the latter of these two cases, where the distal effect of 'that', along with the

definite article in 'the well', is teamed with the verb 'coming', which suggests
a point of view shared by the 'I' enactor and the reader in a position above
the well. This technique is at its most playful in the line 'I wasn't what I didn't
say', which appears almost as a logical puzzle towards the end of 'Hide and
Seek', with the referent of 'what' impossible to locate within the confines of
the poem's text-worlds. Finally, an even more complex conceptual construction
is realized in the poem's single modal-world, which is epistemic in nature: 'I
wouldn't move like that in a field of corn'. 'That' again suggests familiarity here
and a shared point of view with the reader, while the text-world element to
which it refers again remains underlexicalized. Furthermore, 'wouldn't' creates
a remote modal-world through which the reader must try to conceptualize an
as-yet-unrealized, unspecified movement being undertaken by an unspecified
textual enactor, before the negation of this entire scene in relation to the poetic
voice can be understood. The spatio-temporal location of the negated epistemic
modal-world is also, unusually for this poem, generalized through the use of
an indefinite article ('*a* field of corn'), one of only two examples in the entire
text (the other being '*a* stranger's hands'). Polley thus creates yet another series
of negated absences in the poem, but this time renders them all the more mysterious and intangible through their positioning in a remote modal-world with
underspecified deictic parameters.

16.4   Apophasis and whole-text negativity

Throughout 'Hide and Seek', negation functions interanimatively with other
linguistic elements in the same way as all the other key stylistic features of the
text outlined in this chapter so far. Although preceding text-world accounts
of negation have done much to illuminate the pragmatic and conceptual consequences of its use in poetry, I would go further to argue that such accounts
should ensure that the interactivity of negation with other elements of its
whole-text environment are considered if its full complexity as a discoursal feature is to be properly appreciated. In 'Hide and Seek', for example, it is clear that
negation is situated as a crucial component of a much wider poetic and stylistic
motif of absence and loss, which the analysis of examples of negated expressions
in isolation cannot possibly reveal. In literary criticism and theology, poetic
texts which centre around these concerns and explore them through many of
the stylistic means described so far in this chapter have long been recognized as
belonging to a tradition of *apophasis* (see e.g. Franke 2005; Gibbons 2007, 2008;

Katz 2013; Pritchett 2014; Van Winckel 2008). As Gibbons (2007) explains, the term apophasis, from the Greek *phanai*, meaning 'to say', and *apo* meaning 'away from' or 'in opposition to', is used in these disciplines to describe texts which attend to concepts which are present through their absence, or for which no adequate language exists, such as the indescribable nature of God (with St John of the Cross's poem *Dark Night of the Soul* as the definitive example of this). He goes on to point out, however, that apophasis is more complex than the use of simple negation in a given text, but is an 'impulse to proceed by indirection, evoking the impossible or not quite conceivable' (Gibbons 2007: 19). Furthermore, Gibbons argues:

> Apophatic poeticism is an imagining by means of the negative, an entry *into* negative or empty or hidden or invisible space or paradoxically opposite points of thought and feeling. (Gibbons 2008: 39)

Apophasis, then, in poetry and theology, sets out to articulate that which is unarticulatable, or 'that aspect of reality that is an absence', as Gibbons puts it (2007: 22). This broader notion of negativity in poetry, its aims and functions, fits neatly with that put forward by Werth (1999), who argues that a wide range of discoursal components can contribute to an overall conceptual negativity which extends beyond syntactic or morphological constructions. In an analysis of E. M. Forster's novel *A Passage To India*, Werth (1999: 320) includes stylistic features such as negative modification, words with negative meaning, and concessives in a list of linguistic items which he argues contribute to overarching megametaphor of negativity in the text (see also Giovanelli 2013 for a related discussion of nightmare worlds as negation in the poetry of Keats). I would argue that the same sort of whole-text negativity is at work in Polley's 'Hide and Seek' and that the interanimation of a diverse range of stylistic techniques is key to the realization of an apophatic texture extending across the entire poem.

Consider, for example, the nature of the majority of the verbs positioned within the 'I didn't + *verb phrase*' lines in the poem. As noted earlier, there are eleven sentences which begin with this structure in the text and nine of the verbs presented in this way are material supervention processes, in Systemic Functional Linguistics' terms (see Halliday and Mathieson 2004 for an overview, and Gavins 2007 for a text-world application). This means that none of the verbs 'grow', 'constellate', 'hang', 'rust', 'spread', 'leak', 'scratch', 'smell' and 'go to pieces' represent deliberate, intentional actions, but rather present function-advancing processes as happening beyond the 'I' enactor's control or motivation. Even 'wet the bed' can be seen to fall into this category, as something which normally happens involuntarily during sleep. While these processes are not all inherently negative in themselves, their inclusion in a text which is so heavily underscored by other forms of negation and negativity, I would argue, affects their overall force in the poem. In my own reading of 'Hide and Seek', the attachment of such unintentional events to what I would otherwise assume to be an animate enactor functioned as yet another component in the poem's 'persistent aura of unease' (Wilkinson 2013), and led me to conclude that the 'I' of the poem was, in fact, not hiding but dead. This realization further led me to read the near-final lines 'I didn't leak or scratch or smell' as a literal description of a decomposing corpse and to conceptualize a police officer as the 'stranger's hands' in which that corpse similarly literally 'fell to pieces' on discovery. Of course, these text-worlds too are negated like so many others in the text, so that even they remain unrealized and absent situations at the poem's close, and the poetic 'I' remains a distant and ghostly voice, echoing from an ultimately undiscovered location.

16.5   Conclusion

I have sought to demonstrate over the course of the preceding analysis and discussion that style and its conceptual effects function interanimatively and on a whole-text scale in poetic discourse. In particular, I have argued that the apophatic poetics at the heart of Jacob Polley's 'Hide and Seek' cannot be fully understood without proper consideration of the interrelationships between the individual textual features which accumulate to produce the enduring, disconcerting effect of this text. I have suggested that Text World Theory offers an analytical framework which is ideally suited to such an interconnected, textually driven approach. From a text-world perspective, it can be seen that, although Polley's poem shifts deictically from one discrete text-world scene to another, the specific texture of each of these spaces has a contagious effect on the world which occludes it. The cohesive features of the poem identified in the opening sections of this chapter – its repeated syntactic structures, its mixing of three consistent lexical fields, its regular rhyme scheme – all enable the persistence of absence and loss as key themes across all the worlds in the text. However, it is the poem's repeated negations and wider textual negativity which are crucial to the sustenance of the essentially apophatic quality of 'Hide and

Seek'. It is the foregrounding effect of these aspects of the poem which add most to the 'attentional drag', to use Stockwell's (2009: 21) term once again, which endures beyond each world-switch in the poem. Throughout 'Hide and Seek', Polley weaves a vital tension between the text's regularity and constancy and a similarly unremitting poetic and conceptual dissonance which continually threatens to destabilize and corrupt. The further through the poem we read, the more we are invited to seek the undiscovered. The more we seek, the more apparent the ultimate unattainability of the ghostly poetic voice becomes.

Acknowledgement

I would like to thank Dr Jill Robson for her invaluable advice and input, particularly on apophasis and theology, in the early stages of my research for this chapter.

References

Brigham Young University (2015), *British National Corpus.* <http://corpus.byu.edu/bnc/> [accessed 16 September 2015].

Fauconnier, G. and Turner, M. (2003), *The Way We Think: Conceptual Blending And The Mind's Hidden Complexities*, New York: Basic Books.

Franke, W. (2005), 'The Singular and the Other at the Limits of Language in the Apophatic Poetics of Edmond Jabès and Paul Celan', *New Literary History: A Journal of Theory and Interpretation*, 36.4: 621–38.

Gavins, J. (2007), *Text World Theory: An Introduction*, Edinburgh: Edinburgh University Press.

Gavins, J. (2010), '"And Everyone and I Stopped Breathing": Familiarity and Ambiguity in the Text-World of "The Day Lady Died:"', in M. Lambrou, M. and P. Stockwell (eds), *Contemporary Stylistics*, Basingstoke: Palgrave Macmillan: 133–43.

Gavins, J. (2012), 'Leda and the Stylisticians', *Language and Literature*, 21.4: 345–62.

Gavins, J. (2013), *Reading the Absurd*, Edinburgh: Edinburgh University Press.

Gavins, J. (2014), 'Defamiliarisation', in P. Stockwell and S. Whiteley (eds), *The Cambridge Handbook of Stylistics*, Cambridge: Cambridge University Press: 126–211.

Gavins, J. (2015), 'Text World Theory', in V. Sotirova (ed.), *The Bloomsbury Companion to Stylistics*, London: Bloomsbury Academic: 444–57.

Gavins, J. and Stockwell, P. (2012), 'About the Heart, Where It Hurt Exactly and How Often', *Language and Literature*, 21.1: 31–50.

Gibbons, R. (2007), 'On Apophatic Poetics', *American Poetry Review*, 366: 19–23.

Gibbons, R. (2008), 'On Apophatic Poetics, Part Two', *American Poetry Review*, 37.2: 39–45.

Giovanelli, M. (2010), 'Pedagogical Stylistics: A Text World Theory Approach to the Teaching of Poetry', *English in Education*, 44.3: 214–31.

Giovanelli, M. (2013), *Text World Theory and Keats' Poetry: The Cognitive Poetics of Desire, Dreams and Nightmares*, London: Bloomsbury Academic.

Halliday, M. A. K. and Mathieson, C. (2004), *An Introduction to Systemic Functional Linguistics*, London: Continuum.

Harbus, A. (2012), *Cognitive Approaches to Old English Poetry*, Cambridge: D.S. Brewer.

Hidalgo Downing, L. (2000a), *Negation, Text Worlds, and Discourse: The Pragmatics of Fiction*, Stamford, CT: Ablex.

Hidalgo Downing, L. (2000b), 'Negation in Discourse: A Text World Approach to Joseph Heller's *Catch-22*', *Language and Literature*, 9.3: 215–39.

Hidalgo Downing, L. (2002), 'Creating Things That Are Not: The Role of Negation in the Poetry of Wislawa Szymborska', *Journal of Literary Semantics*, 31: 113–32.

Johnson, P. (2012), 'Review: T.S. Eliot Prize Shortlist 2012', <http://www.poetrybookshoponline.com/poetry_portal/review_t_s_eliot_prize_shortlist_2012> [accessed 2 September 2015].

Katz, A. (2013), 'Deconstructing Dickinson's Dharma', *Emily Dickinson Journal*, 22.2: 46–64.

Lahey, E. (2005), *Text World Landscapes and English-Canadian National Identity in the Poetry of Al Purdy, Alden Nowlan and Milton Acorn*, Unpublished PhD Thesis, University of Nottingham.

Lahey, E. (2006), '(Re)thinking World-Building: Locating the Text-Worlds of Canadian Lyric Poetry', *Journal of Literary Semantics*, 35.2: 145–64.

Lahey, E. (2010), 'Megametaphorical Mappings and the Landscapes of Canadian Poetry', in M. Lambrou and P. Stockwell, (eds), *Contemporary Stylistics*, London: Continuum: 157–67.

Lakoff, G. (2004), *Don't Think Of An Elephant!: Know Your Values And Frame The Debate*, White River Junction, VT: Chelsea Green Publishing.

McAuliffe, J. (2013), 'Poets Put Their Best Feet Forward on Matters of Life and Death'. <http://www.irishtimes.com/culture/books/poets-put-their-best-feet-forward-on-matters-of-life-and-death-1.1523400> [accessed 2 September 2015].

McLoughlin, N. (2013), 'Negative Polarity in Eavan Boland's "The Famine Road"', *New Writing: The International Journal for the Practice and Theory of Creative Writing*, 10.2: 219–27.

McLoughlin, N. (2014), 'The Marvellous as We Know It: A Text World Analysis of Seamus Heaney's "Squarings: Lightenings VIII"', *New Writings: The International Journal for the Practice and Theory of Creative Writing*, 11.2: 228–39.

Nahajec, L. (2009), 'Negation and the Creation of Implicit Meaning in Poetry', *Language and Literature*, 18.2: 109–27.

Polley, J. (2012), *The Havocs*, London: Picador.

Pritchett, P. (2014), 'How to Write Poetry after Auschwitz: The Burnt Book of Michael Palmer', *Journal of Modern Literature*, 37.3: 127–45.

Spelke, E. (1990), 'Principles of Object Perception', *Cognitive Science*, 14: 29–56.

Stockwell, P. (2002), *Cognitive Poetics: An Introduction*, London: Routledge.

Stockwell, P. (2005), 'Texture and Identification', *European Journal of English Studies*, 9.2: 143–53.

Stockwell, P. (2009), *Texture: A Cognitive Aesthetics of Reading*, Edinburgh: Edinburgh University Press.

Stockwell, P. (2011a), 'Ethics and Imagination in Literary Reading', in R. Jones (ed.), *Discourse and Creativity*, London: Pearson: 35–51.

Stockwell, P. (2011b), 'Authenticity and Creativity in Reading Lamentation', in R. Pope, J. Swann and R. Carter (eds), *Creativity in Language*, Basingstoke: Palgrave Macmillan: 203–16.

Stockwell, P. (2014), 'Creative Reading, World and Style in Ben Jonson's "To Celia"', in B. Dancygier, M. Borkent, and J. Hinnell (eds), *Language in the Creative Mind*, Stanford, CA: CLSI: 157–72.

Stockwell, P. (2016), *The Language of Surrealism*, Basingstoke: Palgrave Macmillan.

Werth, P. (1999), *Text Worlds: Representing Conceptual Space in Discourse*, Harlow: Longman.

Wilkinson, B. (2013), 'The Havocs by Jacob Polley: Review'. <http://www.theguardian.com/books/2013/jan/04/the-havocs-jacob-polley-review> [accessed 2 September 2015].

Van Winckel, N. (2008), 'The Apophatic', *Poetry*, 192.3: 235.

Index